ArtScroll Series®

Rabbi Nosson Scherman / Rabbi Meir Zlotowitz

General Editors

Perspectives
of the

Published by

Mesorah Publications, ltd

Maggid

Insights and inspiration
from the lectures of

RABBI PAYSACH J. KROHN

FIRST EDITION
First Impression … February 2012

Published and Distributed by
MESORAH PUBLICATIONS, LTD.
4401 Second Avenue / Brooklyn, N.Y 11232

Distributed in Europe by
LEHMANNS
Unit E, Viking Business Park
Rolling Mill Road
Jarow, Tyne & Wear, NE32 3DP
England

Distributed in Israel by
SIFRIATI / A. GITLER — BOOKS
6 Hayarkon Street
Bnei Brak 51127

Distributed in Australia and New Zealand
by **GOLDS WORLDS OF JUDAICA**
3-13 William Street
Balaclava, Melbourne 3183
Victoria, Australia

Distributed in South Africa by
KOLLEL BOOKSHOP
Ivy Common
105 William Road
Norwood 2192, Johannesburg, South Africa

ARTSCROLL SERIES®
PERSPECTIVES OF THE MAGGID
© *Copyright 2012, by* MESORAH PUBLICATIONS, Ltd.
4401 Second Avenue / Brooklyn, N.Y. 11232 / (718) 921-9000 / www.artscroll.com

---

**RABBI KROHN'S ARTICLES IN THIS VOLUME ORIGINALLY APPEARED IN
ZMAN MAGAZINE,
AND THEY ARE REPRINTED WITH THEIR KIND PERMISSION.
WE ARE GRATEFUL FOR THEIR COOPERATION.**

ISBN 10: 1-4226-1184-1 / ISBN 13: 978-1-4226-1184-5

Typography by CompuScribe at ArtScroll Studios, Ltd.

Printed in the United States of America by Noble Book Press Corp.
Bound by Sefercraft, Quality Bookbinders, Ltd., Brooklyn N.Y. 11232

דוד קאהן

ביהמ"ד גבול יעבץ
ברוקלין, נוא יארק

ב"ה

זה יותר מכ... שנה ש... הרב ... יוסף קרא...
נאי דבר ...ני הקהפה ונוסע על קהלות תכ...
...צת תורה. ...שיו אחה בגע... ל... כאה מהי...
הפוס לה... ב... בזר יה... אשר ...כל לקרוא ...
המל...ה "ז...ה דורו ...ה מקיים של... י...ה ...שוה ...
...נפשו יצא ...אב קית הכ...; ...ז שהרי אין מכ...
בני ...צוה ה...ורים ...רות שאים כל...; ...בי הלב ...
"הקהפה". ה...מ...ה ...ורי נ...א ה...סי "הפקפה
הנכונה", ו...ן ...ן ...ו מ...א שהת...רם הוא ה...ה
(כמו "הקהפה מאמון קפ...") הרי ה...ן להיות אפפ שי
באמ...ן ה...ה הוא ...כין מ... אל ... יסוות התורה ו...
...וו...ה ...ל ...עף ב...קהפה. ו...א שאת...אים אא ל...ו...
ע... ב...קהפה... כ... כ... שא...ן ...א...ה י...ו מה ...
שהתרי...ה של ... ...נית ...רית ...בה...קהפה הנכונה

ו...ני מ...ק או... של ... י... ...בת... ה... ל ...רו... ...ת
ישראל ...תקים ...קרי... של "...כ... ...רכין ד...ו" ...בה ...לבל
אשר י...ה י...יל אכ"כ.

אוה...ו ואו...רו
דוד קאהן
...קף ...

Dayan Ch. Ehrentreu
Rosh Beth Din

55 SHIREHALL PARK
LONDON NW4 2QN
TEL: +44 (0) 20 8202 2364
FAX: +44 (0) 20 8203 8942
email: dayan@ehrentreu.com

חנוך עהרנטרייא
ראש בית דין

ששת הימים 41
רמת אשכול
ירושלים
טל: 8551 532 (0)2 972+
פקס: 8552 532 (0)2 972+

כ"ח טבת תשע"ב
23. 1. 2012

Rabbi Paysach J. Krohn's talents are well known worldwide both as an educator and an outstanding lecturer. Eloquent and impassioned Rabbi Krohn writes on many varied subjects which raises in his readers an awareness of Hashems presence and assists them to understand how do deal with day to day issues from a Torah perspective. To have many of his lectures in one volume I have no doubt whatsoever will illuminate people's lives. I feel privileged to extend my heartfelt blessings to such a special person as Rabbi Krohn and pray to Hashem that he should be granted good health and strength to continue his life's work to disseminate Torah values for many years to come.

החותם לכבוד התורה

חנוך הכהן עהרנטרייא

חנוך הכהן עהרנטרייא

קהל עדת יראים

Congregation Adas Yereim
of Kew Gardens, Inc.
122-25 Metropolitan Avenue
Kew Gardens, New York 11415

בס״ד

מכתב ברכה

יום ג׳ לסדר וישב ״והישר בעיני תעשה״

לכבוד ידיד נפשי ציר רגיל בבית דודי

...

TEL. (718) 520-0115
FAX (718) 268-0186

קהל נחלת יצחק ד׳הומנא

CONGREGATION NACHLAS YITZCHOK

141-43 73RD AVENUE
KEW GARDENS, HILLS, N. Y. 11367

בס״ד

NOACH ISAAC OELBAUM
Rabbi
AUTHOR OF SEFORIM
MINCHAS CHEN

נח אייזיק אהלבוים
בעהמח״ס מנחת חן
רב ואב״ד דק״ק נחלת יצחק
בקיו גארדענס הילס, נ. י.

יום שמיני של פסח והגדת לבנך ביום ההוא ומעולם לבן

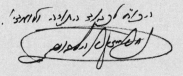

נאום לכבוד התורה והמצוה ולומדיה.

Table of Contents

Author's Preface   11

Acknowledgments   15

Insights of Inspiration

Reflective Enthusiasm   21

From Past Pain to Future Gain   31

Problems and Possibilities in the Secular Workplace   45

Hakaras HaTov   53

Getting a Handle on Anger   61

A Journey to the Poland of Yesteryear   71

Eating and Overeating   81

Money: Part I   91

Money: Part II   99

Seven Strategies for Surviving the Recession   107

Relationships

How Reb Yisrael Can Help *Klal Yisrael*   119

Count Your Blessings   129

Kibud Av V'eim   139

Making Marriage Special: Part I   147

Making Marriage Special: Part II   157

Caught in the Middle: Helping Children of Divorce   167

Caring for Our Elders   177

Forgiveness: Part I   187

Forgiveness: Part II   197

Bitachon in Difficult Times   205

Timely Topics

Shabbos   215

A Living Beis HaMikdash   225

Elul: Pounding on the Door   233

Refining Our Character   241

A Life, Some Shoes, and an Old Baby Bottle   251

Purim, Prayer, and Pulling Together   259

Indices

Index of Personalities   270

Index of Sources   274

AUTHOR'S PREFACE

אֶפְתְּחָה בְשִׁיר פִּי וּשְׂפָתַי...

I open in song my mouth and lips ....

(Recited by the leader of *Birchas HaMazon* at a *bris*)

It is with a heartfelt song and a deep sense of gratitude to the *Ribono Shel Olam* that I present this book to the reading public. The idea that these lectures should be presented as essays was first conceived by R' Yaakov Astor, editor-in-chief of *Zman Magazine*, and its publishers. Since its inception in February 2010, *Zman Magazine* has published one of these essays as its lead article in every issue.

This past summer, on a Motza'ei Shabbos in Camp Munk, R' Gedaliah Zlotowitz proposed that these essays be put together as an ArtScroll book. I was thrilled with the idea. When he told me a short time later that his father Reb Meir agreed, the project began in earnest. I thank Reb Meir and Reb Nosson Scherman for the opportunity to publish this book as part of the Maggid series.

In 1987, when I began recording and filing my lectures, I decided to name the series of speeches אִמְרֵי פִּי, *the expressions of my mouth*, because the word פִּי is comprised of the first letters of my

Hebrew name, פֶּסַח יוֹסֵף. The phrase is from King David's plea, יִהְיוּ לְרָצוֹן אִמְרֵי פִי וְהֶגְיוֹן לִבִּי לְפָנֶיךָ, *May the expressions of my mouth and the thoughts of my heart find favor before You* (*Tehillim* 19:15). I or any other speaker wants nothing more than for our words to be pleasing to the Ribono Shel Olam and to our listeners. It is my fervent prayer, as was King David's, that indeed this will always be so.

My public speaking career began shortly after ArtScroll published *The Maggid Speaks* in February 1987. I guess people felt, "If he can write a story, maybe he can tell one." In truth, I have always felt that a story in a lecture is merely a vehicle to bring home a point but that the essence of the speech consists of the insights and the inspiration that the speaker wishes to convey.

In my talks, I have always tried to build people, not break them; to elevate them, not depress them; to show them how great they can be, not belittle them by telling them they are deficient. The stories I tell are those that I feel that we can all replicate. The stories about Gedolim of today and yesterday are those from which we can learn practical lessons in our *bein adam laMakom and bein adam lachaveiroh*, our relationships with Hashem and our fellows.

I learned this style of speaking from the Maggid of Jerusalem, Rabbi Sholom Mordechai Schwadron (1912–1997). When he first came to America, in the winter of 1964, he stayed in my parents' home for close to six months. It was the first time that I had heard a Maggid, an itinerant speaker, and I saw how people were drawn to him to be inspired by his message. As I explained in the introduction to *The Maggid Speaks,* Reb Sholom could make people laugh, he could make people cry, but more than anything else he could make people change. It is for this reason that in almost every speech I give, I offer practical ways that people can implement the ideas I present. My goal is always to help people change — for the better; for them to become elevated and fulfill their potential.

Growing up, I was fortunate to hear and get to know numerous extraordinary speakers. Thus over time I formulated in my mind what the ideal speech should be. It would blend the passion of Reb Sholom; the eloquence of Rabbi Immanuel Jakobovits; the pleasantness and practicality of my father, Rabbi Avrohom Zelig Krohn; the affection of the Ponevezher Rov, Rabbi Yosef Kahaneman; the fire and enthusiasm of Rav Mordechai Gifter; the clarity of Rav Shimon Schwab; and the creative logic of Rav Yaakov Kamenetzky. I could listen to any of the aforementioned endlessly, not only because of what they represented and who they were, but because of the way they conveyed what was in their hearts and minds. If only I could reach even a fraction of their levels ....

In a homiletical sense, the presentation of these lectures is the implementation of the Torah's expression, רֹאִים אֶת הַקּוֹלֹת *viewing the voice* (*Shemos* 20:15). It is an honor to present my thoughts in this manner, and it is my hope and prayer that you will be inspired by the insights, ideas, and PERSPECTIVES presented on these pages.

ACKNOWLEDGMENTS

Over the past 25 years, many people have given me incredible opportunities in my speaking career, for which I will always be grateful. Though it would be impractical to mention everyone who has ever invited me to speak, I must thank Mr. Michael Rothschild, director of the Chofetz Chaim Foundation, Mr. Eli Slomovits and Mrs. Miriam Schrieber of E&S Tours, Rabbi Leibish Becker and Rabbi Avrohom Nissan Perl of Agudath Israel, and Rabbi Elazar Boruch Bald of Irgun Shiurei Torah for the countless times they have called on me to represent their organizations. I thank Hashem that I have gotten to know these remarkable people.

Much of what I say in public has been filtered through the great perceptive Torah mind of my rebbi, Rav Dovid Cohen. He has been my *moreh derech* for more than four decades and I am blessed that I am able to learn with him every week. My closest friend, R' Yaakov Salomon, has guided me with his keen insight into human nature as to what an audience is ready or not ready to hear. I treasure his friendship and counsel.

Only the Ribono Shel Olam Himself can evaluate the monumental contribution that Rav Meir Zlotowitz and Rav Nosson Scherman have made to His people. Stewarding a team of *talmidei chachamim* and highly proficient writers, editors, and graphic artists, Rav Meir and Rav Nosson have set professional standards of presenting Torah that will be a guidepost for decades to come. Our era has come to be known as the ArtScroll Generation and we should feel proud and fortunate that we are part of it. I am forever indebted that they have published my works.

Many thanks to Rabbi Sheah Brander for the attractive page design and to Mendy Herzberg, who steered the project through from start to finish. Thanks are also due to Eli Kroen and Miss Devorah Bloch for the beautiful cover that showcases their artistic talents, and to Miss Rivky Plittman for the professional layout. Thanks, also, to Mrs. Faygie Weinbaum for her meticulous proofreading.

This book has been enhanced by the deft editing of Mrs. Felice Eisner. In her quiet unassuming manner, her way with the printed word is skillful, clever, and precise. She is a nimble word surgeon whose gentle fingerprints adorn the entire manuscript.

The magnificent pictures that beautify the cover are the fruits of the breathtaking camera work of Mr. Joel Berkowitz of Belle Harbor, New York. He has traveled the world, photographing over a thousand shuls and today has over 100,000 shul photos in his portfolio. His pictures decorate the Munkaczer Rebbe's *succah* every year. I thank him for allowing us to use his photos.

Once again I would like to thank R' Yaakov Astor, editor in chief of *Zman Magazine*, and its publishers for their initiative in transforming my lectures to essays. In a relatively short time *Zman Magazine*, with its thoroughness of research and clarity of reporting, has achieved worldwide acclaim. Its deserved reputation and readership grow with each issue.

Just about everything I do would be impossible without the input and encouragement of my wife Miriam. She is simply the editor of my life. Efficiency is her middle name, organization is her credo, and caring for her loved ones (including me) and her students is the essence of her life. That I can be involved in the countless projects that I love is a credit to her selflessness.

May we be *zocheh* to see *nachas* and *brochah* from our dear children and precious grandchildren and may you see the same from yours.

Paysach J. Krohn   Kew Gardens, New York
Tu B'Shvat 5772   February 2012

Insights
of
Inspiration

Reflective Enthusiasm

David HaMelech says in *Tehillim* (119:60): חַשְׁתִּי וְלֹא הִתְמַהְמָהְתִּי לִשְׁמֹר מִצְוֹתֶיךָ, *I hastened and I did not delay to do your mitzvos.* Rabbi Yehuda Trager, a Rosh Yeshivah in Antwerp, asked, "Why does it use a double *lashon* (a synonymous expression)? If David said, 'I hastened,' doesn't that mean 'I didn't delay?'"

Rav Trager answered: "Imagine going out in the morning and seeing a fellow running for the bus trying to get to yeshivah or to shul on time. You think, 'That fellow is a *zariz*; he's really enthusiastic about running to do mitzvos.'"

However, what you don't know is that he woke up 25 minutes late; that's why he's running, or he got involved in so many things in the morning that he didn't plan accordingly.

David HaMelech says, "I was running to do Your mitzvos — *not because I delayed*, but because I had the proper enthusiasm and excitement."

The *Orchos Tzaddikim* writes that the characteristic of *z'rizus* (enthusiasm) is the jewel of *every middah*. In other words, if we have *z'rizus* we can improve anything about ourselves. However, if a person acts in a lackluster manner — if he has no *z'rizus*, no enthusiasm — he will have a hard time changing his ways.

The *Tur*, Rav Yaakov ben Rav Asher (also known as the *Baal HaTurim*), was the first to write a *Shulchan Aruch*, and of all the words he could have chosen to begin his monumental work, it was from a Mishnah on the topic of *z'rizus*:

יְהוּדָה בֶּן תֵּימָא אוֹמֵר: הֱוֵי עַז כַּנָּמֵר, וְקַל כַּנֶּשֶׁר, רָץ כַּצְּבִי, וְגִבּוֹר כָּאֲרִי, לַעֲשׂוֹת רְצוֹן אָבִיךָ שֶׁבַּשָּׁמָיִם. *Yehudah ben Teima says, "Be bold as a leopard, light as an eagle, swift as a deer, and strong as a lion to do the will of your Father in Heaven" (Avos 5:23).*

Let us then not be lax in studying this vital and all-encompassing *middah*.

Waking Up for Selichos

In 1964, there was a *Knessiah Gedolah* in Jerusalem, sponsored by Agudas Yisrael. *Gedolim* and *rabbanim* the world over would be attending and my father thought that it would be a great opportunity for me to meet many of them. I was 19 at the time and had never traveled overseas, but he felt it was the chance of a lifetime. My uncle, Reb Elimelech Tress, who had been the leader of Agudas Yisrael in America for many years, was ill at the time and could not make the trip. My father suggested that I visit *gedolim, rabbanim,* and *askanim* and ask some of them to record a message on my tape recorder to their friend Reb Elimelech Tress. The purpose was twofold: to present a precious memento to my uncle and to get to know these great people.

I did get to see many of them, although admittedly I didn't have the courage to ask such people as the Steipler Gaon (Rav Yaakov Yisrael Kanievsky), Rav Elya Lopian, or Rav Chatzkel Sarna to speak into my tape recorder. However, Rav Zalman Sorotzkin (known as the Lutzker Rov), Reb Itcha Meyer Levin, and Rav Shlomo Lorincz, the great *askanim* of Agudas Yisrael in Israel, gave me beautiful tape-recorded messages, which my uncle treasured the rest of his life. Indeed, as my father predicted, the trip was a life-changing experience for me.

While there I would write to my parents every day, and they would write back. I still have all their precious letters. (In the 1960's, few people in Israel had phones, so writing was the best way to communicate.) In one of the letters my father wrote, "Paysach, you'll be in

Eretz Yisrael almost until Rosh Hashanah, and I once heard that there is a man who walks around certain parts of Yerushalayim at 4 o'clock in the morning to wake up people for *selichos*. Please do me a favor, find him and record that for me."

My first reaction to the letter was, "How and where was I going to find him, if he even exists?" On top of that, tape recorders in those days were large, heavy, reel-to-reel machines. How was I going to carry around this machine at 4 in the morning, going from place to place, not knowing exactly for whom I was looking?

But it was my father who was asking; he had never been to *Eretz Yisrael* and he was living this trip vicariously through me. Thus, a few nights before I was scheduled to leave *Eretz Yisrael*, I asked another American fellow if he wouldn't mind coming with me to try and find this man.

"You're out of your mind," he said to me.

"I know, but I have to do it for my father. At least I can tell him I tried."

Picture the scene: Two American teenagers, one of them carrying this heavy, reel-to-reel tape recorder, walking through the streets and the tiny alleyways near the Bucharian houses in almost total darkness, at 4 in the morning, trying to find some man singing a song to wake up people for *selichos*!

As we were walking around, feeling pretty ridiculous, but also very anxious, I suddenly heard a voice in the distance. Someone was crying out, "*Shteit oif fahr selichos! Shteit oif fahr selichos!* (Get up for *selichos*! Get up for *selichos*!)"

We ran in the direction of the voice and soon spotted the man. You can't imagine how frightened this fellow was when he saw two tall teenagers running toward him!

"Don't be alarmed," I said. "We're from America," as if that would allay his fears.

We introduced ourselves and I said, "Excuse me, but my father asked if you used a certain *nusach*, if you sang a song when you wake people? And if you do, could you possibly let me record you singing?"

He looked at us, puzzled, but then told us that indeed he was the man we were looking for, and I guess he must have pitied me, since he agreed to comply. He cleared his throat, straightened his *kapote* and began in a loud tenor's voice: "*Yisrael, am kadosh, shteit oif la'avodas haboirei, ratz katzvi v'gibor k'ari la'asos r'tzon avicha shebashamayim. Yisrael, am kadosh, shteit oif la'avodas haboirei* [Israel, the holy nation, arise to perform the service for your Creator. Run like a deer, and be strong like a lion to do the will of your Father in heaven. Israel, the Holy Nation, get up for the service of your Creator]." When he finished he turned to us and said, "Okay?"

It was more than okay. It was incredible!

This is what *z'rizus* meant in an earlier generation.

When I came home and played the recording for my father, he considered it the greatest gift I could have brought him. We listened to it dozens and dozens of times. It was so beautiful.

A year later, Rav Sholom Schwadron came to the house and my father said, "Rav Sholom, I want to bring you back to Yerushalayim for a moment." My father played the tape recording and as he did, Rav Sholom closed his eyes and the tears came streaming down his face.

"When I was 4 or 5 years old," he said wistfully, "I used to hear him singing that *niggun*. He was a young man then. It was so *geshmak*, so beautiful. I would listen to the whole thing and then wrap myself in my warm blanket, and go back to sleep."

From Apples to Jewelry

In *Eretz Yisrael*, fruit that grows in the seventh year is called *pairos shvi'is* and has a certain *kedushah* (holiness). You're not allowed to throw away any part of it, even the peel. Hence you must eat the whole thing, and what you don't eat you must wrap up and put in a special place. According to the Rambam, you aren't allowed to give these fruits to non-Jews (*Hilchos Shemittah v'Yovel* 5:13).

One morning on his way out of his house, a yeshivah rebbi in *Eretz Yisrael* noticed two apples in the refrigerator. He figured he'd eat them later. When he came home for lunch he looked in the refrigerator and saw that the apples were missing, so he asked his wife, "Where are the apples?"

"Oh, I gave them to the cleaning lady."

He was shocked and reminded her that they were *pairos shvi'is* and couldn't be given to a non-Jew. "Where is she?" he asked his wife.

She told him that the cleaning woman just left a few minutes ago, so he ran downstairs to the bus stop where the woman should have been. Someone there told him that the bus had already left. He waited, but the next one was long in coming so he took a taxi to the central bus station, where he knew she had to transfer to a different bus.

He got on that bus and saw the woman sitting in the back. Out of breath, he went over to her and said, "Where is the bag?"

Startled to see him, she replied, "Don't touch me. Don't call the police!"

Then she took out a bag full of his wife's jewelry that she had stolen! They were in the bag being covered by the apples! He had no idea that she had stolen anything, but because of his *z'rizus* for the mitzvah of *shvi'is* he got back the jewelry — and the apples.

Reflective Enthusiasm

In Rabbi Shlomo Wolbe's wonderful *sefer*, *Alei Shur*, he writes that the root of the word *ratzon*, which means "desire," is *ratz*, "running." That which a person desires, he runs after.

His father-in-law, Rav Avraham Grodzensky, once said that at times a *zariz*, someone who is enthusiastic, is prone to mistakes, because when one does things quickly one can trip, fall, or make a mistake. Thus, he said, *z'rizus* is not only with the legs, but also, and sometimes primarily, with the head.

This essay is named "*Reflective* Enthusiasm," because in order to achieve anything with enthusiasm, there has to be a thought process before it. You plan and *then* you act with enthusiasm. Running without thinking can easily lead to mistakes. Of course a person has to have *z'rizus*, but you have to think and plan what you are going to do.

I used to drive with Rav Sholom Schwadron, the Maggid of Yerushalayim, when he was in New York and sometimes I would drive a little too fast. He would always say these three words, which he said in a Sefardic dialect: פְּרִי הַמְּהִירוּת הַחֲרָטָה, *The fruit of rushing is regret.*

The fruit of rushing is regret.

If you rush and don't think about what you're going to do, you'll end up regretting.

Many years later, I discovered that this expression came from a *sefer* called *Mivchar HaPeninim* (*Choice Expressions*), written by the Sefardic *gadol* Rabbi Shlomo ibn Gabirol.

Ivan the Zariz

Many of the *brissen* that I do are for people who are not *frum*. A few years ago a Russian fellow, "Ivan," called me from Manhattan. I don't speak Russian and his English wasn't great. I had a feeling that somehow I wasn't communicating with him, but I tried my best to explain to him, "Ivan, the baby was born Tuesday. We have to do the *bris* next Tuesday, since you count the day of the baby's birth as day one."

"Okay," he said, "can we do at night?"

"By Jewish law we must do it by day, preferably in the morning," I replied.

"Rabbi," he said, "we can't do in the morning. I have work. All my friends have work. I can only do at night or late in the day. What would be the latest we can do it?"

"It really should be done in the morning," I said, "but if necessary we could do it right before sunset." Sunset was 4:30, so we arranged it for 4 o'clock.

That Tuesday I drove from my home in Kew Gardens to Manhattan, parked the car, entered the building for which I had the address, and came to the floor of his apartment. Usually, by the time I get out of the elevator and make my way toward the apartment where the *bris* is to be held, I can hear chatter, laughter, and voices of people at a festive occasion. This time I didn't hear anything. My first reaction was that they were having the *bris* someplace else but forgot to tell me. I knocked on the front door and the grandmother opened it. She was in a housecoat.

"I'm Rabbi Krohn," I said. "Aren't we having a *bris* here today?"

She invited me in to talk to her daughter, who was sitting on the couch with the baby.

"I'm Rabbi Krohn," I repeated. "Aren't we having a *bris* here today?"

"I knew my husband didn't understand!" she said. "He thinks it's tomorrow at 4 o'clock!"

"But I thought I made it quite clear that it's Tuesday."

"I told him to call you last night," she said.

"What are we going to do?" I asked.

"Let's call my husband," she said. "He's in the gym working out."

She called him and handed me the phone. "Ivan," I said, "I'm sorry I wasn't clear enough, but the *bris* should be *today* before 4:30."

I was waiting for him to tell me, "Sorry, Rabbi, come back tomorrow," but instead he said, "How much time do we have?"

"Twenty-five minutes," I said.

"I'll be there."

He came running in, still wearing his gym clothes, asking what he had to do. I told him to freshen up because he would be the *sandek*. We did the *bris* and finished with five minutes to spare before sunset and then I told him, "Ivan, don't tell anybody what went on here today. I'm coming back tomorrow at 4 o'clock when everyone you invited will be here."

The next day I returned and this time, when I got off the elevator, there was a whole cacophony of noise coming from the apartment. I set up as though I would be doing a *bris* and I had them bring out the baby in front of the whole crowd. Then I put my arm around Ivan and said, "Friends, you should know what kind of special friend you have here. Deep down, Ivan is a committed Jew. There had been a misunderstanding, but in reality the eighth day was yesterday. Ivan knew that you were all coming today, but in his enthusiasm to do the mitzvah properly, we did it yesterday with no one here except for Ivan and me, his wife and mother-in-law, and, of course, the baby. You can be so proud of your friend because even though he never had the opportunity of yeshivah training in Russia, his heart told him what was right." I embraced him and everyone cheered.

The festive occasion went on as everyone made a *berachah* over wine. I explained the significance of the ceremony and the baby's Hebrew name and everyone had their bagels and lox (and some vodka). I still cannot get over the *z'rizus* and commitment of Ivan. The man was not religious, yet he understood the importance of doing a mitzvah properly.

When Opportunity Knocks

One of the definitions of a *zariz* is someone who answers a call, seizes an opportunity, and is there in a time of need while others just stand by the wayside.

In 1941, there was a *shochet* in Gateshead, Rav Dovid Drian, who wrote 22 letters to *rabbanim* all over England, pleading with them to please come to Gateshead and help him start a *kollel*. Out of those 22 letters, 18 *rabbanim* didn't even answer him. Three said no. The only one who answered yes was the 51-year-old Rabbi Eliyahu Dessler.

Rabbi Dessler came to Gateshead, started the *kollel,* and raised the level of Torah in northern England and thereby changed the course of Torah history throughout the United Kingdom and even Europe. Why? Because there was an opportunity and he seized it.

Let's think for a moment about people in our generation who have gone with ideas and accomplished incredible things. Is there any Jewish, English-speaking home *in the world* that does not have an ArtScroll *sefer* or book? I have been to many countries throughout the Jewish world and wherever I go there are ArtScroll publications.

ArtScroll was started by two American young men, Rabbis Meir Zlotowitz and Nosson Scherman. How did it begin? A young married man who had no children, Reb Meir Fogel, was *niftar* in 1976. His friend, Rabbi Meir Zlotowitz, wanted to do something *l'zecher nishmaso*, so he, Rabbi Nosson Scherman, and Rabbi Sheah Brander swiftly put together what has become a classic, the ArtScroll *Megillas Esther*, in time for Purim. That's how ArtScroll was started: with *z'rizus*. The rest is history.

Michael Rothschild is the founder of the Chofetz Chaim Heritage Foundation, having been inspired by the Manchester Rosh Yeshivah, Rabbi Yehudah Zev Segal. More than 20 years ago, after I had already spoken numerous times on behalf of the organization, he called me and asked, "How would you like to speak before 20,000 or 30,000 people?" I thought he was joking. What was he going to do, rent Madison Square Garden or Yankee Stadium?

He told me that he had an idea. He would have me speak at BYA (Bais Yaakov Academy) in Brooklyn, have it filmed by Shmuel Borger, the best videographer available, and then, come Tishah B'Av, he would show it in every shul, camp, and Jewish center across the country. This was years ago. Now, these special videos for Tishah B'Av reach *60,000* people around the world.

One fellow believed in himself and changed the way people around the Jewish world think about Tishah B'Av. One person seized an opportunity and he influences tens of thousands *every* year!

One of our greatest problems is that we don't believe in ourselves. We think, "Who am I? What can I do? I'm not significant; no one will listen to me. Am I going to really accomplish anything?"

> **It says in *Tzidkas HaTzaddik*: "Just as you are supposed to believe in Hashem, you must believe in yourself."**

It says in *Tzidkas HaTzaddik*: "Just as you are supposed to believe in Hashem, you must believe in yourself."

A number of years ago at the Agudah Convention, my good friend Yaakov Salomon made a suggestion that there be a place for children who are otherwise on the streets. Two fellows, Rabbi Yitzchak Mitnick and R' Moshe Binik, were in the audience and they liked the idea. They and others eventually opened *Our Place*, which has saved so many youngsters from trouble and turmoil. Indeed, many have returned to authentic *Yiddishkeit*. Of course, it did not hurt that Rav Yitzchak Mitnick was able to challenge every one of the boys to an arm wrestle and win every match! They regarded him as a man of strength and character. No wonder he could inspire them.

> **"Yesterday is history, tomorrow is a mystery, today is a gift of G-d — that's why we call it the present."**

Recently on a trip to Baltimore I met a geriatrician, Dr. Menachem Cooper, who told me he has a patient, Mrs. Yetta Herman, who taught him a little poem that made a lasting impression on him. It's worth repeating: "Yesterday is history, tomorrow is a mystery, today is a gift of G-d — that's why we call it the present."

That's a great thought: Every day is a present from Hashem. Why worry about tomorrow? Who knows what will be then? Whatever happened in the past is done. Make the most of today, seize the opportunities before you! There is much to accomplish! Let's get to it!

From Past Pain
to Future Gain

Rabbi Krohn delivered the followed lecture in the home of Mrs. Sarah Rivkah Kohn, the founder of LINKS, an organization created to give support to teenagers who have lost a parent.

I know from personal experience that when somebody becomes a *yasom* (orphan), emotions become more intensified. Pain is greater, loneliness is sharper, and humiliation is deeper. I know that all of you assembled here tonight can relate to these emotions because you have all gone through what I did.

Yet, on the other hand, friendships are more powerful and achievements are more fulfilling. This topic is such a personal, emotional matter for me that I had to give it in person rather than via phone conference as was originally planned.

As you know, I have written a number of books, now known as the Maggid series, which started with the stories of the *Maggid* of Yerushalayim, Rabbi Sholom Schwadron. My family became very close to him when he came to America for the first time and stayed in our home throughout his six-month visit. My parents were his gracious hosts. However, by the second time he came, my father had passed away. Rav Sholom himself was orphaned as a young boy and was so sensitive to orphans and widows. He treated my mother with the greatest *derech eretz*. It was amazing how he spoke to her and how concerned he was for her.

Rabbi Avrohom Yosef Lazersohn, the leader of Chinuch Atzmai in Israel, told me that he became a *yasom* before his bar mitzvah. He was a nephew of Rav Sholom. At his bar mitzvah, Rav Sholom gave him a *sefer* as a gift. The thing that struck him was the inscription. Rav Sholom at that time had to be over 40, maybe even 50, when he signed it. He inscribed a blessing, and before signing his name, he wrote the words "*Kamoni kamocha* — I am just like you." In other words, even at 40 or 50 Rav Schwadron still felt that he was a *yasom*. That's the message he wanted to convey to this bar mitzvah boy: we're in it together. Once a person is a *yasom* at a vulnerable age, he remains a *yasom* forever. We have to learn how to cope with it, but that emptiness is always there.

> ... even at 40 or 50, Rav Schwadron still felt that he was a *yasom*.

The Surviving Spouse

The *Gemara* states, אֵין אִישׁ מֵת אֶלָּא לְאִשְׁתּוֹ ... וְאֵין אִשָּׁה מֵתָה אֶלָּא לְבַעְלָה, *A man dies only to his wife, and a woman dies only to her husband* (Sanhedrin 22b). What *Chazal* are teaching is that all the pain that orphans and other relatives feel is not as bad as the pain that the spouse feels. A person who loses a spouse suffers forever. Some women and men can get over it. For others the tragedy stays forever.

Therefore, the first lesson that we have to learn is that, as painful as it is to be an orphan, we have to remember that we need to be sensitive and give *chizuk* to the parent who is alive. His/her pain is forever. You'll get married, *b'ezras Hashem*, and have children. However, we must never forget to be sensitive to the surviving parent's pain.

The Phone Call

Every Friday I call a little girl. I've been calling this little girl since she was 10 or 11. She comes from a broken home; her father has no connection to her whatsoever. I call her every Friday to give her a *berachah*. I say the words that fathers bless their daughters with every Friday night, יְשִׂמֵךְ אֱלֹקִים כְּשָׂרָה רִבְקָה רָחֵל וְלֵאָה, *May Hashem make you like Sarah, Rivkah, Rachel, and Leah.*

One Friday, as I was preparing to call her I thought of a question I had never considered before. Every one of the *Imahos* (Matriarchs) had a hard life. Sarah didn't have children for a very long time. Rivkah's husband was blind and she had Esav. Rachel had no children for the longest time and Leah felt she was hated. What kind of blessing is this that we give our daughters in *Klal Yisrael?*

The answer came to me in the *zechus* of this little girl. The reason is that all four *Imahos* overcame their obstacles. They all remained with their *emunah*, their connections to Hashem and their husbands. That's a blessing to every girl in *Klal Yisrael*. No matter what happens in your life, be like Sarah, Rivkah, Rachel, and Leah. Do not let life break you. Build your life and a family and remain connected to Hashem.

[I offered those at the lecture and those listening by phone conference that they, too, could receive a *berachah* every Friday afternoon if they wished. All they needed to do was register once with the organization, LINKS, by dialing 718-305-6080, and every Friday they would hear a recorded *berachah* pertinent for that week. As of now 300 individuals receive calls at 1 p.m. every Erev Shabbos and Yom Tov. If you or an orphaned friend wishes to hear this LINKS *berachah,* you can register by calling the aforementioned phone number.]

Sully to the Rescue

All of you probably know part of the following story, but the last part will likely come as a big surprise. On January 15, 2009, US Airways Flight 1549 took off from LaGuardia airport in New York. Its captain was Chesley Burnett Sullenberger III; everyone called him "Sully." There were more than 150 people on the flight. A minute-and-a-half into the flight, a flock of birds was sucked into the engines of the plane and caused them to stall.

Captain Sullenberger immediately realized that the engines were dead and the plane was now flying only on its takeoff momentum and some auxiliary power. He radioed LaGuardia airport and told them that he had an emergency. He could not even make it back to LaGuardia. The next closest airport was in Teterboro, New Jersey, but he quickly calculated that it, too, was out of his reach.

Captain Sullenberger immediately realized that the engines were dead and the plane was now flying only on its takeoff momentum.

Down below was the great city of Manhattan with its millions of people. He knew that he was going to have to crash-land the plane somewhere. If he tried to land it on one of the highways he probably would kill not only everyone on board but many people on the ground as well. In a split second he made the decision to land the plane in the Hudson River. He knew that in an emergency landing on water, the nose of the plane had to be up and the wings perfectly level. Just a few years previously, a plane tried it, did not land perfectly level in the water, and broke up, killing most on board.

We all know the unbelievable miracle that happened. He called out to the flight attendants to tell everyone to brace for impact, and then landed the plane on water as though he had done it hundreds of times before. Everybody was saved — 150 passengers, plus four crew members. Incredible!

Later, during an interview they asked him how he had the courage and determination to keep his cool. Listen to what he said. When he was very young, his father died and it taught him how precious life was. He made up his mind then that for the rest of his life he will save or enhance any life he could.

Can you imagine? He understood what loneliness was all about. He realized what it meant to be without a parent. And that gave him a certain superhuman determination for the rest of his life to save lives. Isn't that incredible? He envisioned the sadness and tragedy that would befall all the relatives of those on board and that gave him the strength and fortitude to do what he did.

Mrs. Sarah Rivkah Kohn, the founder of LINKS, lost her mother when she was 9. That is one of the reasons that LINKS was started.

She saw the pain of others and with sensitivity and determination created this wonderful organization.

There are so many people out there in pain. Through our own pain we can become more sensitive to someone who is sick or to someone who has lost a family member. If we see a kid at risk, or a child who is challenged and needs tutoring, we can become more sensitive and helpful. Becoming more sensitive to those who still need *shidduchim* can be a by-product of our situation. People who have gone through their own pain have a greater capacity to feel the pain of others, get involved, and follow through with help and concern.

Hashem gave us an opportunity when He gave us our pain, and because of that we'll grow and become better people. When Hashem does something to us, there's a reason. Of course we'd rather that it didn't happen, but once it has happened, we have to learn from the pain and make sure that no one else has to go through this pain alone.

The Anonymous Heroines

Let me tell you a story about two wonderful girls, true heroines, who do not want me to divulge their names. In my opinion, their act should have made headlines in every paper.

These two sisters went paddle-boating in Prospect Park on Chol HaMoed Succos. They noticed a father and his two little boys in a boat near them. The boys were wearing life vests, but the father was not. All of a sudden, a gust of wind blew off the yarmulke of one of the boys, who was perhaps 4 years old, and it fell into the water. He reached to grab it and fell into the water himself.

The father instinctively jumped into the water to save the boy. From where they were, the girls could not see the father or the boy. Then, half a minute later (which felt like a year), the father emerged with the boy, who was coughing and choking. Even though the child was wearing a life vest, he had gone under the water and almost drowned.

However, now the father could not get into the boat. He was afraid that if he hoisted himself in he would tip the whole thing. He didn't have a life vest and was holding on for dear life to that boat.

One of the girls took out her cell phone and immediately called 911. Then they began to paddle toward the father's boat. His face was already pale and he was losing strength. He was probably freezing by now and frightened that he was going to die. These girls had lost their father and were determined not to let the two little boys in the boat lose their father as well.

They pulled their boat alongside his, but couldn't lift him up. Instead, they positioned their boat in a way that he was able to keep himself afloat by holding onto both crafts. Meanwhile, he was losing strength. After what seemed like forever, the exhausted father finally somehow hoisted himself into the boat where his children were. As he was lying on his back, the girls thought he had died because they saw how shocked, pale, and frightened he had been.

After what seemed like an eternity, a helicopter appeared, as well as a police boat. They escorted the man's boat to shore where *Hatzolah* was waiting. Everyone was so busy that no one ever asked how this man had been saved. Only these two sisters at the scene knew. Only they knew that they had the determination to help because of what they had gone through; they didn't want another child to suffer as they had suffered.

In my humble opinion, what a *zechus* for their father! What a *kibud av v'eim*! What a tremendous mitzvah! Nobody knows who they are and I am not at liberty to reveal their identity. The lesson here is that wonderful people took their *tzaar*, their pain, saved a life and made sure a family did not become orphaned.

Reb Elchonon

Many *yesomim* and *yesomos* feel sorry that they can't fulfill the mitzvah of *kibud av v'eim*, whether it was a father or a mother who passed away. I want to share something with you.

Rav Elchonon Wasserman, *hy'd*, was head of the yeshivah in Baranovitch. He had the opportunity to ride out World War II safe in America, but voluntarily returned to Europe in 1939 to be with his students, despite the Nazi threat (which eventually took his life). His son, Rabbi Simcha Wasserman, *zt'l*, told me that there is no picture of his father smiling. He was always very serious. Who could blame him, trying to avert the coming Nazi whirlwind in the tense years between world wars and then during the Holocaust? It was a terrible time for *Klal Yisrael*.

In my recent book, *In the Spirit of the Maggid*, I relate the story of how Rav Elchonon was once in Chicago and was teaching a little girl who had lost her father how to say *Modeh Ani*. Today, she is Rebbetzin Nechama Doba Groner, principal of the Bnos Yisroel School for Girls in Flatbush. Rav Elchonon taught her the *aleph-beis* and *Shema* as well. He used to walk her up and down the porch, making sure to smile for this little *yesomah*. He went out of his way to be friendly to her because she had no father.

When Rav Elchonon would go to England, Rabbi Asher Shternbuch took him around to collect money. Sadly R' Asher passed away at a young age. I can tell you from personal experience how my house changed after my father, Rabbi Avrohom Zelig Krohn, passed away. My father was a tremendous *tzaddik* and *baal chessed*. The house was always busy with people constantly coming in and out for advice, encouragement, and moral support. However, after my father was *niftar*, *rabbanim* felt uncomfortable coming to the house and the many guests who had come in the past suddenly stopped coming, fearing it would be too much for a widow to handle. The house changed.

Because he realized this, every time Rav Elchonon went to England he made sure to visit Rebbetzin Devorah Shternbuch. She had a teenage daughter, Leah, a *yesomah*, who collected money for his yeshivah and Rav Elchonon corresponded with her. Can you imagine the *gadol hador* taking his time to do this? I saw a letter he wrote on the stationery of his Yeshivah Ohel Torah, in Baranovitch.

> *To the orphaned children of my dear friend, R' Asher,*
>
> *I very much want to know how each of you are doing and how the learning is going [for the boys]. I want to tell you something. A person can fulfill the mitzvah of kibud av v'eim even after a father or mother passes away. If a person does mitzvos, learns Torah, makes berachos aloud, answers amen — everything he does fulfills the mitzvah of kibud av v'eim, because the parent in Shamayim wants the children to be good. Every mitzvah they do is a mitzvah of kibud av v'eim. The parent is honored in Shamayim.*

I want to tell you another thing. Yesomim and yesomos have a special zechus to ask Hashem more than others to have rachmanus on them. It says in Tehillim (68:6) that Hashem is the father of all the orphans.

What *chizuk* and what compassion!

Kibud av v'eim is a mitzvah a person can do even after a parent passes away. No one should feel remorse that he/she hasn't done enough. He/she has done plenty and he/she can continue to do more even after a parent's passing.

Rav Schwab on Bitachon

I want to share with you something very personal. I was 21 when my father passed away. I was the eldest of seven children, and when I was 20 my father was already very sick.

I was in Yeshiva Torah Vodaas at the time. My father was a *mohel* and during his illness he made sure I learned *milah*. I often accompanied him, especially during summers, to learn how to do *brissen* but it never occurred to me that, at 20, I'd have to learn it quickly to support my mother and younger brothers and sisters. I was in denial and didn't want to believe it. I thought my father would get better.

One Shabbos, my brother Kolman and I were guests of Rav Shimon Schwab, *zt'l*, the rav of the Washington Heights community. (He had been my father's rebbi in Yeshiva Ner Yisroel.) We stayed in his house for Shabbos, because it was near the hospital where my father was a patient. After Mussaf, we went to the hospital and then when we came back to eat the meal, Rav Schwab asked me how my father was.

"I have *bitachon* he'll be well," I replied. I'll never forget his firm, instructive comment.

A stern look came over his face and he said, "*Bitachon*, faith in Hashem, doesn't mean your father will get better. Faith means that Hashem has a master plan and, hopefully, one day you'll be able to understand it. Sometimes terrible things happen, but that doesn't mean we shouldn't have *bitachon*. *Bitachon* means that we have faith in Hashem, and until *Mashiach* comes we can't know why a terrible thing had to happen. *Bitachon* means we don't give up. And that is why we must constantly give *chizuk* to one another."

The Secret of Happiness

I saw a great expression yesterday: The happiest people don't necessarily have the best of everything. They just make the best of everything they have.

> **The happiest people don't necessarily have the best of everything. They just make the best of everything they have.**

Isn't that a great expression? That's our role. We don't have everything. We no longer have that parent. Nevertheless, we have to make the best of it.

How do we make the best of it? I once heard this wonderful *vort* from Rav Pam, *zt'l*: People are always looking for the city of happiness, but they don't realize that it's in the state of mind.

> **People are always looking for the city of happiness, but they don't realize it's in the state of mind.**

That's what we need to focus on. Will we allow ourselves to be broken and sad? We all go through a period of grief, but eventually we need to make the best of what we have, not feel that we need to have everything.

The Wings of a Bird

Rabbi Mattisyahu Salomon taught a beautiful idea. The *Midrash* (*Vayikra Rabbah* 11:8) compares *Klal Yisrael* to a bird. "Just as a bird can't fly without wings, so, too, *Klal Yisrael* can't do anything without its *gedolim*."

Rav Mattisyahu asks, "What does the *Midrash* mean that a bird can't get around without wings? It certainly can. It can hop along from place to place!"

However, he answers, the *Midrash* says that a bird can't "fly" — *pore'ach* — without wings. *Pore'ach* also means "to blossom" — to grow and shine and to fulfill your potential. If a bird wants to

> ***Pore'ach* also means "to blossom" — to grow and shine and to fulfill your potential. If a bird wants to soar high, it needs its wings.**

soar high, it needs its wings. So, too, if we want to soar, we need a relationship to a *gadol*.

Every one of us — every family — must have a Rav, Rebbe, or Rosh Yeshivah to ask questions of. If you can't ask the question, ask your parent to ask it. Either way, you need to have a *gadol* with whom you have a connection. It doesn't have to be Rav Yosef Shalom Elyashiv or Rav Aaron Leib Shteinman; they are hard to reach. The idea is that everyone has to have somebody that, in effect, connects him to *Har Sinai*. When you have a Rav, Rebbe, or Rosh Yeshivah to whom you can ask your questions, open up your heart to, and get guidance from, then you'll soar. Then, you'll fly high. Then, you'll blossom. That's what the *Midrash* tells us.

Bedamayich Chayi

The Klausenberger Rebbe lost his wife and 11 children during the Holocaust. Can you imagine that *gehinnom*! They asked him, years after the war, how so many Holocaust survivors were able to rebuild their lives. The Rebbe said the answer is two words: בְּדָמַיִךְ חֲיִי.

We say these words on two different occasions: at a *bris* and in reading the *Haggadah*. The literal meaning is, "In your blood you shall live." The Rebbe explained that at a *bris* the *mohel* says it because the night the Jews went out of *Mitzrayim* they couldn't eat the *korban Pesach* unless they had a *bris milah*. Imagine a man who just had a *bris*. There's some blood, pain, and weakness. And then shortly after the *bris*, he has to run out of *Mitzrayim*!

בְּדָמַיִךְ, *in your blood* (in the *zechus* of the blood of *bris milah*) — חֲיִי, *they "lived."* That's why we say it at a *bris*.

Why do we say it at the *Seder*? We know that a few days before the first *Pesach*, the Jews slaughtered sheep, and sheep were worshiped as gods in *Mitzrayim*. Under normal circumstances the Egyptians would have killed the Jews for doing so. Here, though, the Jews were *moser nefesh*; they risked their lives, and the Egyptians did nothing. בְּדָמַיִךְ, in the *zechus* of that bloodshed in the *schechting* of the sheep, חֲיִי, they merited to live.

The Rebbe explained, "When Aharon lost his two children, the *pasuk* describes his reaction as, וַיִּדֹּם אַהֲרֹן, *Aharon was quiet* [*Vayikra*

10:3]. בִּדְמָיָךְ shares the same root as וַיִּדֹּם, 'quiet.' In their quietness, חָיִי, 'they lived.' "

Of course we can focus on the negative, and a person who has *tzaaros* can focus on the *tzaaros*, saying things like, "How could Hashem do this to me?"

However, בִּדְמָיָךְ, if a person is quiet, similar to the word וַיִּדֹּם, and only focuses on the positive, then חָיִי, he can live.

We all have a lot of good. We have our lives. There's much to be grateful for. Of course, we went through *gehinnom* and a difficult time, but בִּדְמָיָךְ חָיִי. Focus only on the positive: on the wonderful parent we do have, on the friends that we have, on the mentors that we have, on the siblings that we have, on the wonderful support of LINKS. In *Modim*, say "thank You" for LINKS.

Gratitude

R' Chananya Chalak told me this story. He heads *Ezer Mizion*, a great medical organization in *Eretz Yisrael* that distributes medicines, prescriptions, and medical advice to people who can't afford them. He told me that someone from Europe called and said he wanted to come to see him and give him a donation. Eventually they met in Chananya's office in Jerusalem.

Afterwards, Chananya asked if he had *davened* Maariv yet. He said no, so Chananya suggested that they go to the *Kotel*. They got there and saw someone *davening* with all his heart and with his hands raised to the sky. Their hearts went out to him. As they observed this gentleman, Chananya remarked, "Look how the fellow is *davening*. We have to help him. Whatever he needs medically, I'll help him. Whatever he needs financially, are you ready to help him?"

"Yes, anything," came the quick reply.

After he finished *davening* they went over to him and said, "Good evening, Reb Yid. How are you doing?"

"*Baruch Hashem*, everything is fine."

"We'd like to help you out."

"What do you mean? Everything is fine."

"My name is Chananya Chalak. I have a very large medical organization here in *Eretz Yisrael*. Anything your family needs, medically, we can help. If it's not medical, but financial, my friend here can help you."

"No, everything is fine."

"What do you mean? We saw you *davening*. You *davened* like the world was coming to an end."

"Let me tell you, then. Last night, my wife and I married off our youngest child. Tonight, I came to the *Kotel* to say 'thank You' to *Hashem*."

Imagine — that's how the fellow *davened* when he was saying, "thank You"!

That's what we have to do. We need to have *hakaras hatov*. Of course we went through difficult times, there's no question about it, but we must begin to look at all the good that we have in this world.

Gozer U'mekayaim

When the Skulener Rebbe, Rav Eliezer Zusia Portugal, was in Romania, he and his wife raised hundreds of children in their home. Many of them didn't have parents. The Portugals were absolutely remarkable people. It wasn't only orphans whom they raised, but at times if a *bachur* didn't want to go to the army, he would come to the Rebbe and hide in his house. The Rebbe would accept him because he knew if the *bachur* went to the army he'd end up without any semblance of *Yiddishkeit*.

One day, someone informed the authorities that the Rebbe was hiding boys who were evading the army. The authorities came and put the Rebbe in jail. He sat in that tiny cell convinced he would die there.

They say that his *Shemoneh Esrei* took more than half an hour each day. When the Rebbe came to *Baruch She'amar* — and specifically to the words, גּוֹזֵר וּמְקַיֵּם, *He makes a decree and fulfills it* — he wondered how it fit there. *Baruch She'amar* begins by thanking and blessing Hashem for all the good things in life — and then it says גּוֹזֵר וּמְקַיֵּם. A *gezeirah*/decree is a terrible thing. What does it mean that He makes it and fulfills it? The Rebbe was so angry at himself for never thinking of this question before. He had been *davening Baruch She'amar* all of his life. Hashem decrees a terrible thing and fulfills it. How does that fit in with the rest of the upbeat, positive *tefillah*?

The Rebbe then said, "Hashem, don't take me out of here until I think of the answer." After a while the answer came to him. Hashem makes a *gezeirah* — and וּמְקַיֵּם — simultaneously gives us the קִיּוּם, the "strength," to make it through that difficult time.

That's how it fits into the theme of *Baruch She'amar*. Even though, for whatever reason — we won't know until *Mashiach* comes why we had to go through that difficult time — nevertheless, Hashem is גּוֹזֵר וּמְקַיֵּם — He gives us the strength to withstand the *gezeirah*, to not be broken by it, to live through the terrible time and hopefully even grow from it. גּוֹזֵר וּמְקַיֵּם.

Hashem has given each of us the strength and the fortitude to carry on in life. May we give from that strength to one another so that we can lead lives in which we all will be productive, inspirational, and committed to the *Ribono Shel Olam* and His people.

Problems and Possibilities in the Secular Workplace

In the *Shemoneh Esrei* that we recite every day of the week, we ask for things we need: wisdom, forgiveness, healing, the rebuilding of Yerushalayim, etc. One of the most important things we can ask for is *berachah*, "blessing." And indeed when we ask for *berachah*, we ask over and over and over again, using it as our request for *parnassah* (*Bareich Aleinu*). If you *daven nusach Ashkenaz*, you ask for *berachah* four times; if you *daven nusach Sefard*, you ask for *berachah* six times.

Why do we ask so many times for *berachah* specifically during the request for *parnassah*? It occurred to me that perhaps because, in truth, *parnassah* is a curse. Hashem cursed Adam (*Bereishis* 3:19), בְּזֵעַת אַפֶּיךָ תֹּאכַל לֶחֶם, *By the sweat of your brow you will have to eat bread*. You will have to sweat to make *parnassah*. Therefore, every day we say to *Hashem*, You gave us this *k'lalah*, this curse; please give us *berachah* and take away that *k'lalah*.

And the truth is that it's a terrible shame. We could have had it so easy.

The *Gemara* says in *Sanhedrin* (59b) that we had a wonderful opportunity to acquire a helper, but it was lost. If the *nachash* (snake) hadn't been cursed, everyone would have had two good snakes as servants to do anything they wanted. Rav Yaakov Kaminetzky, *zt'l*, writes (*Emes L'Yaakov, Bereishis* 3:14) that before it was cursed, the *nachash* had intelligence like that of a human being. It was able to speak and would have taken care of all of our *parnassah* needs. But when the *nachash* was cursed, Rav Yaakov explains, its *seichel* (humanlike intelligence) was taken, too. It was cursed to crawl on its belly and we were left בְּזֵעַת אַפֶּיךָ תֹּאכַל לֶחֶם. Now we have to sweat to make money.

Antagonism, Ignorance, Obscenity

The curse of בְּזֵעַת אַפֶּיךָ תֹּאכַל לֶחֶם has been expanded today. It's not only the men who are cursed by having to go out to make *parnassah*, but many women must work outside the home as well. Besides the obvious immorality and contaminated atmosphere in the typical secular workforce, a person faces more subtle forms of challenging influences all the time. I'll give you examples of three types: demeaning antagonism, ignorance, and obscenity.

Antagonism:

Doctors in their residency are required to be on call in the hospital certain times during the year. Numerous doctors have told me about the clashes they have had with irreligious Jews overseeing them. For example, a religious obstetrician I know told me that when she was in a hospital, the director, an irreligious Jew, made her come in on Yom Kippur.

She had no choice but to come in, but she insisted that she be placed in the labor and delivery section. (She felt that the *pikuach nefesh* element involved in delivering a baby gave her a more sound reason *halachically* to be there.) Still, she couldn't avoid confrontation. As she was in the doctors' lounge on Yom Kippur, an irreligious Jewish doctor was sipping coffee. "It's Yom Kippur today," she said to him.

"You know," he replied snidely, "I don't think that lightning is going to strike me if I have another sip of coffee." She couldn't imagine a non-Jew speaking to her in such a disrespectful manner. That's an example of antagonism from an irreligious Jew.

Ignorance:

Here is an example of ignorance. I have a friend who is a psychologist, R' Byrech Lehrer. The first position that he ever had as a psychologist was in Ridgeway, Pennsylvania, which proudly calls itself elk country. They have a tradition that on the first day of the hunting season, school is closed so fathers and sons can go hunting.

It was nearing Rosh Hashanah and R' Byrech's wife was expecting a baby. The closest shul to Ridgeway was two hours away in Williamsport, but since his wife was expecting, he had to stay in Ridgeway. He purchased a *shofar* in Williamsport and brought it back to Ridgeway, elk country, and practiced blow-

> **"You must be a great hunter. Your moose calls are terrific."**

ing *shofar* every day. One day a fellow calls him and says, "You must be a great hunter. Your moose calls are terrific." That's ignorance. While it's not as bad as antagonism, it can wear on a person.

Obscenity:

The last subtle, (really, not-so-subtle) negative influence I want to mention is, unfortunately, all too common in the general workplace today. Indeed, it is so deeply ingrained in the culture that while even non-Jews of earlier generations who were not particularly righteous would be appalled at it, those of more recent generations think nothing of it. I'm talking about the use of obscenities, *nivel peh*.

There is a very frightening *Gemara* (*Kesubos* 8b) that says, כָּל הַמְנַבֵּל פִּיו וּמוֹצִיא דְּבַר נְבָלָה מִפִּיו, אֲפִילוּ נֶחְתַּם לוֹ גְזַר דִין שֶל שִבְעִים שָנָה לְטוֹבָה – נֶהְפָּךְ עָלָיו לְרָעָה, *Even if a person is destined to have 70 years of good, it will all be torn up and turned to bad if he uses nivel peh.* We don't know why there are so many *tzaaros*, but the *Gemara* is telling us that a person who becomes so used to *nivel peh* that it becomes part of his everyday speech, *chas v'shalom*, is putting at risk a lifetime of potential good.

People who would never talk like that in shul or at home find that their vocabulary suddenly becomes more "colorful" in the workplace. It's a slippery slope.

The entire secular workplace is a slippery slope. How can people who perforce operate there deal with it?

Strangers in a Strange Land

We need to take our cue from Yaakov Avinu. In essence, he dealt with the problem of working in the "secular workplace" when he lived with his father-in-law, Lavan, a master crook, fraud, and con man.

Yet, after living with Lavan for 20 years, Yaakov could say, עִם לָבָן גַּרְתִּי, *I sojourned with Lavan* (*Bereishis* 32:5). As *Rashi* explains, עִם לָבָן גַּרְתִּי וְתַרְיַ״ג מִצְוֹת שָׁמַרְתִּי, *I lived together with Lavan, but guarded all 613 mitzvos.*

Rav Yaakov Kaminetzky asks: How was Yaakov able to keep תַּרְיַ״ג מִצְוֹת in Lavan's work environment?

He said the answer is in the words: עִם לָבָן גַּרְתִּי. Yaakov says he was a *ger* (root of *garti*). He was a "stranger." He was different. He was distinctive. If you consider yourselves different from the people you work with — עִם לָבָן גַּרְתִּי — then you guard the *mitzvos* — וְתַרְיַ״ג מִצְוֹת שָׁמַרְתִּי (the words גַּרְתִּי and תַּרְיַ״ג consist of the same letters).

I Am a Jew

Rabbi Yissachar Frand told me a very interesting story. Somebody came to visit the Brisker Rav, Rav Velvel Soloveitchik. During the conversation, the Brisker Rav asked him, "What are you?"

"I'm a lawyer," the fellow said.

"What are you?" the Rav asked again.

"Rebbe, I'm a lawyer."

"That's not how a Jew is supposed to answer that question," he explained. "A Jew is supposed to answer what Yonah answered the people when they asked him, מַה מְּלַאכְתֶּךָ, *What is your job*, what do you do?, Yonah answered, עִבְרִי אָנֹכִי, *I am a Jew*" (*Yonah* 8:9).

That's how a Jew answers: not that I'm a lawyer, accountant, or doctor. That's how you earn *parnassah*. That's not who you are. You are an עִבְרִי.

Avraham was called an עִבְרִי, the *Midrash* (*Bereishis Rabbah* 42:8) tells us, because the world was on one side and he was on the other side. He was not afraid to stand out as different. When you walk into the workplace, you are a *ger*: you are distinctive, different, and separate. You are an עִבְרִי. If you have that in your mindset, then you will make *gedarim* (protective fences) and understand that no matter what you see there, you are not like them. What you do for a living is not what you are.

A while ago I had the opportunity to go to Antwerp. I went to (now-defunct) Sabena Airlines in JFK. Everyone was checking in and it was very crowded. I felt uncomfortable. Then a representative from the airline came around and asked people if they were checking in to first class, business, or economy.

"Where I sit doesn't make a difference," I told him. "I'm a first-class guy."

"I like that," he said. "Go check in at first class." (However, he didn't give me a first-class ticket but allowed me to check in with the first-class passengers.)

What I do or where I sit — does it affect who I am? I'm an עִבְרִי. It doesn't make a difference how I bring in *parnassah*.

I have a very close friend, a pulmonologist, who went to a medical conference. Five Jewish doctors and 20 non-Jewish doctors were going to be there. The caterer was going to obtain airline meals for these five doctors until one of the doctors said to the caterer, "I will pay you to have all the dishes look the same so that we shouldn't appear different." (He was going to have the airline meals placed on plates that looked like all the other plates in the catering hall.)

As soon as this doctor left, my friend called the caterer and said, "I'll pay you double, but our plates should be different from the other plates. I don't want to camouflage the fact that we are different. Let them know we eat on this kind of plate and they eat on that kind of plate."

They Know

And don't think you can hide it. No matter where you go in the world, they know you are a Jew. Whether you have a beard or not, whether you are wearing a yarmulke or not — they know.

Somebody told me a story about the time he attended a business conference at Bayer Pharmaceutical, the company that makes Bayer aspirin. It was a major conference held in Germany, with representatives from all over the world in attendance. This fellow was the only

Jewish person at the convention and decided to not wear his yarmulke.

After he arrived, he went to the dining hall where the guests had gathered. It was an absolutely magnificent hall. The company had even hired a violinist who strolled around the crowd and played classical music. This fellow happened to appreciate classical music, and when he saw the strolling violinist, he sat down at his own table but kept his eye riveted on the violinist. Suddenly, the violinist caught the eye of this fellow, stopped playing the piece by Strauss, and instead started playing the Israeli song *Hava Negilah*.

Can you imagine? In the middle of Germany? He was sitting there without a yarmulke. How did that musician know he was Jewish?

They know. They know. You can't hide it.

The Tollbooth

As long as we can't hide it, we might as well do our best to make a *kiddush Hashem* and live up to who we really are.

Some of you may know my friend Yidel Kleinbart from Borough Park. Yidel's wife was expecting their fifth child. Labor for a fifth child is not like for a first child: it usually happens very quickly. One morning, she announced that it was time to go to the hospital, which was Mt. Sinai Hospital in Manhattan. It was 8 a.m. at the height of rush hour.

They got into the car and the traffic was not moving — but the baby was. When Yidel made it to the Brooklyn Battery Tunnel and saw the long line of cars, he turned into the bus lane where traffic was moving swiftly. When he got to the tollbooth he didn't even pay the toll.

On the other side of the tunnel a New York City policemen was waiting for him, because they had already radioed ahead that someone had skipped paying the toll. "What are you doing?" the cop asked. "Where are you rushing?"

He pointed to the back and said, "My wife is expecting any minute. I have to get to Mt. Sinai."

"Why didn't you tell us?" the policeman said. "We would have gotten you a police escort. Go!"

Baruch Hashem, they came to Mt. Sinai on time, the baby was born, and everyone was healthy. That night, Yidel returned via the same Battery Tunnel. When he got to the tollbooth, he took out two coins and was about to give them to the toll collector, when the toll collector asked, "What is this?"

"I was here this morning," Yidel replied.

"Oh," the toll collector replied. "What did your wife have, a boy or girl?"

"You know?"

"Yes."

"How?"

"Because," the tollbooth collector said, "they told us a guy like you would surely come back and pay."

Isn't that amazing? He had driven by the tollbooth in a flash but they must have noticed his distinctive hat, yarmulke, or perhaps even his wife's head-covering. In that second they made a decision: this is a religious Jew and he will come back and pay! That is being *m'kadesh Shem Shamayim*. That is how we should deal with the fact that they know who we are.

A Fused Life

Let me end with a thought.

A *talmid* once wrote a letter to Rav Yitzchok Hutner and said, "Rebbi, I think I'm living a double life. I live one way in the outside world, and in my home I live a different way."

Rav Hutner replied with a brilliant insight. He said if a person rents a room in one house and then rents a room in another house, that's a double life. But if somebody has two rooms in one house, that's not a double life. That's a broad life (Letter no. 94).

He reinforced the point with a beautiful insight. The *Gemara* (*Berachos* 13b) says: כָּל הַמַּאֲרִיךְ בְּאֶחָד, *One who says the Shema and extends his saying of the word echad* — מַאֲרִיכִין לוֹ יָמָיו וּשְׁנוֹתָיו, *his days and years are lengthened.* Rav Hutner said you have to be מַאֲרִיךְ בְּאֶחָד, you have to stretch (מַאֲרִיךְ) that lifestyle that you live with at home to include the lifestyle you live outside the home. Your life in the secular workforce and the life in your home should be one of *kiddush Shem Shamayim*. There has to be a fusion. כָּל הַמַּאֲרִיךְ בְּאֶחָד, if you are מַאֲרִיךְ in this *achdus*, in this fusion of life, to make everything that you do honest *al pi Torah*, then you will be מַאֲרִיכִין לוֹ יָמָיו וּשְׁנוֹתָיו.

Let us hope that all our *tefillos* will be answered and all the specific *berachos* that we ask for regarding *parnassah* should come to fruition. And the *berachah* should not only be that we should have *parnassah,* but that we should be able to be *m'kadesh Shem Shamayim* in such a way that the atmosphere of *chol* should become an atmosphere of *kodesh*.

Hakaras HaTov

I once had the opportunity to meet a young *Sefardishe talmid chacham,* a *maggid shiur* in Yeshivah Rishon L'Tzion in *Eretz Yisrael,* Rav Shmuel Tyri. He told me a very interesting incident that he heard from his Rosh Yeshivah, Rav Chaim Meir Rothman. It dealt with a father and son living in the coldest regions of Siberia who got into a terrible argument concerning the one coat the family owned.

"I'm the one who should be allowed to wear this coat," the father said. "I'm old. I'm frail. I could get sick. I could die. I need it more than you, my son."

"No," said the son. "I'm the one who should have that coat! I'm the one who's outside working in the field. It's freezing out there. The winds are horrible. I am the one supporting the family. I'm the one who deserves the coat!"

Both the father and son decided to ask their Rav to settle the argument. The Rav listened to each side and then said, "I've never heard of such an argument between a parent and child. I don't know of anything like this in *Shulchan Aruch.* I must think about it. Give me two days, then come back and I will have a decision for you."

Before the two days passed, the father started thinking. "The truth is that my son is right. I am old and I stay at home. I'll wrap myself in another few extra blankets. My son is out in the fields and is freezing. He should have the coat."

At the same time, the son started thinking. "The truth is that my father is right. My father is an old man. He devoted his entire life to me. He's the one who should have the coat. Our home is not well insulated. I'll take some logs and build a fire at the worksite and I'll be warm. My father should have the coat."

"Father," the son said, "you have it."

"No, my son," the father said, "you should have it."

And now they were involved in a new argument. When they came before the Rav, he saw that they were presenting totally opposite views of what they had been claiming before!

"Wait a minute, I will be right back," the Rav said. He went back to his room, returned with a heavy fur coat, and gave it to them. "Here," he said with a smile, "now you have two coats, one for each of you."

They thanked him profusely and then before they left, the son said, "Rebbi, I hope you don't mind my asking, but I assume that you had this coat two days ago. Why didn't you give it to us then?"

The Rav replied, "When I saw that each of you was saying, 'I can't share it. I have to have it for myself.' I decided that I, too, must have my coat. I simply can't share it with others. But now that I see that you and your father are saying, 'I don't need the coat, it's more important that the other person has it.' I, too, felt that I could say about my own coat, 'I don't have to have it, let someone else have it.'"

I believe that this is the lesson David HaMelech is teaching in *Tehillim* (121:5), ה' צִלְּךָ, *Hashem is your shadow.* If you share and give, Hashem will act as your shadow. He will share and give. However, if, *chas v'shalom,* a person is stingy and holds back from giving to others, then Hashem is going to act to him in that same way.

> "Hashem is your shadow." If you share and give, Hashem will ... share and give.

A Jew Says "Thank You"

Every morning, when a person wakes up, the very first words he says are *Modeh ani,* Thank You. *Hakaras HaTov.*

Sefer Tehillim has 2,527 *pesukim*. The very last *pasuk* reads, כֹּל הַנְּשָׁמָה תְּהַלֵּל קָהּ, *Let the entire soul praise Hashem*. It is as if David HaMelech is telling us, "I wrote 2,527 *pesukim*; however, it all comes down to this: Your entire *neshamah*, your entire essence, has to praise Hashem."

The *Midrash* (*Bereishis Rabbah* 14:9) expounds on this *pasuk* by telling us: עַל כָּל נְשִׁימָה וּנְשִׁימָה צָרִיךְ לְקַלֵּס לְבוֹרְאוֹ ... *On every simple breath [of life], one must pray and be grateful to his Creator.* Most of the time we don't think about it; we simply take for granted that we're living. However, *Chazal* emphasize the importance of appreciating every breath of life. It is the essence of who we are.

We are called *Yehudim* — Jews — which comes from the word *hoda'ah*, "thanks." When Leah had her fourth child, she said, "Now, this time I'm going to thank Hashem," and she called her son Yehudah (*Bereishis* 29:35). The *Sforno* says that the essence of the name Yehudah is the expression of gratitude. That is why we are called *Yehudim*. A Jew says, "Thank you."

The Truth

Rav Mordechai Neugroschel of Jerusalem is a brilliant *talmid chacham* who has recorded more than 700 *shiurim* on various topics. He has a radio show every week, and people from all over *Eretz Yisrael* call him with questions. He teaches in various schools and is a renowned worldwide lecturer.

In 1996, his father-in-law was very sick and was in the Tel Hashomer Hospital, outside Tel Aviv. Rabbi Neugroschel planned to stay with his father-in-law the entire night. One of the religious nurses in the hospital recognized him and said, "Rabbi, you have to give *shiurim* tomorrow. There is nothing you can do for your father-in-law. Why not go home? We'll take care of him. Someone will be with him all night."

"No. He's *my* father-in-law," he replied. "I have to be here. There is no one like a family member when one is alone in a hospital."

In the morning, another family member came to the hospital and took over for him. Rabbi Neugroschel went to a local *minyan* and started driving back in his van to Yerushalayim. It was rush hour and traffic was at a crawl as he made his way up the long hills to the Holy

City. When you're barely moving in traffic and you are tired, your eyes begin to close. Rav Neugroschel, who had been up all night, was fighting to stay awake when suddenly he realized that his van was veering off the side of the road … tumbling down a cliff, rolling over and over, finally halting as it crashed on its side against a tree.

Baruch Hashem he was wearing a seat belt, but he was locked inside. People who saw the van go over the side of the road ran down to the smoking car, somehow managed to yank open the door, and pulled him out. He was stunned, bruised, and scratched, but he was alive.

People tried to reassure and comfort him as police and emergency equipment were called. As they were waiting for the emergency services to arrive, one gentleman offered some unsolicited advice, "Whatever you do, don't tell the police that you fell asleep. You'll get fined, they'll take away your license, and you won't get car insurance anymore."

A few minutes later, a policeman came over to Rav Neugroschel and asked, "What happened?"

Disregarding the well-meaning advice he had just received, Rabbi Neugroschel said, "Officer, I want you to know I've been driving for close to 20 years. I never fell asleep while I was driving! But my father-in-law is very sick, and I was up the whole night with him at the hospital. I felt that was the right thing to do, so I stayed right next to him and this morning I drove back to Yerushalayim. It's obvious, officer, that I must have fallen asleep."

The secular Israeli officer told him, "The mitzvah saved your life. I'm not going to give you a summons."

Only in Eretz Yisrael!

Afterward, Rav Neugroschel told me, "Do you know why I told the truth? Not simply because of the Torah's command of מִדְּבַר שֶׁקֶר תִּרְחָק, *Keep far from falsehood* [*Shemos* 23:7]. I told the truth because of *hakaras hatov*. Imagine somebody does you a favor and saves your life, and then asks you to do him a favor. Of course, you would do anything for him! The *Ribono Shel Olam* just saved my life. And now, two minutes later, He's asking me, 'Obey My laws, say the truth.' Of course I had to say the truth."

Now that's *hakaras hatov!*

If we realized all the miracles that happen to us every minute — עַל כָּל נְשִׁימָה וּנְשִׁימָה — then, when Hashem asks us to do something, it's not a question of

> **It's not a question of *frumkeit*. It's a question of *hakaras hatov*.**

frumkeit. It's a question of *hakaras hatov*. He has done and is doing so much for us that the least we can do is comply with His wishes.

Queen Wilhelmina

I would like to share with you one of the most remarkable stories I have ever heard. This story begins in 1908.

In that year, the queen of the Netherlands, Queen Wilhelmina, a deeply religious person, decided to vacation in the town of Marienbad, which then was in Hungary, but today is part of the Czech Republic. She had a small number of people in her entourage as this was not an official royal trip.

When she came to the train station in Marienbad, there was a tremendous crowd at the other end of the station. "What's going on here?" she asked. She was told that a great *Chassidishe Rebbe* had just arrived in Marienbad and that a crowd had come to welcome him. As a religious person, she understood what a rabbi was, but she had never heard of a "*Chassidishe Rebbe*."

"Just what is a *Chassidishe Rebbe*?" she asked. "What does he do? Who is he?"

The people told her that it was the great Munkaczer Rebbe, Rav Tzvi Hirsch Spira (1845–1914), and that he was known as one whom people would visit to get advice and blessings. She was told, "Thousands of people tell him of their pain, anguish, and problems. They ask him to pray on their behalf and in his wondrous ways he is able to help them."

As she heard this, she quietly reflected on her own tragic situation. She was the last in the line of her family's royalty, her three half brothers had died, and upon her eventual demise the royal family lineage would cease to exist. The doctors told her that there was very little chance that she could have children. She and her husband Prince Hendrik were duly concerned about the continuation of the monarchy in her family. When she heard who the Munkaczer Rebbe was, she thought that maybe she could get a blessing from him.

The queen and her entourage left the train station but later that day she asked one of her attendants to try to arrange for her to meet the great sage privately. The attendant sought out the rebbe's *gabbai* (assistant), and word came back to the queen that night that the rebbe would see her. The next evening, without public knowledge of his whereabouts, the Munkaczer Rebbe was brought to the secluded area of a beautiful park just outside the city that had been designated as the meeting place. Queen Wilhelmina was accompanied by two attendants, and the rebbe came with two *bachurim*. Seated on two park benches, on that quiet summer evening, the majestic rebbe and the cultured queen began their conversation.

She spoke candidly to the rebbe and explained her torment about not having a child to carry on the monarchy. The rebbe listened attentively and

> The rebbe saw her pain and told her through an interpreter that by next year there would be a child.

saw her pain. He told her through an interpreter that she need not worry for by next year there would be a child and her monarchy would continue. He used the expression, עַד כִּי יָבֹא שִׁילֹה, indicating that her monarchy would continue until *Mashiach* comes (see *Bereishis* 49:10). The next year, 1909, the queen had a daughter and named her Juliana. Juliana was the only child she would have. Thirty-nine years later, in 1948, Juliana became queen of the Netherlands.

That's the end of the first part of this story.

The second part deals with a *talmid chacham*, Rav Yaakov Tzvi Katz, who was taken with his family from Hungary to the Bergen-Belsen concentration camp. There, his 18-year-old son, Shmuel, was tragically killed. The Nazis took 12 *sefarim* that Rav Yaakov Tzvi had in manuscript form and burned them. Somehow he survived. After the war, Rav Katz wanted to go back to Hungary, but couldn't. It wasn't a place for Jews after the war. Where could he go? Many Jews thought that the Netherlands would be an alternative. He wrote a letter and applied for an immigration visa to the Netherlands. They told him that they were only taking people who could contribute to their country. When they inquired about his job, he said that he was a rabbi, and they replied that they had plenty of rabbis.

Rav Yaakov Tzvi Katz then wrote a letter in Yiddish to Queen Wilhelmina. His son, Rav Moshe from Stamford Hill, England, explained to me why he wrote it in Yiddish: so that nobody else should understand it. It would have to be translated and be given directly to the queen.

He wrote, "To the honorable Queen Wilhelmina, I am sure you remember the intense meeting in Marienbad back in 1908. You were so worried and concerned that your monarchy might not continue. You met with the great Munkaczer Rebbe, who gave you a blessing. You may remember there was a boy there who had to translate the rebbe's words from Yiddish. I was that boy. I was the one who transferred the rebbe's blessing and gave you the message to have confidence in the future. I brought you the news that you would indeed have a child."

He then went on to plead in the letter that in recognition of his bringing her that great news that she allow him to be accepted into her country.

The translated text was brought to the queen in her palace. She read and reread the letter and then made it her personal agenda to see to it that he was granted immigration papers swiftly. I was told that on the train to the Netherlands, when Dutch police saw a telegraphic visa from the queen, they took him from where he was sitting and placed him in first class.

He went to Amsterdam to the *Nidchei Yisrael Yichanes* shul where he became the Rav and served there for more than 17 years. He wrote a *sefer* that Rav Dovid Cohen showed me: *Leket Kemach HaChadash*. In the *hakdamah* he writes, "I have tremendous *hakaras hatov* to Queen Wilhelmina. I give her my blessing that the royal line of her and her daughter, Queen Juliana, continue, עַד כִּי יָבֹא שִׁילה." Indeed, as the Munkaczer Rebbe blessed the queen, the monarchy continues in her family. Her granddaughter, Beatrix, is now the present queen.

Focus on the Good

We have to learn the literal meaning of *hakaras hatov*. Literally, *hakaras hatov* means to recognize that there is good in this world.

This is almost impossible when one listens to the news today. As a test I listened to the news as I was preparing this talk, and most of it was negative. The topics varied but there was barely a news story that would bring a smile to one's face. A hurricane will hit Florida, police shot a boy who aimed a water gun at them, schools are overcrowded, kidnapping is a growth industry — if someone goes to Pakistan, the Philippines, Brazil, or Ecuador, he has to be very careful, because he might be kidnapped. SNET — the Connecticut phone company — is on strike, the Lincoln Tunnel is under construction — there will be traffic delays for the next few weeks, and the New York Mets lost again.

We tend to focus on the bad. *Hakaras hatov* means to focus on the good. Let us not take for granted that we can walk and talk and think and breathe. Those who have spouses, jobs, homes, children, grandchildren, and time to learn should be invigorated by their opportunities. Even if one has some of the above and not all of the above, there is what to be grateful for.

Do not put down this article without making a commitment to recognize the good that Hashem does for you. Think about something good in your life, focus on it for a few moments, and then be grateful to Hashem. He will bless you in return.

Getting a Handle on Anger

The *Mishnah* in *Avos* (2:15) teaches, Rabbi Eliezer says, יְהִי כְבוֹד
חֲבֵרְךָ חָבִיב עָלֶיךָ כְּשֶׁלָּךְ, וְאַל תְּהִי נוֹחַ לִכְעוֹס, *Let your fellow's
honor be as dear to you as your own and do not anger easily.*
At first glance, it looks as if Rabbi Eliezer is teaching two things: 1.
to be sensitive to another person's honor and 2. not to quickly lose
your temper. The Bartenura, however, explains that it is actually one
lesson: He notes, "When is it possible to always give honor to others?
Only if you don't anger easily, for if you lose your temper quickly, it
will be impossible not to end up shaming others."

Rabbi Eliezer is telling us that if we want to honor our friends, we
have to begin to understand how to contain the fire within us; how to
get a handle on our anger.

The Frog Principle

The Steipler Gaon (*Birchas Cheretz*) in *Parashas Va'eira* teaches
an important principle about anger. The *pasuk* (*Shemos* 8:2) says: וַיֵּט
אַהֲרֹן אֶת יָדוֹ עַל מֵימֵי מִצְרָיִם וַתַּעַל הַצְּפַרְדֵּעַ וַתְּכַס אֶת אֶרֶץ מִצְרָיִם, *Aharon
stretched out his hand on the waters of Egypt and frogs came up
and covered the whole land of Egypt.* Rashi cites a *Midrash* that says

it was actually only one frog that emerged (the *pasuk* uses the word הַצְפַרְדֵּעַ in singular) ; however, people became angry and hit it — and it split into two frogs. Then they hit those two frogs again and they became four ... then eight ... 16 .... You would think they would have stopped by now. But they continued hitting. Then there were 32 ... and 64 ... and 128 ....

The same thing was happening in every house. They could not control themselves! That is why the frogs ended covering the whole land of Egypt.

Couldn't they just control themselves? Didn't they realize what was happening?!

No. That is what anger is all about! Anger is about losing control. You lose your ability to think rationally and continue doing things that are harmful. And not only are these outbursts harmful to others, but even to you yourself.

Anger Leads to Catastrophe

Rabbi Sholom Schwadron, the Maggid of Jerusalem, told me this story that he heard from a *tzaddik*, Rabbi Chaikel Meletzky. Rabbi Chaikel was a *melamed* for many years. When he was 48, he contracted a terrible disease and one of his legs had to be amputated. For the rest of his life he was confined to a wheelchair.

He lived in a place called *Brody's Haiser* (houses) in Yerushalayim, where he would regularly wheel himself out to the courtyard to get some fresh air and to learn. A motto he always told his children was: "Never be involved in a *machlokes* [argument]." He even wrote that in his will as one of his final instructions to his family.

He went so far as to tell them, "If you are in the middle of *Kriyas Shema* and a *machlokes* breaks out in shul, walk out! Even in the middle of *Kriyas Shema*! Under no circumstances should you be involved in a *machlokes*."

One day in the courtyard, he heard a young woman arguing with an old man. "I'm the one who deserves the apartment," the woman was saying. "I have younger children. I have my whole life ahead of me."

"What do you mean?" the old man said. "I was on the list way before you."

"But you're an old man," she yelled at him.

"Nobody knows how many years they have left," he said back.

R' Chaikel couldn't take it any longer and went back into his house, unwilling to listen to any more of this quarrel. This incident took place at the end of the 1940's, when it was common for Arabs to randomly throw bombs and grenades into different Jewish areas in Yerushalayim.

A few days later, R' Chaikel was sitting in his house and was about to wheel himself outside when suddenly he heard a grenade go off in the courtyard. When he wheeled himself outside he saw that his son had been hit by shrapnel.

It just happened that an ambulance was going through the street at that moment. He yelled and got the attention of other people. They signaled the ambulance to stop and take his son to the hospital.

As he was getting into the ambulance, he looked back and saw the other people who had been hurt by this grenade. It was the old man who had been yelled at the other day. Though injured, he lived to tell the story. Lying on the ground not far away was the young woman who had done the shouting. She was dead!

Years later, at this son's *sheva berachos*, R' Chaikel told this story in poetry form. He ended the story as though he were quoting the old man: "Don't be so hot, let your temper turn cold / for no one knows who is really young or old."

That young woman thought she was going to live forever or at least outlive the old man. However, she was mistaken.

Anger Leads to Catastrophe

At the beginning of the Torah, we are taught what terrible things can happen because of anger. Kayin and Hevel brought offerings to Hashem, but Hashem didn't turn to Kayin's offering. Kayin became very angry and his countenance fell. Hashem turned to Kayin and asked: לָמָּה חָרָה לָךְ ... הֲלוֹא אִם תֵּיטִיב שְׂאֵת, *Why are you so annoyed...? Improve and you will be forgiven* (Bereishis 4:6-7).

In the next *pasuk* the Torah tells us that they were in the field and וַיָּקָם קַיִן ... וַיַּהַרְגֵהוּ, *And Kayin rose up ... and killed [his brother Hevel]* (ibid. 4:8). What does it mean that Kayin *rose up* and killed Hevel?

The *Midrash* tells us that Kayin started to become angry at Hevel and attacked him, but Hevel was stronger. Then, the *Midrash* says, Kayin said to Hevel, "Don't kill me. Our father only has two sons." Hevel had *rachmanus* and let him go.

The next *pasuk* tells us that when Kayin rose up, he killed Hevel! But he had just begged him not to kill anyone because, "Our father has only two sons." That was a logical statement and he should have abided by it. But Kayin was so drunk with anger that even the logic that he himself had just uttered moments earlier had no impact upon him. He got up from the ground and killed his brother.

The *Kli Yakar* derives a great lesson from this episode, teaching us how arguments start. The *pasuk* says וְהֶבֶל הֵבִיא גַם הוּא מִבְּכֹרוֹת צֹאנוֹ וּמֵחֶלְבֵהֶן, *Hevel also brought of the firstlings of his flock and from their choicest* (ibid. 4:4). Why doesn't it say that Kayin brought and Hevel brought? Why does it say that Hevel also brought?

The *Kli Yakar* says that Hevel saw that Kayin brought a *korban* and said to himself, "I'll do the same thing." In other words, he did it out of jealousy. (Hevel may never have had the idea of bringing a *korban* to Hashem had Kayin not introduced this concept.)

That's how anger starts: with jealousy as a root cause.

This is so relevant! Don't we know of people from the same family where some of the siblings are wealthier? They have nicer homes and can dress their children better. What happens? Some of the siblings are jealous of the others, and make comments behind their back to other family members. All of a sudden, a terrible argument starts. How did it all begin? The answer is: with jealousy.

Don't we know certain families who are jealous of other families? One family may wonder with pain, "How did they merit marrying off all of their children? They aren't more special than we are, so how did they do it?" Jealousy and anger set in and soon one family is making comments about the other family and starts to hate them. Why? It all starts with jealousy.

Sometimes we witness a person being honored and we might be inclined to think, "Why is he getting honored and I'm not?" So we start making comments, and with those comments comes anger.

Why Shaatnez?

The *Midrash Tanchuma* (*Bereishis* 9) states, "What is the reason that we don't wear *shaatnez*?"

Hashem says, "Kayin brought from the linen and Hevel brought from the wool — and it was the combination of linen and wool that brought death to the world." Hence it makes no sense that we would wear clothes that remind Hashem of those terrible times.

What an eye opener!

My rebbe, Rav Dovid Cohen, told me that the Arizal teaches that there is only one person who is allowed to wear *shaatnez*; in fact, he has to wear *shaatnez* (see *Shemos* 39:29): the *Kohen Gadol*. He wears *shaatnez* because, similar to Aaron HaKohen, he is one who is an *oheiv shalom v'rodeiph shalom*, one who loves peace and pursues peace. As such, he undoes what transpired between Kayin and Hevel and thus can wear what others cannot wear.

Indeed, the way to make up for anger and jealousy is to become people who love peace and run after it.

Rabbi Sholom Schwadron would often cite the wonderful teaching of Rabbi Shlomo Ibn Gabirol (an early Sefardic Rishon): פְּרִי הַמְּהִירוּת הַחֲרָטָה, *The fruit of acting quickly is regret.*

If You Rush, You Will Regret

We must learn to take it easy. Many times we react with words or deeds so quickly that by the time we realize what we have done, harm has already transpired. Years ago I performed a *bris* in a shul that was only five houses from where the

> **The fruit of acting quickly is regret.**

grandparents lived. As I was about to start the *bris* I realized there was no wine. Wine is on the list of items that I tell parents to prepare in advance; however, sometimes things are forgotten, and this time they forgot the wine.

When I asked the father of the baby for the wine, he became infuriated with his brother-in-law who had been asked to bring it. The father turned to him and yelled, "It's your fault. You were supposed to bring the wine. Go quickly to my father-in-law's home and bring wine."

"I don't know where he keeps the wine," the brother-in-law said, red-faced.

"It's in the basement by the door. Go quickly and bring it," the father responded.

The brother-in-law ran to the home and made a dash toward the basement. He picked up a gallon jug and brought it to the shul just in time for the *rabbanim* to start reciting the blessings.

The truth is that when I saw that jug of liquid I noticed it was yellow, but I figured it was Tokay wine or some other fancy wine. One of the *rabbanim* made the blessing and then when he finished he handed the *becher* (Kiddush cup) to the father to drink.

The father drank from the *becher* and spit it out, screaming "What is this? It's not wine!"

It was motor oil!! His father-in-law had stored motor oil in an empty wine bottle!

Everyone started howling and laughing, but I was frightened because I had given some of the "wine" to the baby! The custom is to place a dab of wine in the baby's mouth at the recitation of the words, בְּדָמַיִךְ חֲיִי. Frantic, I quickly called the pediatrician who laughed at the incident and told me. "Don't worry; it's okay. No harm was done, but don't forget to bring him in for the 5,000-mile checkup."

If you rush, you are going to regret.

Patience

Rabbi Chaim Ozer Grodzensky was once giving a *shiur* in his home to a group of *bachurim*, when suddenly a man came up the stairs, an *am ha'aretz*, and interrupted the *shiur*. "Can a *Kohen* take a divorcée?" he asked.

Everyone knows that a *Kohen* cannot marry a divorcée! It is an open *pasuk* in the Torah! All the *bachurim* became angry at this man, but R' Chaim Ozer turned quiet, thought for a minute, and said, "Yes, a *Kohen* can take a divorcée."

The *bachurim* couldn't believe it! The man was very happy and left.

The *bachurim* could no longer concentrate on the *shiur*. How could their rebbi have said something that was against an open *pasuk* in the Torah?! R' Chaim Ozer saw that they were upset and said to them, "*Bachurim*, don't you understand? Don't you realize that he's a wagon driver who is a *Kohen* and there's probably a divorcée standing outside who wants a ride with him. He once heard that a *Kohen* can't take a divorcée, but he didn't realize it specifically means he can't marry her. But in his case all she wants is a ride to another place in his wagon. So a *Kohen* can 'take' a divorcée, just as he asked. Go downstairs and see for yourselves."

Sure enough, they went downstairs and there was the wagon driver with a divorcée whom he was taking as a passenger in his wagon.

That's how a leader of *Klal Yisrael* behaves. He has patience for every person.

Soft Words Turn Away Anger

Many of you know Mrs. Ella Adler of Brooklyn. She and her husband Yanky had a *tzaarah* that no one should know of. Her son, Michoel, seven weeks after his bar mitzvah, passed away.

Shortly afterward, on a Friday afternoon, she was in the Department of Motor Vehicles with her elder daughter. She took a number and they told her that the wait time was about three hours! Instead of wasting time she took out her *siddur* and she started *davening*.

When she reached *Shemoneh Esrei*, she looked around for an empty room in which she could *daven*. She found one, went inside, and started her *Shemoneh Esrei*. Naturally, her *tefillos* were filled with tears. As she got up to *Shema Koleinu*, a woman employee of the DMV walked into the room and yelled, "What are you doing here?"

She couldn't stop in middle of *Shemoneh Esrei*, so she continued without responding. But the woman started cursing, "Get outta here! What are you doing in this office?!"

But she could not stop *davening*. The woman started yelling right in her face, so Mrs. Adler pointed to the *siddur* and then to her mouth, indicating that she couldn't talk.

The woman did not buy it, grabbed Mrs. Adler by the arm, and literally swung her across the room. Mrs. Adler landed against the wall with a thud. She thought to herself, "I have *every* right to scream back at this woman ...." But she didn't.

Rather, she said in a calm voice, "Why did you do that to me?" and then she began crying. "You can't possibly know what I've gone through these past two months." Then she started crying again and told her that she had lost a son, and she had other children at home, and how very

> "You can't possibly know what I've gone through these past two months."

difficult it was for everyone, and how very little time she had to herself today to pray and talk to G-d and so on ....

The woman listened and then said, "Well, you don't have to pray here. Go pray any place else."

Even then Mrs. Adler didn't yell back, but said calmly, "I don't know what religion you are, but I'm Jewish and this is how we pray to G-d." Then she burst into uncontrollable tears and walked out of the office back into the waiting area.

Two or three minutes later this woman walked out of her office and came over to Mrs. Adler, put her arm around her, and said, "I'm really sorry. I'm also Jewish." And they started crying together. When the crying subsided they got into a serious conversation.

An hour later, Mrs. Adler finished her business at the DMV and left.

Shortly afterward, she attended a *shiur* delivered by Rav Shaya Cohen, who often speaks about the importance of *kiruv*. She went over and told him the story.

"You have to go back to this woman and talk to her," he told her.

Indeed, she found the woman at the DMV office and brought her a pamphlet that she had written in memory of her son. Touched, the woman said to her, "Mrs. Adler, I want you to know that this past Friday night I went to a synagogue. I haven't gone in the longest time, and I prayed to G-d that He should forgive me and I prayed for your son."

Incredible!

The lesson of this great story is what Shlomo HaMelech said in *Mishlei* (15:1): מַעֲנֶה רַּךְ יָשִׁיב חֵמָה, *A soft answer turns away anger.* Mrs. Adler could have exploded. If anyone had a right to, she did. Instead, she used soft language and thereby turned away anger. Perhaps this Jewish woman will come back and do *teshuvah*.

Dr. Meir Wikler, who has years of experience as a marriage counselor, once told me the three most important words in marriage. "It's not the three you are thinking of," he said with a smile. "Rather, they are: 'I was wrong.'"

Those are the most important words in marriage and in every other relationship. If you say, "I was wrong," to your spouse, rebbe, or friend, even when you don't feel that you were wrong, you reduce the resentment of the other person and it shows you have learned that "Soft words turn away anger."

> **The three most important words in marriage are … "I was wrong."**

If you talk softly, the other person can't possibly continue his anger. May we all learn to control the fire within us, so that our attitude will foster friendship, understanding, and tolerance. This in turn can bring about unity in our families, communities, and in *Klal Yisrael* so that we merit to see *Mashiach* in our time.

A Journey to the Poland of Yesteryear

Over the last seven years, Rabbi Paysach Krohn has led summer tours to various cities in Eastern Europe.

His first travel book, Traveling With the Maggid: A Journey to Great Torah Centers of Yesteryear, *published by ArtScroll/Mesorah in 2007, dealt with his travels to Lithuania and Belarus, history, divrei Torah, and episodes of the Gedolim who lived in those areas, such as the Vilna Gaon, Rav Chaim Ozer Grodzinsky, the Alter of Kelm, the Alter of Slabodka, the Ponevezher Rav, Rav Shimon Shkop, and others.*

In a recent speech, he detailed some of his experiences during a trip to Poland. These experiences and others will eventually be part of his second "Travel" book, b'ezras Hashem.

When the name Rav Meir Shapiro is mentioned, the first two things that come to mind are *daf yomi* and the remarkable yeshivah he built in Lublin. Indeed, as we stood in the majestic Yeshivah Chachmei Lublin building, the feelings of awe and sadness were overwhelming. It had been turned into a medical college, but recently the Lauder family purchased it, returning it to Jewish hands.

To picture the yeshivah, imagine a state capitol building with tremendously tall pillars, a building with endless rooms; a building that literally dwarfed any other yeshivah building in Europe. To give a talk in the same room where Rav Meir Shapiro gave his *shiurim* was both stirring and humbling.

The building looks as if it had been built to exist forever. Sadly this great Torah institution lasted only nine short years, from 1930-1939. Tragically, Rav Meir Shapiro himself passed away at the age of 47, a mere four years after the inauguration of the yeshivah.

What happened? How could a yeshivah and an idea that were so long in planning disappear in such a short time?

The reason he wanted to build such a magnificent yeshivah was that he saw that Polish boys, many from very fine families, were falling by the wayside. Secularization of Polish youth was rampant between World War I and World War II. There was little *chashivus haTorah* among many Polish boys. Rav Meir Shapiro wanted to change that and sought to build a yeshivah that would restore prestige to Torah the way it was meant to be. It was the first European yeshivah with a dormitory, and the awesome physical presence of the building would be a sign of its prominence.

When the cornerstone of the building was first laid in 1924, 30,000 people attended the ceremony. When they had the *chanukas habayis* in 1930, close to 100,000 people attended, including people from all over Eastern Europe.

Rabbi Fishel Schachter, *shlita,* a well-known *maggid shiur* and *darshan,* tells that the Chortkover Rebbe, Rav Yisroel Friedman, was not happy with the huge gala event that was being planned. "Why do you have to make such a great event?" he protested. "Why do you need 100,000 people? Why does everyone have to know about it?"

Sources point to the Chortkover Rebbe's view of the occasion. *Rashi (Shemos* 34:3) explains that the first *Luchos,* which were given with great fanfare, created an *ayin hara.* Rashi adds, אֵין לְךָ יָפֶה מִן הַצְּנִיעוּת, *there is nothing better than modesty.* Similarly, *Midrash Tanchuma (Ki Sisa* 31) also notes that the first *Luchos,* given with tremendous pomp, were eventually broken. Therefore, when the second *Luchos* were given, Hashem instructed Moshe to do it with *tzniyus* — and they lasted much longer than the first *Luchos.*

Undoubtedly, Rav Meir Shapiro understood these sources as well as anyone, yet he replied, "Hashem knew the first *Luchos* were going to be broken, and He still did it that way, because He felt that one has to take a stand for the glory of Torah. The fact that Hashem had the event written in the Torah shows the *mesiras nefesh* one must have for Torah!"

It would seem that Rav Meir Shapiro knew in his heart that possible calamity could happen because of the publicity, yet he felt it was worth it for the glory of Torah. It would seem to me that only a person of such stature could make that evaluation. We are not on that level. We must heed the words of the *Midrash Tanchuma* and of Rashi. We must keep a low profile. If Hashem blesses us even with a small amount of success, we should not publicize it.

There are many whom Hashem has blessed with wonderful children and grandchildren. Don't talk about it. If you make a good business deal, don't tell everyone. If you want to give *tzedakah*, give it quietly. No one has to know. Don't make that fancy *chanukas habayis* for your brand-new, gorgeous home. It only creates jealousy. Keep a low profile. If you are able to take a vacation, you don't have to tell everyone where you are going. Keep a low profile. It safer, that's for sure.

The Greatest Marbitz Torah

Another stop we made on the tour was in Cracow. Rav Chaztkel Sarna, the Rosh Yeshivah of Yeshivas Chevron in Jerusalem, was once sitting with a group of *talmidei chachamim* and posed a question to them. "Who do you think was the greatest *marbitz Torah* in the last 100 years?"

Many of the *talmidei chachamim* ventured a guess. Some mentioned the Chofetz Chaim, others undoubtedly said Rav Meir Shapiro, while others suggested Rav Chaim Soloveitchik.

"I disagree with all of you," said Rav Chatzkel. "The biggest *marbitz Torah* of all was Sarah Schenirer."

Indeed, where would we all be without our mothers and wives encouraging their husbands and children to learn Torah?

Sarah Schenirer was born into a family of Belzer Chassidim. During World War I, her family fled Cracow and ended up in Vienna. One day she decided to go to what someone told her was "an Orthodox shul." She entered and saw that the Rav, Rabbi Moshe David Flesch, who had been a *talmid* of Rabbi Samson Raphael Hirsch, was about to give a *derashah*. He was wearing a regular modern suit and hat. She had never seen a rav who looked like that. She was used to a rav with a *shtreimel* and a *kaputah*. A woman in the *ezras nashim* saw her reaction and whispered, "Just wait till you hear one *derashah* from him."

Rabbi Flesch spoke about Yehudis, the heroine of Chanukah, and said that the battle for Jewish survival goes on today. "We need women in *Klal Yisrael* to fight this battle," he proclaimed with fervor. Sarah Schenirer was so taken by that one *derashah* that it literally changed her life — and the lives of generations of women after her.

Vienna is a big city. Her parents had been scrambling to find an apartment anywhere in the city, like so many other people from Poland who were desperate to resettle in a religious neighborhood. *Hashgachah pratis* led them to find an apartment near this shul so that their daughter Sarah would come to hear this rav. This, unto itself, is a great *mussar* lesson. Hashem directs our every step, and only after time can we realize the purpose of His orchestration.

Quite often young men seeking to be accepted into a specific yeshivah in *Eretz Yisrael* are disappointed that they were rejected, for whatever reason. This happens as well with girls seeking to attend a particular seminary in *Eretz Yisrael*. There are those who wanted to find a house in a particular neighborhood and "unfortunately" had to settle on living someplace else. We don't realize that Hashem is הַמֵּכִין מִצְעֲדֵי גָבֶר, *the One Who leads us every step* of the way exactly to where we're supposed to be. More often than not, the boy finds the perfect *rebbi* and *chavrusa* in the yeshivah he did not want to go to. The girl in the "unwanted" seminary is introduced to a new friend, whose brother she eventually marries. The neighborhood you did not want to consider has the rav and the schools for your children that enhance your life. We can never know. We must only try our best and see where *hashgachah pratis* leads us. Nothing is by chance.

Count Your Days; Make Your Days Count

In many elementary-school yeshivos and Bais Yaakovs, the walls themselves are part of the *chinuch*. You walk down the corridors of these Torah institutions and you see pictures of *Gedolim* as well as *divrei Chazal* and *pesukim* adorned with beautiful artwork. In the Bais Yaakov of Montreal, I once saw a *pasuk* decoratively displayed on a wall, a sight that became etched within me: לִמְנוֹת יָמֵינוּ כֵּן הוֹדַע (*Tehillim* 90:12). The simple meaning is that David HaMelech asked Hashem to inform him how many days (and years) he had left so that he could pace himself to accomplish all he had to do in his lifetime. However, Sarah Schenirer understood the verse homiletically in a unique way:

לִמְנוֹת יָמֵינוּ , *to count your days*, כֵּן הוֹדַע, *you have to know*.

In other words, in order to make sure that not a day of your life is wasted, you have to "know" what you did and keep yourself accountable for all you did that day. Make *every day count!*

I would suggest if one wants to do a *chessed* every day, or learn a certain amount of *mishnayos* a day, one should keep a notebook and write it down. The fact that you force yourself to keep a record of what you have done and what you are trying to accomplish will itself compel you to keep it up. If you decide that you will study a *perek* of *Tanach* every day, write down your accomplishments in a little notebook and soon that notebook will become one of your most treasured possessions.

The *Sefas Emes,* Rav Yehudah Arye Leib Alter, died when he was only 58. His son, Rav Avrohom Mordechai Alter, the *Imrei Emes*, was talking to his brother, R' Betzalel, at the funeral and remarked, "At least our father had *arichas yamim* [literally, "length of days"].

"What do you mean?" R' Betzalel said. "He was only 58!"

"I didn't say *arichas shanim* [length of years]," the *Imrei Emes* replied. "I said he had *arichas yamim* [length of days]."

There is a great difference between *arichas yamim* and *shanim*. Not everybody merits *arichas shanim*. Not everyone will merit living many years. However, every one of us can see to it that he has *arichas yamim* ("length of days") by making every day count, making the most of every day.

Majdanek

From Lublin we traveled a short while to the nearby town of Majdanek. It was here that one of the worst Nazi death camps was situated.

It is impossible to describe the experience of walking into a gas chamber to stand under the very shower heads where less than 70 years ago Jews were gassed to death. They had been told to write their names on the clothes in order to retrieve them afterward. Surely there were those who suspected that it might not be a regular shower. We cannot possibly understand their fright.

Are there lessons to be learned here?

Rav Mattisyahu Salomon once pointed out an important lesson from the words of Yaakov Avinu when he heard that Yosef was still alive: ...וַיֹּאמֶר יִשְׂרָאֵל רַב עוֹד יוֹסֵף בְּנִי חָי, *And Yisrael said: "How great! My son Yosef is still alive ..."* (*Bereishis* 45:28).

Rashi understands the word רַב, *How great,* to mean, "How great is my joy that my son is still alive." The *Midrash* (*Bereishis Rabbah* 94:3) understands רַב differently: "How great [a *tzaddik*] is my son Yosef! He overcame so many troubles and obstacles and remained true to his holy standards." Yaakov was saying, "רַב כֹּחוֹ שֶׁל יוֹסֵף בְּנִי, *Yosef my son is much greater than I am*, because he had so many problems and *tzaaros* and yet he still remained a *tzaddik*."

To me that is the lesson in Majdanek. Let us remember all those people who had *emunah* and *bitachon* in these terrible moments; all these people who did mitzvos under the most difficult situations. They are רַב — they are greater than we can ever hope to be. By standing in these areas we realized that we were standing where great people lived and died.

And as we stand in awe of these people, we should understand as well that around us, in our shuls and neighborhoods, there are many people who live very difficult lives, for whatever reason. They didn't choose it; Hashem chose it for them. How should we view these people? We should say רַב. They are greater than we are! They come to *shiurim* even though they are in tremendous pain. They may have kids at risk, be struggling with *parnassah* — whatever it is. Nevertheless, they still come to *daven*; they come to learn. We have to look at them with deep awe and respect. Never look down at those who have problems. To the contrary, if they are observant even under difficult circumstances they are indeed great.

Bread and Kiddush Hashem

Many of us are familiar with the noted writer, historian, and editor of Agudath Israel's *Dos Yiddishe Vort*, Rabbi Yosef Friedenson. He went through the camps and *baruch Hashem* survived. He often tells of a young man in his barracks, Binyamin, who when he *davened* Shacharis in the morning, would exclaim out loud with gusto, אַשְׁרֵינוּ, מַה טוֹב חֶלְקֵנוּ, וּמַה נָּעִים גּוֹרָלֵנוּ, וּמַה יָפָה יְרֻשָׁתֵנוּ, *Happy are we! How good is our portion, how pleasant is our lot, and how beautiful is our inheritance!*

Imagine! There, in the barracks, starving and facing another day of the most brutal slave labor, a young man was able to exclaim אַשְׁרֵינוּ! He felt fortunate to be a Yid even under those circumstances.

Rabbi Friedenson tells the story that one day the Germans ordered Binyamin and him to clean out the barracks where the Poles stayed. Under the bed of a gentile named Yanik, they found a piece of bread. Rabbi Friedenson turned to Binyamin and said, "Let's share it."

"But we have the opportunity to make a *kiddush Hashem*," Binyamin said.

Imagine! They were starving. Who was going to know the difference? Would anybody have had a complaint that these two men shared a piece of bread under those circumstances? But Binyamin said that they could make a *kiddush Hashem*, so he put the bread in his pocket and later gave it to Yanik.

The next day, another Pole came over to Rabbi Friedenson and told him that he saw how he and Binyamin had given back the bread. "You people are good people," he said.

Tomorrow, before we go out into the world, let's ask ourselves: Are our actions those that would make a *kiddush Hashem*?

Shema Yisrael for the Last Time!

When we were in Majdanek standing under those showerheads, I mentioned that, unquestionably, as the gas began pouring out of the showerheads, people realized they were about to die. Many screamed. Surely many said the *Shema*. What are we thinking when we say the *Shema*?

Rav Elchonon Wasserman told the following incident. The Chofetz Chaim had a son-in-law, R' Tzvi Hirsch Levenson, who was the Mashgiach of the yeshivah. After a while Rav Levenson wanted to spend more time on his own learning and give over some of his responsibilities to others. Listen to what the Chofetz Chaim told him.

The Torah says we have to love Hashem בְּכָל לְבָבְךָ, וּבְכָל נַפְשְׁךָ, וּבְכָל מְאֹדֶךָ., *with all your heart, your soul, and with all* מְאֹדֶךָ (*Devarim* 6:5). What does מְאֹדֶךָ mean? Most people are familiar with the *Chazal* that interprets it as money or resources. A person has to be willing to love Hashem not only with all of his heart and soul, but with all of his money and resources as well. However, the Ramban (ibid.), says that מְאֹדֶךָ comes from the word מְאֹד, *very*, which means whatever you consider *very* important in your life, you must be willing to give up for Hashem.

The Chofetz Chaim said to his son-in-law, "I know that money isn't important to you. Therefore, the words בְּכָל מְאֹדֶךָ can't mean money in your case. מְאֹדֶךָ really means whatever you consider important, and you consider learning Torah the most important thing. Therefore, that's what you have to sacrifice at this point. There comes a time where you have to give up even some learning to do something for *Klal Yisrael.* And I feel that leading the yeshivah and guiding the *bachurim* is now your primary purpose."

Therefore, we can think of two things when we say the word מְאֹדֶךָ. Whether it's money or something that is *very* important to us — that's what we have to be willing to give up for the sake of Hashem.

We all paused for a moment and then with broken and contrite hearts recited the *Shema* as never before.

Sheves Achim

On the afternoon that we visited the concentration camp of Auschwitz, we also traveled to Lizhensk and the burial place of the Rebbe R' Elimelech.

After a grueling few hours in Auschwitz, the Rebbe's hometown of Lizhensk was a welcome respite. In preparation and anticipation for *davening* at his *kever,* which is enclosed by golden iron gates, we began feeling a sense of *ahavas Yisrael* and the joy of *chassidus.* On the bus we let loose with tremendous song and (if you can believe it) began dancing on the bus. I explained to everyone an interesting way of understanding the famous verse, וְאָהַבְתָּ לְרֵעֲךָ כָּמוֹךָ, *You shall love your neighbor as you love yourself (Vayikra* 19:18). Just as you accept and love yourself, even though you have faults, accept your friend in that same manner. Just because another person has some faults is not a reason to dislike him. You, too, have faults and you still like yourself.

And indeed on the wall in the room where the Rebbe's *kever* lies, there is a huge poster with the famous prayer of the Rebbe Reb Elimelech which includes his famous exhortation, תֵּן בְּלִבֵּנוּ שֶׁנִּרְאֶה מַעֲלַת חֲבֵרֵינוּ וְלֹא חֶסְרוֹנָם, *Please [Hashem], give us the capacity to focus on the virtue of our friends and not on their fault ....*

That's what *ahavas Yisrael* is all about and what the life lessons of these trips are all about.

Eating and Overeating

E verything in life is a test. One of the most available and challenging tests is food. Listen to these incredible statistics from an article I saw:

> Americans waste 27 percent of the food available for consumption. 96.4 billion pounds of the 356 billion pounds of edible food in the United States was never eaten, which means that 30 million tons of food is wasted each year. In England, people toss away a third of the amount of food they buy. In Sweden, 25 percent of the food people buy is wasted. The Department of Agriculture estimated that if we would recover 5 percent of the food that is wasted in America, we could feed four million people a day. If we recovered 25 percent of the food that we waste in America, we could feed 20 million people.

For the most part food is, *baruch Hashem*, available to us in America and in other Western countries. But that only makes the test more challenging. Food can elevate us or cause us terrible harm.

In Golders Green, London, I met a wonderful fellow, Mendy Tajtelbaum, who told me about his late father, R' Yitzchok Dovid

Tajtelbaum, a wealthy Jew who gave a substantial amount of money to the Gerrer Rebbe to build up the Jewish section of Arad in the southern part of Israel. Mendy once heard a story about his father, but was hesitant to ask him about it because it concerned the concentration camps. However, he eventually found the courage to ask if it was true. He had heard that when his father was in Auschwitz and was given his bread ration every morning, he would cut it in half. He would keep only one half for himself and distribute the other half, bit by bit, to other inmates who were starving!

His father said it was true, but he wanted to explain where he had learned that trait.

He told his son that he grew up in a little town in Poland called Sheps. In those days there were no refrigerators or freezers, so a person could only prepare enough food for the day. He said that one cold, snowy night his mother made a thick soup for supper, with pieces of chicken and vegetables. He was one of nine children and he watched as his mother served her husband and then the children.

As she was about to serve herself, there was a series of loud knocks on the door. One of the children opened the door and a poor beggar covered with snow and slush barged in. He smelled awful and exclaimed in Yiddish, "*Gibtz essen!* (Give some food!)." The mother told him to go into the other room and wash up first. While the fellow was washing up, the mother took an empty bowl and went around to each child, removed a spoonful of soup from each of their bowls and put it into the empty bowl. She also took from her own and her husband's bowls as well. By the time the poor man returned to the room, he had a full bowl of hot soup. R' Yitzchok Dovid Tajtelbaum learned from his saintly mother.

That's using food in an elevated manner.

I have no doubt that the *Ribono Shel Olam* blessed R' Yitzchok Dovid with wealth because he understood what it meant to be charitable to others. In Auschwitz he implemented the lesson he remembered from what he had witnessed years earlier and Hashem rewarded him.

Which Came First?
The Apple or the Berachah?

In 1965, on the first Friday night that he was in America, Rav Sholom Schwadron, the *Maggid* of Jerusalem, spoke in the home of my parents, Rav Avrohom Zelig and Hindy Krohn, to a mesmerized crowd of people in Kew Gardens, New York. He told classic stories that evening, but there was one that I will always remember. It was a magnificent story about Rav Aharon Karliner, the first Stoliner Rebbe.

Rav Aharon was sitting at the head of a *tisch* on a Motza'ei Shabbos, surrounded by many enraptured chassidim. Someone gave the Rebbe an apple. Slowly he recited the *berachah* aloud and then ate the apple. The chassidim were in awe at what they had just seen.

A little 8-year-old boy, Yankele, was sitting in the back. He too watched what transpired and thought, "Why is everyone in awe? The Rebbe makes a *berachah* and eats an apple; I do that as well."

Rav Aharon Karliner looked toward the back and caught little Yankele's facial expression. He realized that the little boy was not as awed or impressed as the attending chassidim were. The Rebbe thus called Yankele to come forward and said to him in a whisper, "I want to ask you something."

Everyone was wondering what the Rebbe was telling the child. "Yankele," the Rebbe said, "What's the difference between you and me? I make a *berachah* and eat an apple and you also make a *berachah* and eat an apple."

"Rebbe," Yankele answered, "I wasn't going to say anything, but I was wondering the same thing. What *is* the difference?"

"I'll tell you," the Rebbe said lovingly. "When I get up in the morning, I see the beautiful world: the clouds, the sky, the trees, and everything that Hashem created. It's so beautiful that I want to make a *berachah* to thank Hashem. But one can't just make a *berachah* for no reason. So I wash *negel vasser*, then I *daven*, then I take an apple and make a *berachah* and eat. However, when you wake up, Yankele, the first thing you think of is that you are hungry. You want to eat something. But you know your mother won't let you eat without a *berachah*, so you, too, have to wash *negel vasser*, *daven*, and then you take an apple and make a *berachah* and eat. So we both take apples, we both make *berachos,* and we both eat. However, there is a great difference between you and me. I eat the apple so that I can make the *berachah.* You make the *berachah* so that you can eat the apple."

> "I eat the apple so that I can make the *berachah.* You make the *berachah* so that you can eat the apple."

Most of us can surely admit that we are like Yankele: we make the *berachah* so that we can eat the apple. The apple is the priority. However, for the Rebbe the apple (or any food, for that matter) was only the means to the end; the priority was making a *berachah.*

Here, in a different way from the mother in Sheps, the Rebbe elevated food. He used it as a vehicle to make a connection to Hashem.

Yeshurun Became Fat

In *Devarim* (32:15), Moshe warns *Klal Yisrael,* וַיִּשְׁמַן יְשֻׁרוּן וַיִּבְעָט, *Yeshurun became fat and kicked* — they became obese, which symbolizes the idea of excessive materialism leading to assured rebellion. Yeshurun is a reference to *Klal Yisrael.* Rav Samson Rafael Hirsch points out that this is the first time in the Torah that the Jewish people are called Yeshurun. Why here?

The answer is that they were now going into *Eretz Yisrael* and were no longer going to have the daily gift of Heaven-sent manna. They were going to have their own fields that they could develop and experience abundance for the first time. And a sudden abundance of good things, especially after coming from the empty desert wilderness to the fruitful land of milk and honey, can lead people to forget Hashem.

That is why, says Rav Hirsch, the name Yeshurun was used here for the first time. Yeshurun means "straight, just, upright." Moshe knew it would be hard for the Jewish nation to remain "upright" when they would have an abundance of blessing. He, therefore, used the term Yeshurun to remind them who they really were and what they represented. They had to live up to this name when they would be tested with plenty.

How true. Look at Jews in America, England, and other prosperous Western lands. Despite relative wealth and comfort, it is in these lands that there is more assimilation than ever before. How can that be? Shouldn't these people feel more gratitude toward Hashem and strive to do His mitzvos?

The answer lies in the fact that when a person has too much, he becomes rebellious, intimidating, and self-assured. Thus, though food can be elevating, it can also bring out the most negative spiritual behavior.

Rabbeinu Bechaya in his *sefer Shulchan Shel Arbah* gives us an incredible insight as to the spiritual dangers of overeating. He notes that when one overeats and drinks too much, it can lead to haughtiness and the capacity to do [horrible] things that normally would not be done. He writes that the brothers sold Yosef only after they ate and drank, as it says וַיֵּשְׁבוּ לֶאֱכָל לֶחֶם וַיִּשְׂאוּ עֵינֵיהֶם וַיִּרְאוּ וְהִנֵּה אֹרְחַת יִשְׁמְעֵאלִים, *They sat to eat food, they raised their eyes and they saw, behold — a caravan of Ishmaelites … (Bereishis 37:25).* He then adds a startling thought. "That is the reason why the Torah instructs us, וְאָכַלְתָּ וְשָׂבָעְתָּ וּבֵרַכְתָּ, *You will eat, and you will be satisfied, and bless Hashem (Devarim 8:10),* for one must make an immediate connection to Hashem with *bentching* after eating, otherwise the satiation could lead to haughtiness and sin."

A Berachah L'vatalah

Food is challenging in so many ways. Many of us fight a daily battle simply not to gain weight. And so many of us are losing this battle.

According to a study done in 2004, 66 percent of adult Americans are overweight or obese. Now in 2011 it's probably even greater.

Truthfully, I did not want to speak about this topic. I will share something personal. Years ago, before my eldest daughter was married, I made up my mind that I was going to lose a certain amount of weight before the wedding, and *baruch Hashem* I did. I walked every day, was careful about my intake of food, and accomplished my goal. More recently, when my grandson was about to become bar mitzvah, I made up my mind once again that I would lose weight (it was more than 14 years since my daughter's wedding and I had gained a few pounds), so that I could dance easily and look good for the pictures. And once again, *baruch Hashem*, I accomplished the goal!

But then, after the *simchahs*, I regained the weight I had lost! I felt bad and resolved to do something about it, but for whatever reason did not accomplish what I intended. Then the Brooklyn Task Force asked me to give a talk about overeating. How could I? Shouldn't a speaker practice what he preaches?

I asked my rebbi, Rav Dovid Cohen, for some advice and he told me he had a great story to tell. "Use this story," he said, "and everyone (including you) will get the appropriate message."

In a city far from New York, a certain prominent woman was asked by the *menahel* of the Bais Yaakov to be the guest of honor at the upcoming ladies' dinner. She refused. The *menahel* asked her why she wouldn't do it. He gave her the reasons that she deserved the honor. "After all," he said, "all your daughters have attended the school; you are so beloved in the community, and you and your husband have provided the school with much financial assistance."

The woman replied that she was overweight and was too embarrassed to be the focus of attention. The *menahel* told her the dinner was in three months and he gave her a *berachah* that by then she would lose all the weight she wanted and would be proud to be seen in public. She listened and then agreed.

Three months later the dinner took place; however, she had not lost an ounce! Unflinchingly, she got up to speak and said, "You should all know, I did not want to accept this honor. I felt I was overweight and did not look good. However, the *menahel* gave me a *berachah* that I would lose the weight by the time the dinner was here, so I want all of you to know you are all looking at a *berachah l'vatalah*."

In reality we have to be serious about our weight. So many diseases occur because of excess weight. Heart attacks, diabetes, strokes, and even some forms of cancer occur more frequently in people who are overweight. However, many of these are preventable. When you think about it, what right do we have to overeat and possibly cause a spouse or children, heaven forbid, to sit *shivah*? Did you ever think of it that way? Isn't it awful? We have to be able to push away those extra franks-in-blankets, pastries, and cheesecake desserts.

What We're Starving for

Why aren't we careful? Is it really a lack of self-control?

Rabbi Avraham Peretz Friedman of Passaic, New Jersey, is a multitalented individual. He has served as a rabbi in various communities, has authored books on marriage, and even lectures often for the FBI. He once showed me an article he wrote but never printed: "You Shall Eat and Be Satisfied: The Torah Approach to Healthy Eating." In it he asks, "Is it a lack of self-control that causes us to overeat?" He answers emphatically, "No."

And the proof? Would any of us eat something *milchig* an hour after we ate *fleishig*? Would any of us eat *chametz* on *Pesach*? Would any among us eat before Ne'ilah on Yom Kippur?

We see that we can all control ourselves if we have to. If it's not a question of self-control, then what is it?

We're starving — but it's not for food. We're starving for something — and food fills that void. What is it that we are starving for?

Rabbi Friedman told me that he used to lecture in Durham, North Carolina, on "Self-Esteem through Jewish Spirituality." He would discuss why people crave food. Once, after a lecture, a man who was more than 100 pounds overweight told him, "I am filled but not fulfilled!"

People seek comfort, security, reassurance, and feelings of importance. Food often gives them that satisfaction. Therefore, people will often eat *even though they are not hungry!*

However, our souls also crave — for connection to Hashem. And that is why Hashem gave us food: to make that connection to Him. By making a *berachah* before and after eating, our souls fulfill their craving.

If we would take the time to understand the benefits of food — if we would stop to admire the color, texture, and beauty of food — we would feel so much more grateful to Hashem for the food we are privileged to eat. Food should be eaten slowly. It should be savored and appreciated. Remember, Hashem could have made it that our diet would be motor oil or gasoline.

Rav Chatzkel Levenstein once said, "People recite *Birchas HaMazon* because they believe it is the *frum* thing to do. Yes, it is a mitzvah to *bentch*, but we must know that an integral part of *Birchas HaMazon* is the element of *hakoras hatov*, gratitude to Hashem for the food and for its appearance, and many people don't even think about that." (See *Ohr Yechezkel, Middos*, p. 327.)

The Limits of Exercise

How are we going to change? Many people think it's through exercise. Yes, we should exercise, especially before we eat, because it helps us digest the food better. However, exercise is never enough.

There are many who exercise on a treadmill for a considerable amount of time. They build up an appetite and when they are done, they feel they're entitled to a reward and they head straight for the refrigerator. The calories add up, even if you exercise. If you don't minimize the calories, exercise won't help you lose weight.

In order to change we have to accept something: We cannot eat all we want, whenever we want.

Advice From a Well-Being Coach

Rabbi Eli Glazer and his wife, of Baltimore, Maryland, started a wonderful organization called *Soveya*, which means "satiated." They both were once very overweight and lost more than 100 pounds each. He almost died due to his weight and subsequently started this program that is now being brought to day schools all across the country. He lectures in yeshivos while his wife lectures in Bais Yaakovs, and they are proving to people, through individual counseling as well, that a person can really change. (They can be reached at 888-876-8392. Check their website www.soveya.com.)

In Brooklyn today there is a gentleman who is dedicating his life to helping men lose weight. His name is Tzvi Goldberg. If you contact Tzvi he will guide you through consultations and daily encouraging emails on your progress ... or lack thereof.

My favorite message of his is: "Who needs perfect? Celebrate direction, not perfection."

This should be hung on every refrigerator. It's not a question of perfection; nobody can be perfect. It's a question of direction.

Tzvi claims, "When a person eats because of emotional triggers, because of stress, or because of anger or boredom, it's a sign that his life lacks meaning and food is only temporarily pro-

> **When you eat because of emotional triggers, because of stress, or because of anger or boredom, it's a sign that life lacks meaning and food temporarily provides that meaning.**

viding that meaning. Those are steps in the wrong direction."

Incredibly, there is no charge for his service! This is not a misprint. Tzvi does not charge.

His rallying cry is, "It's not your weight so much as where you carry the weight that matters most to your health. Studies have linked a larger waist size to higher risk of heart attack, cancer, diabetes, and dementia." (He can be reached at tg.wellness. coach@gmail.com. Women have their own resource by contacting Goldie at

> **It's not your weight so much as where you carry the weight that matters most to your health.**

kschasuna@gmail.com. Here, too, there is no charge for her advice.)

Rabbi Yisroel (Jerry) Gross of Brooklyn lost 60 pounds with Tzvi's help and has kept it off for years. He even ran the 26-mile New York Marathon under the banner of *Soveya* to get the message out that indeed people can change.

You're a Jew — Think Before You Chew

The *Meshech Chochmah* (*Bereishis* 2:16) points out that "Hashem told Adam, מִכֹּל עֵץ הַגָּן אָכֹל תֹּאכֵל, *Eat from every tree in the Garden!* Food was not only meant to satiate the body it would also satiate Adam's soul." (It was only from the Tree of Knowledge that Adam could not eat.) He cites the *Yerushalmi Kiddushin* (4:12): *At the final Judgment one will have to give an accounting for not having eaten everything that he saw.* (See *Mesillas Yesharim*, Chapter 13.)

I am not here to tell you not to eat. It's the most natural thing to do. Just do it in moderation. Eat slowly. You're a Jew — think before you chew.

We have a responsibility not only to ourselves but to our families and friends. May Hashem bless all of us that we be able to see each other 20 pounds lighter with *Mashiach* in Yerushalayim.

Money:
Part I

Does it handle you or do you handle it?
A lecture on dollars and sense

When Avraham Avinu sent Eliezer to find a *shidduch* for Yitzchak, the Torah introduces the episode with these words, וַיֹּאמֶר אַבְרָהָם אֶל עַבְדּוֹ זְקַן בֵּיתוֹ הַמּשֵׁל בְּכָל אֲשֶׁר לוֹ, *And Avraham said to his servant, the one who ruled over everything that he had* ... (*Bereishis* 24:2). The simple meaning is that Eliezer was in control of all of Avraham's possessions. The *Kli Yakar*, however, tells us that the phrase "ruled over everything that he had" refers to Eliezer's possessions. He ruled over his money; money did not rule over him.

Rav Avraham Pam would often quote this *Kli Yakar* when he spoke about *shidduchin*, since he felt that those who were controlled by money could not be counted on to act appropriately in *shidduch* matters. The *Kli Yakar* writes that anyone who runs after money is someone whose money rules over him. He has no control. Avraham trusted Eliezer because he (Eliezer) had the proper perspective on finances. Thus, he could be trusted to find a proper *shidduch* for Yitzchak.

The *Midrash* (*Koheles* 1:13) tells us that that no person leaves this world having fulfilled even half of his desires. Anyone who has $100 wants $200. Anyone who has $200 wants $400. By nature, we want to make more money and hold onto as much of it as we can for as long as we can. If we do not work on ourselves, this all-too-human nature can overwhelm us.

When the Vilna Gaon was planning a trip to *Eretz Yisrael* (sadly, he never made it to his destination), he wrote a letter to his family that included these words, "Do not be obsessed and impressed with riches and honor. This world is compared to those who drink salty water. They drink endless amounts and are sure they will be satiated, but in reality it only makes them thirstier."

Many of our grandparents and great-grandparents came to America because it was referred to as the *goldene medinah the Golden Land.* Many people felt that if they only could make a good salary today they would have security tomorrow.

> For countless people, the American dream became the American nightmare.

But sadly, for countless people, the American dream became the American nightmare. Money was not the answer to their happiness and today there is a serious lack of money. We read every day that thousands of jobs have been lost. Even when jobs are created, many require less skill and pay less. Today we live in difficult financial times. Who ever heard of banks going bankrupt? Who ever heard of financial institutions going under? We live in a society obsessed with the dollar.

Without proper *hashkafos* one can easily be adversely affected by the dollar. Both the "haves" and the "have-nots" must be aware how to handle their financial situation.

The Tough Sale

The *Gemara* (*Shabbos* 31a) tells us that when a person goes up to *Shamayim* after 120 years, the first question he will be asked is not how many mitzvos he did or even how much Torah he learned. But

> "Were you honest in business?"

rather, נָשָׂאתָ וְנָתַתָּ בֶּאֱמוּנָה, *Were you honest in business?*

They will not ask how much you made in commissions; how many suits, cars, or dresses you sold; how many walls you decorated; how many properties you managed. They will ask, "Did you fabricate lies about your competition? Did you pay your bills on time? Did you inflate the deductible on the insurance? Were you honest in your dealings with others?"

R' Elya Dushnitzer was a *mashgiach* in the Lumzher Yeshivah in Petach Tikvah, Israel. The Chazon Ish once said that R' Elya was one of the *lamed vav tzaddikim* (36 righteous people) upon whom the world stands. When R' Sholom Schwadron, the Maggid of Jerusalem, was a teenager, he learned in the Lumzher yeshivah. He told the following story:

R' Elya had an orchard of orange trees. The orchard was not his originally. He bought it from his son, R' Asher, who had received it as a *nadan* (dowry). The orchard was not producing well, so R' Elya took it off his son's hands. As R' Elya grew older he accumulated many debts. "How can I die," he said, "owing so much money? I have to sell this orchard and use the money to pay my debts."

He always told people, "Please *daven* for me — please tell the little children in the yeshivah to *daven* that I should be able to sell this orchard."

A year later, one of his *talmidim* went into business and started selling various properties. A fellow from America came and said to him, "I want to buy an orchard."

"Oh, my rebbi is trying to sell an orchard. Let me hook you up with him."

He phoned R' Elya and arranged a meeting. When they arrived, R' Elya said to them, "I want to tell you a *Gemara* in *Bava Metzia* (29b): 'If a father left a lot of money to his son and the son wants to make sure the money will go down the drain, he should hire workers and *not* look after them.' If a boss hires workers but does not oversee them, they will not do a good job and he will lose his money in no time."

R' Elya then turned to the businessman, "You want to buy this orchard? Will you be living in *Eretz Yisrael* or America?

"America."

"Then I can't sell you this orchard. It's ridiculous. The workers will not take care of it and you'll lose all your money."

"No, rebbi," the man said, "I want to buy it anyway."

"Then I am obligated to tell you that in the northwest corner of the orchard there are a few orange trees that the sun does not reach and therefore oranges don't grow. I want you to know that."

As the *talmid* was watching this, he began to understand why the orchard had never been sold.

"Don't worry," the businessman told R' Elya, "I want to buy it anyway."

"Oh, I forgot to tell you about the southwest corner," R' Elya reminded himself. "On the southwest corner there are a lot of rocks and stones ... and the ground sinks in. Therefore, nothing can grow there either."

"I want to buy it anyway."

Suddenly the man looked at his watch, took out a pill, and swallowed it. "I have a little heart condition," he explained.

"A heart condition?" R Elya asked in surprise. "And you want to buy this orchard? It could give you aggravation. There is no way I'm selling it to you. Hashem should help you to have a *refuah sheleimah.*"

No matter how much the man begged, R' Elya would not sell the orchard to him.

R' Sholom Schwadron would often ask, "Why did Hashem make this man go through all this trouble only to fail at his attempt at buying the orchard?" R' Schwadron then explained that *Hashem* wanted him to get a *berachah* for a *refuah sheleimah* from a *lamud vav tzaddik.*

As a footnote to the story, in the end R' Elya eventually sold the orchard. But there is no doubt that R' Elya Dushnitzer was someone who came to *Shamayim* and was able to give a positive answer to the question, נָשָׂאתָ וְנָתַתָּ בֶּאֱמוּנָה, *Were you honest in business?*

If You Think That's Difficult ...

A young man once came to R' Yisrael Salanter and said, "Rebbe, I have to quit my job."

"What's your job?"

"I'm a *shochet.*"

"Such a *heilege* [holy] job in *Klal Yisrael.* Why do you want to quit?"

"Exactly for that reason. I feel such an *achrayus*, sense of responsibility. What if my *chalif* (*schechitah* knife) isn't perfect? What if I have to check the lungs and I don't do a perfect job? I'll cause others to eat *treif*. What if the butcher pressures me to tell him that the animal is kosher even when it is not? I can't have that on my conscience."

"Then what do you want to do?" R' Yisrael asked.

"I'll be a plain, simple businessman."

"That's easier?" R' Yisrael said. "Do you have any idea how many things you have to be mindful of in business; how much should be on your conscience? Look at what you have to worry about if you go into business: לֹא תִגְנֹב [do not steal], לֹא תַחְמֹד [do not covet] [*Shemos* 20:13,14] לֹא תְכַחֲשׁוּ [do not say anything untrue] [*Vayikra* 19:11], לֹא תִגְזֹל [do not rob] [ibid. v. 13], לֹא תַעֲשֹׁק [do not cheat] [ibid.; *Devarim* 24:14], and much more. There are 10 times as many *aveiros* in business as in *shechitah*!"

Treife Food, Treife Money

The Manchester Rosh Yeshivah, Rav Yehuda Zev Segal, once said something very frightening in the name of R' Menachem Mendel of Riminov, a *talmid* of the Rebbe Reb Elimelech of Lizhensk. R' Menachem Mendel asked, "Why do we find that at times a child seems to be going on the right *derech* and then suddenly in his teen years he goes off the *derech*?" [I want to add a personal note here before you read his startling answer. We have no right to judge any child or any family. We can only reflect on ourselves. There are many reasons that children go off the *derech*, and the Riminover merely suggests one of them. We must think of his answer in terms of our own immediate family and not those of others.]

The Riminover suggested that the reason is

> The literal *kashrus* of the food itself was not in question. Rather the food was purchased with *treife* money.

that in very many cases, it comes down to *treife* food — but not the type of *treife* food you are thinking of. This food had a perfectly good *hechsher*. The literal *kashrus* of the food itself was not in question. Rather, the food is spiritually *treif* because it was purchased with *treife* money.

When people use *treife* money — money they were not supposed to earn; money they procured from cheating in business or in some other fashion — and buy food for their family, they contaminate the spiritual lifeblood of their own children. When the children eat food that is spiritually *treif* it contaminates the נְשָׁמָה (soul) and מוֹחַ (mind). That is why otherwise wonderful children can, *chas v'shalom*, go off the *derech*. They have been fed *treife* food.

To reiterate, this is not to criticize anyone who, *chas v'shalom*, has children like that; it's not our right to judge. There are hundreds of reasons why children can go off the *derech*. But a person has to ask himself, *What kind of food am I giving to my children? Is it being purchased with treife money? Am I contaminating my own family?*

By the Sweat of Your Brow ...

Rabbi Yissachar Frand told a wonderful story witnessed by R' Chaim Yaakov Goldvicht, a Rosh Yeshivah in *Eretz Yisrael*. Rav Goldvicht would introduce the episode by explaining in a unique way the words that Hashem said to Adam after he sinned. Hashem scolded Adam and said (*Bereishis* 3:19), בְּזֵעַת אַפֶּיךָ תֹּאכַל לֶחֶם, *By the sweat of your brow you will eat bread*. The simple meaning is that now Adam (and the rest of mankind) would have to "sweat" to make a living; *parnassah* would not be easy.

However, Rav Goldvicht explained that the phrase can be understood as two points of information. First: there would have to be sweat and toil; that is בְּזֵעַת אַפֶּיךָ. No one can get away without working to make a living. Second: one must know that the *parnassah* that does come can often surface by other means and not necessarily as a direct result of the toil. Hence, תֹּאכַל לֶחֶם ("you will eat bread") is an independent statement. He then gave an example.

In 1948, before Israel became a state, Rabbi Goldvicht was in a grocery store when a little girl came in and asked for a *machberet* (a notebook). The storekeeper, who stocked hundreds of items beside food, looked around and turned over the store until he found that little *machberet*. It took him 10 minutes. However, the profit margin was very little. He made 10 cents on it.

Two minutes later a British soldier came in and wanted a Parker pen, which was, at the time, an expensive, top-of-the-line pen. The shelves in this store were piled with all kinds of odds and ends that the grocer sold. It would have been almost impossible to find a thin pen among the dozens of items that were strewn around. Yet he found it immediately, because he had seen it when he was looking for the *machberet* for the little girl. He got the pen, charged the soldier full price, and made himself a nice profit.

R' Goldvicht said, the בְּזֵעַת אַפֶּיךָ was the *machberet*, and תֹּאכַל לֶחֶם was the Parker pen. Indeed, we have to work and sweat, but that's not always where the *hatzlachah* will come from.

The *Maharsha* (*Kiddushin* 82a) says something frightening: Without work you cannot rely only on *tefillah*. You have to get out there and get a job. If somebody is unemployed, he should not stay home. He has to go out and get a job. *Tefillah* alone is not enough. Of course, he adds, Torah study must be one's priority and that is what should take up most of his time, but a job is of utmost importance.

The *Gemara* tells us (*Niddah* 70b): What should a person do to become wealthy? He should conduct business honestly. Many people tried that, the *Gemara* suggests, but it did not help. So the *Gemara* suggests to *daven* to the One to Whom all wealth belongs. That, too, did not always work, the *Gemara* says. It concludes that you have to have both. You have to work with honesty and *daven*.

The *Gemara* (*Kiddushin* 82a) also tells us that every father should train his son in a career that is easy and clean, and he should *daven* because every type of career has wealthy and poor people. There are many people selling furniture and making a fortune. There are people selling dinette sets and not making any money. There are artists who make a fortune and many who cannot put bread on the table. Many people are selling peanuts and popcorn and making a fortune; many are selling peanuts and popcorn — and that is what they are making: peanuts and popcorn.

The *Gemara* tells us that poverty does not come from the job. Everything is according to your *zechusim* and *Siyata D'Shmaya*. That is what we have to remember. It is not the job. Do not think, if only I were in computers I'd have made a fortune. You'd be making the same "fortune" you are making today. It is all depends on your *zechusim*.

A Few Recommendations

Let me close with some suggestions that may lead us to financial stability.

■ Rabbeinu Bachya tells us that *baruch* does not mean only "blessed," but *bereichah*, "a wellspring." When you recite a *berachah* you are not only thanking Hashem, but praying, "Hashem, please give to everybody from this infinite wellspring of Your blessing." In this light we can understand what *Chazal* meant (*Berachos* 35b) when they taught that if one eats food and does not make a *berachah* he is stealing not only from Hashem but also from *Klal Yisrael*. He is stealing from *Klal Yisrael* because he gave up the opportunity to pray that *Klal Yisrael* should receive from the wellspring of blessing that Hashem possesses.

■ *Chazal* (*Bava Basra* 25) teach that if you want to acquire wisdom/intelligence keep your feet a little to the right side when you *daven* the *Shemoneh Esrei*, which is the south side of the shul. However if you want to get rich, keep your feet a little to the left, the north side of the shul. The reason is that in the *Beis HaMikdash*, the *menorah*, which represents Torah, was on the south side. However, the *Shulchan*, which represents food/*parnassah*, was on the north side. Thus, the south side (right side) points to wisdom; the north side (left side) points to wealth.

■ Finally, may we all be *zocheh* to be "happy with our lot." That attitude is the key to emotional stability, which is surely more important than financial stability in the long run.*

---

*For more insights on the right approach to financial matters, see "Money, Part II" (p. 99) and "Seven Strategies for Surviving the Recession" (p. 107).

Money:
Part II

Does it handle you or do you handle it?
A lecture on dollars and sense

Too often people judge and evaluate each other by the amount of money they have. People should be defined by the amount of Torah they learn, the quantity of *chessed* they do, the *yiras Shamayim* they have, and the *ahavas Yisrael* they display. Rav Sholom Schwadron, the *Maggid* of Jerusalem, decried the Yiddish question, "*Vifel is er vert?* — How much is he worth?"

"What people are really asking," said Rav Sholom, "is 'how much money does he have'? But they don't say that. They use the euphemism *vert* [value or worth]. However, money does not evaluate a person's worth in this world or in the next."

These days, when money is tight and *parnassah* is hard to come by for many people, it is appropriate to evaluate our attitudes and sensitivity toward money and financial responsibilities.

Your Attitude Determines Your Altitude

The Baal Shem Tov told a beautiful story that puts the challenges of *parnassah* into their proper perspective. There was an old man, a water carrier, who was shlepping water up a hill to deliver it to the residents who lived there. That's how he made his living. Somebody said to him, "Reb Yid, how are you doing?"

"What do you mean, how am I doing?" came the bitter reply. "I'm 70 years old and have no savings. I have to shlep this water up the hill. It's so hard. I would've thought that by my age I could have retired already. But here I am, shlepping water. That's how I'm doing!"

The next day, someone else met this same water carrier doing the same thing he had been doing the day before and asked, "Reb Yid, how are you doing?"

This time he said, "Wow, look at me. *Baruch Hashem*, I don't have to ask anybody for help. I can shlep my own water and carry it up the hill. I am self-sufficient. I don't have to worry that my children will have to support me. It's wonderful."

What was the difference? The Baal Shem Tov clarified the water carrier's view by explaining a seeming disagreement between Rav Meir and Rav Yosi in *Rosh Hashanah* 16a. Rav Meir held that we are all judged on Rosh Hashanah; however, Rav Yosi held we are judged every day. The Baal Shem explained that on Rosh Hashanah we are judged as to how much money we will make the upcoming year. However, on a daily basis we are judged as to what mood we will be in to accept that particular amount allotted to us. In other words the same person can have the same amount of money on different days of the year, but at one time he will be thrilled with his lot and at another time he will be despondent.

I can relate to those feelings. As a *mohel*, some days I think to myself, "What a great job! I have the opportunity to be working around happy people who are celebrating a momentous occasion in their lives. I have the best job in the world. And, on top of that, I get bagels and lox *every* morning."

Then at other times I think, "What kind of profession is this? You can never plan a vacation because one never knows what boys will be born this week, forcing me to be here next week. I never know my schedule more than eight days in advance. In the 'girl season' I wait impatiently for my phone to ring. When I was younger I used to worry, 'Maybe people want an older *mohel*,' and now that I am older I worry at times, 'Maybe people want a younger *mohel*.'"

(The truth is, though; I love and am very proud of my profession as a *mohel*. The event is holy; one has the opportunity to usher a newborn into the *Bris shel Avrohom Avinu*, and many times there are opportunities for great *kiddush Shem Shamayim*.)

But that is what the Baal Shem meant. On Rosh Hashanah you are judged and it is decreed what you will receive the entire year. But every day you are judged on your mood, on your attitude: How do you look at what you have?

The Wheel of Fortune

Chazal (*Shabbos* 151b) tell us that R' Chiya once said to his wife, "When a poor man comes to the door, don't forget to give him money, because maybe someday our own children will have to knock on somebody's door for money."

"What!" she said. "Do you want to curse us? Why are you saying that?"

"I'm not the one telling it to you," he replied. "It's a *pasuk* (*Devarim* 15:10): נָתוֹן תִּתֵּן לוֹ וְלֹא יֵרַע לְבָבְךָ בְּתִתְּךָ לוֹ כִּי בִּגְלַל הַדָּבָר הַזֶּה יְבָרֶכְךָ ה' אֱלֹקֶיךָ, *Give to the poor man, for in return* (בִּגְלַל) *for this matter, Hashem your G-d will bless you ....*" The word בִּגְלַל means "circle" (from *gilgul*). R' Chiya continued, "Nobody holds onto money forever." The wheel of fortune is constantly turning. Those at the top one day can just as easily be at the bottom the next day, and vice versa, those who have no money can rise to wealth and riches.

> The wheel of fortune is constantly turning.

There is a fascinating *Midrash* (*Bamidbar* 22:8) regarding money and possessions. The *Midrash* asks why possessions are called נְכָסִים. The *Midrash* answers, שֶׁנִּכְסִים מִזֶּה וְנִגְלִין לָזֶה, *Because they vanish from one and go to another.* נְכָסִים are נִכְסִים, "they become hidden." No one holds onto them forever.

The *Midrash* continues: Why is money also called זוּז? שֶׁזָּזִים מִזֶּה וְנוֹתִין לָזֶה, *They* [money and financial holdings] *move from one to the other.* זוּז indicates movement.

The *Midrash* teaches further that money is also called מָמוֹן. Why? It stands for, מָה אַתָּה מוֹנֶה?, *What are you counting?* Do you think you will hold onto it forever?

מָעוֹת, which also means money, stands for, מַה לָעֵת?, *What are you making a big deal of? Something that is only for a [short] time.* People do not hold onto their money forever.

Be a Yielding Person

R' Akiva once asked R' Nechunya HaGadol, "How did you merit to live such a long life?"

"וַתְרָן בְּמָמוֹנִי הָיִיתִי, *I was generous with money,*" he replied (*Megillah* 28a).

The *Sefer Chassidim* (323) writes something remarkable. "It is better to be a friend of an *am haaretz* who is yielding with his money than to be a friend of a *talmid chacham* who is stingy."

We have to be careful not to be stingy. We have to be kind and generous with our money. Give a bigger tip, a nicer gift.

A young woman from Queens was dating a young man who hailed from out of town. He did not have a car, so the girl's family said he could borrow their car for the evening. They went out once … twice … three times. After four times, their relationship was over. About a week later, the parents of the girl received a letter in the mail with a $50 ticket. A traffic-camera had taken a picture of the car going through a light on Queens Boulevard. The parents realized that this had happened while this young man was taking out their daughter. They could have called the young man and told him he was obligated to pay the ticket, but they decided not to call him. They paid the $50. I think that was very generous.

Debt and Tzedakah

The *Sefer Chassidim* (454) informs us, "If you owe money to people, do not dispense money to numerous charities until you have paid your debts." If you owe money to others for services they rendered, for something you purchased, or for money you borrowed, it seems that the money you have is essentially not yours. It belongs to the people to whom you owe money.

If one owes money, he must readjust his standard of living and not live with luxuries and non-essentials to which he may have become accustomed. That third suit or that extra dress will have to wait. The car he plans to buy may have to be downsized from the one he had been driving until now. Paying back debts must be a priority.

There are many who owe money and simply disregard their responsibilities. During Ne'ilah on Yom Kippur, as the *baal tefillah* repeats the *Shemoneh Esrei*, he says, "You [Hashem] reach out a hand to willful sinners .... You taught us to confess ... our sins, לְמַעַן נֶחְדַּל מֵעוֹשֶׁק יָדֵינוּ, so that we can withdraw our hands from robbery." In 1916, the Chofetz Chaim asked his congregants, "Who is guilty of robbery here in our shul? Are we not all honest and *ehrlich*? What do these words, לְמַעַן נֶחְדַּל מֵעוֹשֶׁק יָדֵינוּ, mean to us?"

The Chofetz Chaim's answer shocked everyone. "The person who took out a loan and did not repay it — he is the one who is guilty of *geneivah* [robbery]."

If one has an outstanding debt and sees that he will not be able to pay on time, he is duty-bound to call the party to whom he owes the money and assure him that the money will soon be forthcoming. Or, even better, he should offer to make a small payment as a gesture of good will.

Charity Starts at Home

Listen to this frightening *Sefer Chassidim*. He writes (324) of a wealthy man who was known to give *tzedakah* generously to the poor. A *chacham* said to him, "Everything that you are giving to the poor is not צְדָקָה, but a צְעָקָה [a crying shame]. You have a brother and relatives who are poor. You have to give to them first!"

How many of us have relatives that are starving, brothers and sisters that do not have food to eat or are out of a job? Do we give them money? We will give first and most generously to all the *mosdos* where we get honor and glory, but not them. If you have relatives who are financially in debt, monetarily down, you have a responsibility to give to them *first*.

The Kapishnitzer Rebbe, Rabbi Avrohom Yehoshua Heshel, once made a special trip to Manhattan from his home in Brooklyn to visit one of his chassidim in his office. When the Rebbe entered the front vestibule, the secretary rang the chassid in the back office and said, "You won't believe this, but I think your rabbi is here."

He came running out and called, "Rebbe! What are you doing here? I just saw you this morning in shul. I feel terrible. Why did you have to come? You should have called and I would have come to you."

"No," the Rebbe said. "I need you now, so I decided to come to you."

"Please sit down. Rebbe, what can I do for you?"

"I'm collecting for a family. *Nebach*, they're very broken. No money, huge medical bills, tuition bills, and food bills."

"*Oy*, Rebbe, that's all you need? You could have called me and I would've brought the money to you."

"No, the right thing is that I need you, so I have to come to you."

"Rebbe, to whom should I make out the check?"

"Make it out to your brother!" he told him.

What a lesson that was! The Rebbe went out of his way to drive home the point to this fellow. That is a lesson that we all have to remember. Each of us has family members who are down and out. They have to be our priority.

Bread and War

It once struck me that the middle letters of the Hebrew word מִלְחָמָה, "war," are ל, ח, and מ, which spell לֶחֶם, "bread," symbolizing perhaps that putting bread on the table is a war, a battle.

> **Putting bread on the table is a war, a battle.**

When I shared this thought with my brother-in-law, R' Yehuda Abraham, he said, "There are indeed many words that mean both food and battle."

He mentioned the following: the word טֶרֶף in *Tehillim* (111:5) means "sustenance" or "food." However, it also means to "tear to bits" (See *Bereishis* 37:33, טָרֹף טֹרַף יוֹסֵף). The word מְזוֹנוֹת or זָן means "sustenance." A similar compound word, כְּלֵי זַיִן, means "ammunition."

The Torah tells us that Yaakov Avinu said, "... יֵשׁ שֶׁבֶר בְּמִצְרָיִם, ... *there are provisions [food] in Egypt*" (ibid. 42:1). Interestingly שֶׁבֶר, from *shevirah*, also means "breaking."

מִחְיָה, as in עַל הַמִּחְיָה, means "sustenance," but מְחִיַּית עֲמָלֵק means "wiping out" or "fighting" Amalek.

When Moshe saw the burning bush, he realized, ...וְהַסְּנֶה אֵינֶנּוּ אֻכָּל,

... the bush was not consumed (*Shemos* 3:2). The word אָכַּל, "consumed," has the same letters as אכל, "food."

The lesson from all these words — *lechem, teref, mezonos, shever, michyah,* and *ochel* — is that making a *parnassah* is like being on a battlefront. One needs "ammunition." His time becomes "consumed." He has to "fight off" competition. He has to "break open" new venues of income, etc.

As in any war, there are victors and casualties. Those whom Hashem blesses with "victory" must be sensitive to those who are, for the moment, "casualties." Indeed, the *Ohr HaChaim* writes (*Devarim* 15:7) that the reason there are poor people in this world is to test how the wealthy will respond to their needs.

Nobody Else Has to Know

Those who are blessed and are able to live comfortable lives must be sensitive to those who cannot live as they do. The Torah tells us (ibid 8:12), פֶּן תֹּאכַל וְשָׂבָעְתָּ וּבָתִּים טֹבִים תִּבְנֶה, *Lest you will eat, be satiated, and build big, beautiful houses*. The word טֹבִים is missing a ו. Why? Because these houses are not really good.

When you build a big house in an area where not everybody has a big house, it is painful to others. And, *chas v'shalom,*

> **Blessing comes when you act discreetly.**

it can be harmful to the person himself. For as *Chazal* teach (*Taanis* 8b), אֵין הַבְּרָכָה מְצוּיָה אֶלָּא בְּדָבָר הַסָּמוּי מִן הָעַיִן, *Blessing is found only with things that are hidden from the eye*.

Keep a low profile. Do not tell everyone where you are going on vacation. Do not tell people what luxuries you can afford. Do not talk about your wealth. Real *berachah* comes about when we do things discreetly, with modesty and sensitivity.

Rav Yaakov Galinsky tells a whimsical story. There was a fellow who was building an ostentatious house in Rav Yaakov's neighborhood. No house in the area was even half the size of this one going up. One day Rav Galinsky went over to the fellow and said, "Excuse me, but you see this window that you are installing? I think it should be over a little bit, two feet to the right. And you see this decorative design over the door? I don't like the style. I think you should get a different one."

The owner became very angry with Rav Galinsky and said, "Why are you telling *me* what to do? This is my house and I'll build it however I please."

"It may be your house, but you're not going to see the outside of it very much. You'll be living inside. I'm going to see it every day and every night because I walk down this street very often, and it looks like you are trying to impress the passersby, so as a passerby I want to inform you that I would be more impressed with a different style design. Therefore, do it the way I want it."

I can't imagine that this story actually happened, but Rav Galinsky was trying to bring out a point. If you are building, do it in a way that is modest.

Through having the proper attitudes and *hashkafos* toward money, as well as abundant sensitivity to the plight of those less fortunate, may we merit to preserve our wealth and develop real wealth, the wealth of a Torah-true life both inside and outside our homes.

Seven Strategies for Surviving the Recession

W e are at a crossroads in history, not only for the Jewish people, but for the world at large. The financial crisis affects *every* one of us the world over.

Rabbi Yechezkal Levenstein, the legendary *Mashgiach* in the Ponevezh Yeshivah, once stepped into a taxi driven by a secular Israeli. Surprisingly, the driver opened up and volunteered the following story:

> A number of years ago, a group of friends and I had finished our service in the Israeli army and decided to go on a safari in South Africa. One morning, my friend decided to stroll about on his own. Five minutes later we heard him yelling for his life.
>
> We ran over and saw that a boa constrictor had wrapped itself around him and was crushing him to death. First we took sticks and started hitting the snake. Nothing happened. Then we took rocks and hit it. Still nothing happened! It was wrapped around him as tightly as *ever*.
>
> One person told our poor friend, "You're going to die! Say '*Shema*!'"

The fellow started saying *Shema* — and, miracu-
lously, the snake loosened its hold and slithered away.

"What happened to that fellow?" Rabbi Levenstein asked
the taxi driver.

"Rabbi, what do you mean? The next morning, he put on *tefil-
lin* for the first time in seven years. Then he signed up in yeshivah,
became religious, married, and now has children."

"And what about you?" he asked the taxi driver.

"Rabbi, the snake wasn't wrapped around me."

The Message Is for You

Anyone who thinks that the financial situation is not going to affect
him is like that taxi driver. Even if you
have not yet been personally touched
by the financial crisis, the message is
for you too.

> Even if you have not yet been personally touched by the financial crisis, the message is for you too.

There are many people who have
been able to maintain the same standard of living they had until now.
However, only a fool would think that it will always stay that way and
that the effects of the recession will never touch him.

When was the last time you walked into the office and said, "Thank
You, Master of the World, that I have a job"? When was the last time
someone bought an SUV or went on vacation and said, "Thank You,
Hashem, that I can afford this vacation with my family"?

Even if someone has not been personally affected by the recession — yet — there is a message for him. Do not take anything for
granted. And if you have been affected by the recession, the message
is even stronger.

How should we approach these difficult times? I am not going to
talk budgeting or taking a job that may be below your status and educa-
tion. That talk has its place. However, what I want to talk about now is
the spiritual perspective, which is the most important perspective and
the only one we have full control over anyway. I would like to suggest
seven different strategies to help survive this recession. Indeed, if we
do them properly we will not only survive, but thrive.

Strategy #1: Make That Connection

The Meiri (to *Nedarim* 49b) says: "Even though a person is judged on Rosh Hashanah regarding his livelihood (as well as his very life) he should pray every single day without fail for his livelihood."

Rabbi Shimon Bar Yochai was asked why Hashem only gave enough manna for each day. If He was already sending manna, why not give enough for the whole year? Because, Rabbi Shimon Bar Yochai answered, no one would ever talk to Hashem. If someone has all his needs taken care of, he is never going to reach out to Hashem. That is why the manna came every day and not all at once. It prods us to make the connection.

Make that connection to the Master of the World! And make it every day!

In fact, there are four places where we can make that connection just in morning prayers alone. They are propitious moments — opportunities — that appear every day.

The first is in the verse … פּוֹתֵחַ אֶת יָדֶךָ, *You open Your hand …*, which is part of *Ashrei*. This is so important that if it is not said with proper concentration it has to be repeated.

The second place is in *Bareich aleinu* (in the ninth blessing of the *Shemoneh Esrei*), which is the blessing for livelihood. However, not only should you be praying for yourself but you should also be praying for others, because if you have others in mind your prayers will be answered first (see *Bava Kamma* 92a).

The third place may surprise some of you. In the ArtScroll *Siddur* (and in most other *siddurim* today) under the blessing *Shema koleinu* (in the sixteenth blessing of the *Shemoneh Esrei*), there is a beautiful personal prayer for livelihood. Be sure to say it at least once a day.

The fourth place is also found in most *siddurim* today: After *Aleinu* there are additional prayers. Among them is a special prayer for livelihood. I try to never miss saying it.

Strategy #2: Birchas HaMazon

Sefer HaChinuch (#430, toward the end) says: "Anyone who is careful in *Birchas HaMazon* [the blessing after a meal] will have his sustenance come to him with honor his entire life."

If most of us were honest with ourselves, we'd admit that we are probably not as careful as we should be in *bentching*. We are even likely skipping words. We fool ourselves into thinking we know it by heart. Do you want sustenance with honor your entire life? Start saying *Birchas HaMazon* slowly and carefully from a *siddur* or a *bentcher*.

Strategy #3: Standing for the Mitzvah of Giving Tzedakah

Here is another thing many people are not careful about. It is even mentioned in the *Shulchan Aruch*: During Shacharis, stand at וַיְבָרֶךְ ... דָּוִיד, *And David blessed ...,* and then give *tzedakah* when you come to ... וְהָעשֶׁר וְהַכָּבוֹד מִלְּפָנֶיךָ, וְאַתָּה מוֹשֵׁל בַּכֹּל, *And wealth and honor come from You, and You rule everything ....*

Why do we stand up at *Vayivarech David*? According to Rabbi Yaakov Kamenetzky, it is because people are doing the mitzvah of walking to the center of the shul and giving *tzedakah*. In other words, giving *tzedakah* is one thing, but giving honor to those engaging in the mitzvah of giving *tzedakah* is another. Giving *tzedakah* is so great that we stand to honor those engaged in it. What a way of sensitizing ourselves to this great mitzvah!

Tomorrow there should be a whole group of people standing for וַיְבָרֶךְ דָּוִיד — and then walking to give *tzedakah*.

Strategy #4: Giving Tzedakah More Generously Than Ever

Chazal teach (*Gittin* 7a) that if a person sees that money is tight, he should give *tzedakah*. What does the *Gemara* mean, "give *tzedakah*"? If money is tight, how can one give *tzedakah*?

The answer can be illustrated with the story about a farmer who walked into the post office one day with a heavy package. The postal clerk weighed it and told him it was too heavy.

"What do you mean, 'it is too heavy'? What am I supposed to do?"

"You've got to put on more stamps."

"More stamps?" the farmer said indignantly. "That's going to make it heavier!"

He did not understand that it was the stamps that were going to carry it.

It's the same with *tzedakah*. If a person sees that his money is tight, he should give *tzedakah*! Giving *tzedakah* will merit him to make more money.

I heard another story from a collector who visited a certain well-to-do man every year. This time he happened to come to him literally on the day that Bear Stearns went under and the fellow lost a fortune. Furthermore, since he hadn't invested in Bear Stearns, but in a company that invested in Bear Sterns, he had no idea until that evening that his whole retirement fund was now gone.

It was at that moment that the collector came to him as usual and asked for money.

"I just can't give you what I gave you last year!" he told him. Then he explained to him about Bear Stearns.

"Okay, I'm sorry," the collector replied. "Whatever you want to give me is fine."

The man wrote out a check and handed it to the collector, who did not want to embarrass him, so he folded the check without looking it and exited the front door. Once outside, he looked at the check — and it was double the amount the man usually gave!

He immediately went back inside and said, "Excuse me, but maybe you don't remember what you gave last year. You doubled the amount this year!"

"Of course I remember," he replied. "I can't give what I gave last year — I've got to give more! I need more merit! That's why I have to give more now!"

Strategy #5: Keep a Low Profile

My mother always used to tell me: Blessing comes when you keep a low profile. The *Gemara* in *Taanis* (8b) indeed teaches just that: אֵין הַבְּרָכָה מְצוּיָה אֶלָּא בְּדָבָר הַסָּמוּי מִן הָעַיִן, *Blessing happens only with things that are hidden from the eye.*

If you have a great job and can take vacations, do not talk about them. All it is going to do is cause an *ayin hara* and create jealousy, which is almost sure to cause the eventual loss of the blessing.

If you merit having a livelihood, especially in these difficult days, do not talk about it. If something good happens in your life, there is only one person that you should tell it to who is guaranteed to be happy for you: your mother. No one else. Not your brother-in-law. Not your sister-in-law. No one!

I have another secret for you: If you have a beautiful home, do not make a lavish *chanukas habayis*. Not in today's times. All it will do is cause people to say, "Where'd you get those curtains? Where'd you get that beautiful sink? Where'd you get the towels? Why don't I have it?" it will lead to jealousy and, *chas v'shalom, ayin hara*

If you have anything that is going well for yourself in your life, keep quiet. Follow the advice of *Chazal* (and the advice of my mother): Keep a low profile.

Strategy #6: Honesty

The *Gemara* (*Niddah 70b*) tells us: "What should a person do to become wealthy? Be honest in business."

The *Gemara* then adds, "Many people tried this, but it did not help. What then should a person do? Be honest *and* pray to Hashem for your livelihood."

Prayer will help people *get* the money, but honesty in business is the way people merit to *keep* their money. Everyone knows the famous teaching (*Shabbos 31a*) that the first question a person will be asked after he passes from this world is: נָשָׂאתָ וְנָתַתָּ בֶּאֱמוּנָה, *Were you honest in business?* That is the *first* question.

If a person is not honest in business, not only does he lose his money, but he corrupts his children.

Many years ago, I was a counselor in camp. One day a fellow co-counselor and I shared a day off and decided to visit our friends in other camps. Before doing so, he wanted to call his mother to tell her that he was not able to visit her.

Now this was 35 years ago, long before cell phones. It cost money to make a long-distance call, and my friend did not want to pay it, so he decided to try a trick that was all too common. He would make a collect call and convey a message to his mother *through the unsuspecting operator* in a way that told his mother not to accept it.

"Operator," he said, "I'd like to make a person-to-person call to Mrs. Ich Kum Nisht" (Yiddish for "I'm not coming").

The operator waited for a second, and then said to him, "*Far vos kumstu nisht?*" ("Why aren't you coming?"). This was an operator in Liberty, New York!

You think you can get away with things, but you can't.

Rabbi Yehudah Winder, a noted *talmid chacham* and first-grade rebbi, told me an amazing story. A child in his class had a loose tooth. "Don't touch it," Rabbi Winder urged. "You'll only make it bleed."

Of course, this only made the child touch it more. Sure enough, it fell out and his mouth was bleeding.

"Go wash your mouth and then come back to class."

At lunchtime Rabbi Winder saw another child walking around with this child's tooth. "What are you doing with his tooth?!" he asked.

Listen to what the first-grader said: "My father gives us a dollar for every tooth that comes out. His father only gives him 50 cents. So we made a deal. I'll go home and show my father his tooth, get the dollar, and split it with him!"

Of course, he didn't consider that his father just might be smart enough and ask him to open his mouth to see where the tooth came from.

I cannot tell you how many times I heard Rav Pam quote the well-known saying of the *Maharsha* (*Kiddushin* 82b): "There are those who make their money with *chillul Hashem* through dealing dishonestly with non-Jews. This is nothing but a 'mitzvah that comes about through an *aveirah*' and the money is not going to last."

Have we really been honest in business?

Rav Shimon Schwab once told a group of accountants: "*The New York Times* is wrong when they write 'the Orthodox fellow was caught cheating.' He's not Orthodox! What makes him Orthodox? Those who

> **Those who resort to cheating, dishonesty, and fraud are irreligious.**

resort to cheating, trickery, dishonesty, and fraud may have the outward appearance of being God-fearing Jews. However, in fact, they're irreligious!"

It is not the outside that makes one religious. If he's not honest, he's not religious — and he's going to lose his money!

Strategy #7: Achdus

Not long ago, I had the opportunity to pray at the gravesite of the Rebbe R' Elimelech of Lizhensk in Poland as I took more than 100 people there in the summer. There is something incredibly special about *davening* there. Thousands of people go there every year.

Listen to what the Rebbe R' Elimelech wrote over 200 years ago: "In the time of *Mashiach*, fighting and baseless hatred will become rampant. And because of this, the channels of abundance and livelihood of the Jewish people will be disrupted."

What foresight! We do not have enough respect for one another. We categorize one another and only look favorably upon those in our category. That is why we have a recession today, according to Rebbe Elimelech of Lizhensk. We do not get along well enough with our fellow Jews.

"However," the Rebbe says, "from the great pressure that people will feel, Torah scholars and the God-fearing will be aroused to make an effort to tell all the Jewish people to make peace among themselves, and from this," he concludes, "the redemption will come."

In Summary

We have to pray with fervor, but it is not only a question of our daily prayers; we have to concentrate to say *Birchas HaMazon* slowly, word by word.

Additionally we should give *tzedadah* during the *tefillah* of וַיְבָרֶךְ דָּוִיד at the words וְהָעשֶׁר וְהַכָּבוֹד מִלְּפָנֶיךָ, וְאַתָּה מוֹשֵׁל בַּכֹּל, *And wealth and honor come from You, and You rule everything.* We must also realize the importance of giving *tzedakah* — even when things are tight.

> **Keep a low profile. If you have been blessed with anything special, do not flaunt it.**

We should keep a low profile. If you have something special, *don't* flaunt it.

Remember the importance of honesty and integrity. An honest person will merit holding onto his hard-earned money.

Last, but certainly not least, we have to do better at getting along with fellow Jews of all stripes. That, according to the Rebbe Reb Elimelech, will help bring the *Geulah* (Redemption).

Many of us have gone through difficult times, but Hashem, in His great kindness, gives us the strength to endure. May we realize that we have the strength, live up to our tests, and see the fruits of our spiritual labors bear the most beautiful material and spiritual results.

Relationships

How Reb Yisrael Can Help *Klal Yisrael*

I n the beginning of *Lech Lecha*, Hashem says to Avraham, "I will make you a great nation; I will bless you, and make your name great" (*Bereishis* 12:2). Hashem then adds two words, וֶהְיֵה בְּרָכָה, *and you shall be a blessing*. Rav Samson Raphael Hirsch underscores the importance of these words by explaining that they were not merely Hashem conferring more endowment to Avraham, but rather they were a directive to Avraham, a guidepost pointing out the way he must live his life!

Hashem was saying to Avraham, "Your directive is to become a blessing for the rest of the world!" Rav Samson Raphael Hirsch comments that in these two words, וֶהְיֵה בְּרָכָה, lies the monumental task of a Jew in this world. The *Sforno* also understands these words to be instructional: Hashem was telling Avraham to reach perfection and teach it to the world.

In *Shemos* 3:4, the Torah tells us that when Moshe saw the incredible sight of a bush that was burning but not being consumed, he was סָר לִרְאוֹת, *he turned aside to see* the remarkable sight. Immediately after that, the Torah says that וַיִּקְרָא אֵלָיו אֱלֹקִים, *Hashem called to him*. It seems that because "he turned aside to see," he merited that Hashem spoke to him. However, the *Midrash* (*Shemos Rabbah* 1:27) wonders what is so unusual about Moshe's act. Anyone would turn to see a tree on fire (just as they would turn to see a Hatzolah ambulance with its sirens blaring). If someone realizes there is something unusual going on, he turns to see it.

However, the *Midrash* explains that it was not just that Moshe turned to look at the bush, but that סָר לִרְאוֹת — he "turned from his own affairs" to see the pain of *Klal Yisrael*. He was concerned for his fellow brothers and sisters; that's why he merited that Hashem called to him. סָר לִרְאוֹת is a description of his personality.

In *Ohr Yechezkel* (Vol. 4, page 101), Rav Chatzkel Levenstein writes that we see from the *Midrash* that Moshe's *zechus* to become a leader was not that he was a great *chacham*, but that he felt the pain of *Klal Yisrael*.

> Moshe's *zechus* to become a leader was not that he was a great *chacham*, but that he felt the pain of *Klal Yisrael*.

We must learn how to become people of וְהְיֵה בְּרָכָה, people who are סָר לִרְאוֹת — who turn from our own affairs and look to ease the pain and the anguish of others.

סָר לִרְאוֹת *People*

Rabbi Naftoli Yehuda Mandelbaum, z'l, of Baltimore, was a wonderful rebbi who, sadly, passed away one *Lag B'Omer* on an outing with his *talmidim*. There was a boy in his class who was getting straight *alephs*, but was not accepted by his peers. When the boys would go out to the park Sunday afternoon, they never included him. Rabbi Mandelbaum soon realized it was because the child didn't know how to ride a bike.

The next Sunday he went with this child and taught him how to ride a bike! In reality, the boy's father should have done that! The mother should have done that! But the rebbi was סָר לִרְאוֹת: he saw the problem and went out of his way to teach the boy how to ride a bike. He did not have to do that. His job was being a rebbi and to bring out the best in every child in class and he was already doing that with this boy. However, the rebbi was a סָר לִרְאוֹת.

The legendary Agudah activist Rabbi Shlomo Lorincz, from *Eretz Yisrael*, told me about the time he had typhoid fever in 1951. He was taken to the Asutta Hospital in Tel Aviv a few days before Yom Kippur and was nervous that the doctor would tell him that he had to eat on Yom Kippur. Sure enough, that is exactly what the doctor told him. He was so upset that he told his wife to go to the Chazon Ish and please ask him what he should do. He did not want to rely on the doctor.

Mrs. Lorincz told me that the Chazon Ish told her that if this doctor, whom the Chazon Ish knew, said that her husband had to eat, then he had to eat. She went back and told her husband. He was devastated. He felt worse about that than he did about his illness, because this was the first time in his life that that he was not going to fast on Yom Kippur.

Erev Yom Kippur, three hours before *Kol Nidrei*, the Chazon Ish suddenly and unexpectedly showed up in his room. Rav Lorincz said that he almost fell out of his bed from surprise. The Chazon Ish told him, "With regard to Yom Kippur, the Torah tells us, וְעִנִּיתֶם אֶת נַפְשֹׁתֵיכֶם, *And you shall afflict yourselves* [*Vayikra* 23:27]. Affliction here means 'fasting.' And on Yom Kippur one must be happy with that, as he is fulfilling the mitzvah.

"However," said the Chazon Ish, "the Torah also says, וְנִשְׁמַרְתֶּם מְאֹד לְנַפְשֹׁתֵיכֶם, *And you shall greatly beware for your souls* [*Devarim* 4:15]. Just as you have to be happy to do the first mitzvah, you have to be happy to do the second mitzvah as well. On this Yom Kippur, your mitzvah is to be happy by eating."

Rabbi Lorincz told me that the Chazon Ish had to take three buses to get there and it took him more than an hour to go each way! And he did that before *Kol Nidrei*! But that's exactly what somebody does when he is a סָר לִרְאוֹת.

> We can provide those needs, satisfy those yearnings, and alleviate that pain.

There are needs in *Klal Yisrael*. There are yearnings in *Klal Yisrael*. And there are pains in *Klal Yisrael*. We can provide those needs, satisfy those yearnings, and alleviate that pain. We just need people of וְהָיָה בְרָכָה and סָר לִרְאוֹת.

The Chofetz Chaim Asks to Speak Again

When Rav Sholom Schwadron first came to America, he stayed for six months at my parents' home in Kew Gardens, New York, and became close to our rav, Rav Yaakov Teitelbaum. One evening after

Maariv, Rav Teitelbaum told the following story to Rav Sholom, who repeated it many times.

In 1923, there was a *Kenessiah Gedolah* held by Agudas Yisrael that was attended by great Torah luminaries such as the Chofetz Chaim, the Chortkover Rebbe, and Rav Isser Zalman Meltzer, among others. On the first afternoon of the historic session, the Chofetz Chaim was honored to give the opening speech. At night, though, the Chofetz Chaim asked that he be given permission to speak again.

People were surprised. What could have been so important that the Chofetz Chaim felt that he had to speak again? Surely, there were other great *talmidei chachamim* who were scheduled to speak. However, this was the Chofetz Chaim asking, so the organizers acquiesced.

"I spoke this afternoon," the Chofetz Chaim said to his audience, "and I told people to go out to be *mekareiv Yidden*. Later I heard people in the hall quote the *Gemara* in *Bava Metzia* (107b) that says, 'קְשׁוֹט עַצְמְךָ וְאַחַר כַּךְ קְשׁוֹט אֲחֵרִים, *first, perfect yourself — and then you perfect others.*' Hence they feel they can't be *mekareiv* others until they, themselves, are perfect."

The Chofetz Chaim then told this parable: A man built a city and when it was done they made a great party for him. At the party they served some supposedly delicious tea, but the man complained and said, "The water in the tea is awful. It has so much sand in it."

"It's your fault," they told him, "You built the city along the seashore and so our water has sand particles in it."

"Have you never heard of a strainer?" he asked them defiantly. "Next time you need water, use the strainer; it will get the particles out."

Two weeks later, he heard that a fire had raged through the town and burned down many of the buildings. The man came running and asked, "What happened? Why didn't you put out the fire? There is plenty of water here!"

"It's your fault," they answered. "We were going to use the water to put out the fire, but then we remembered your orders that we use a strainer to filter the water first. By the time we did that, half the town burned!"

"If a fire is raging," the man shouted, "you use any water that you can!"

"This should be our approach," said the Chofetz Chaim. "If the fire of *apikorsus* [heresy] and *amaratzus* [ignorance] is burning, you use any water that you can."

Thus, even Jews who are not totally knowledgeable in Torah but still have enough within them to teach others who know less than they do are obligated to do so.

Partners in Torah

Every single man and woman reading this right now can teach Torah to somebody else. I want to introduce you to a program where you can satisfy the yearning of thousands of people who are looking to learn Torah. And you don't even have to leave your house. All you have to do it is call Partners in Torah. Listen to what can be accomplished by your own telephone in your own house.

There was a young man, David, a Sefardic fellow in *Eretz Yisrael*. He had no connection to anything Jewish. He was running around the whole world trying to find himself. He ended up at the University of Alaska studying computers; he had a brilliant mind. One day, he heard about Partners in Torah. He called and they set him up with Avraham Steinberg, a *bachur* learning at the time in Yeshivah Shaar HaTorah in Kew Gardens, New York.

The minute Avraham began speaking with this young man over the telephone, he realized that he was bright and decided to teach him *Nefesh HaChaim*, a very deep *hashkafah sefer,* written by Rav Chaim Volozhiner. David was hooked. It spoke to his soul. Soon he went back to *Eretz Yisrael* and today he is in Yeshivah Kaf HaChaim. He is there only because Avraham Steinberg and others learned with him on the telephone. He was at the University of Alaska! How much further away can one be?

There is a girl whom my wife taught many years ago [in Shevach High School], Nechama. Today, this girl is a married woman with children. She learns with a woman in the Young Israel of Las Vegas. Can you imagine a Young Israel in Las Vegas?

I wanted to hear firsthand from the woman in Las Vegas what it was like to learn with Nechama, so I called her.

"You should know," she told me, "that Nechama has changed my life. Today I keep *kashrus* — not only in the house, but out of the house, too. Today we're *shomer Shabbos*, and Shabbos means so much to us."

Many of you will be hesitant to get involved with *kiruv* because, "What if they ask questions that I won't be able to answer?"

This question was posed to my very close friend, Yaakov Salomon, one of the stalwarts of Aish HaTorah. He said, "These people are not looking to trap you. If they are calling Partners in Torah, they want to learn."

"Here is a piece of advice," continued Yaakov. "Saying 'I don't know' is good *kiruv*. If you don't know, then the person feels, 'Oh, I asked a great question. They're going to get back to me.' And then you find the answer. There are answers for everything."

Rebbetzin Esther Reisman, wife of Rav Yisrael, *shlita* — as if she does not have enough to do between a large family and the classes she gives — learns with a woman named Michelle, who attends the University of Fairbanks in Alaska. (I don't know why Alaska has so many people wanting to participate in Partners in Torah!)

I decided to call Michelle and ask her firsthand what they were learning.

"Oh, Mrs. Reisman sent me some wonderful books that we're learning."

Of course, I immediately was thinking that among those books must surely be one of the Maggid books. After all, they are inspirational.

"What books did she send you?" I asked.

"*Love Thy Neighbor,* by Rabbi Pliskin. That's what we're learning."

Okay, strike one. But two more strikes to go.

"What's the second book that she sent to you?"

"*The Bamboo Cradle.* We read that and it's very inspirational."

Strike two, one more.

"What's the third book?"

"I'll tell you, but I can't pronounce that word — T, Z, A, D, D, I, K."

"Do you mean the book, *A Tzaddik in Our Time*?" I asked apprehensively.

"Yeah, that's what it is. What does that word mean?"

"A *tzaddik* means a very righteous man. The book is about Rav Aryeh Levine and it's a wonderful book."

After we finished our conversation, I said, "Do you know that I also wrote some nice books? I would be happy to send some to you."

"I would be forever grateful," she said.

So that week I sent out four *Maggid* books: two to Michelle and two to Mrs. Reisman!

The phone number for Partners in Torah is 1-800-STUDY-4-2; or 1-800-738-3942. Call them. Don't delay. You're going to make a difference in somebody's life somewhere in the world (and it doesn't have to be Alaska). You will be able to inspire someone, and you will change in the process. (You can also register to be a mentor or a student by logging on to www.partnersintorah.org)

[In 2004, after the passing of his dear friend, Shmuel (Sammy) Homburger in London, Rabbi Krohn delivered the *sheloshim* (30-day) Memorial *hesped*. He proposed the formation of a Partners in Torah-type program throughout England, *l'zecher nishmas* Sammy. Mr. Dov Harris and his dynamic committee made PaL (Phone and Learn) a reality. Today over 700 people throughout the United Kingdom learn as PaL study partners. To sign up in England as a tutor or partner call 08000-J-LEARN (553-276) or contact PAL at WWW. phoneandlearn.org]

Turning Our Pain Into Gain

Everyone has suffered pain. Think back to the pain that you've had in your life.

Did anyone reading these words ever go through a broken engagement? If you did and you were fortunate enough to find your true *zivug* (marriage partner) afterward, and you hear of someone who had a broken engagement, call them and give them *chizuk*! Tell them it's not the end of the world. Things can and often do work out for the best.

Did you ever go bankrupt? If you've heard of someone else who suffered bankruptcy, call them and tell them how you handled it. Take your pain and transform it into somebody else's gain.

Did you become a *yasom* (orphan) at a young age? How many people have called me to comfort other *yesomim* or *yesomos* because I became a *yasom* at 21, the eldest of seven children? You take that pain that you have or had, and you transform it into somebody else's gain. (Today there is a great organization in Brooklyn, called LINKS, started by Mrs. Sarah Rivkah Kohn, for children who lost a parent in their teenage years; see p. 31.)

My *mechutan*, Max Perlstein, is an accountant. Every time he does work for a company, he checks to see if there is an opening and then he calls Binyomin Babad at PCS (Professional Career Service). Everyone should have the number at PCS, 718-436-1900, because the people there are always helping people find jobs. Mr. Perlstein was instrumental in many people getting jobs that way. (Today, two of the people to speak to at PCS are Moshe Tyberg and Avraham Kahn; Reb Binyomin Babad is working elsewhere.)

Dozens and dozens of families have been saved. There was a young fellow whom Reb Binyomin sent for a job interview for a position offering a salary of $45,000. Unfortunately, the company did not need him at the time. However, six months later, the gentleman who had interviewed him called Binyomin and said, "I'm leaving, but I was so impressed by that fellow you sent me, I want him to take my job."

That job was $75,000 a year. It's unbelievable! If you know somebody who needs a job or has a job available, call PCS!

Reb Binyomin told me that someone called him a while ago and said, "Thank you so much for getting Yosef Goldman [fictitious name] the job in that company."

"Excuse me," Binyomin said, "but I don't recognize you. Are you the boss of the company?"

"No."

"Are you a co-worker?"

"No."

"Who are you?"

"I'm his neighbor. And I saw what was happening to his family when he didn't have a job. You saved his life!"

Davening for Others

Isn't it interesting that most of the words in the middle part of the *Shemoneh Esrei*, where we ask Hashem to grant our needs, are plural: חָנֵּנוּ ("Endow *us*" with wisdom), הֲשִׁיבֵנוּ ("Bring *us* back" in repentance), רְפָאֵנוּ ("Heal us"), בָּרֵךְ עָלֵינוּ ("Bless us" with sustenance). It is because we are obligated to *daven* for each other, not only ourselves. I believe this is all part of סָר לִרְאוֹת and וֶהְיֵה בְּרָכָה.

Davening for others is advantageous, as the *pasuk* tells us, בְּהִתְפַּלְלוֹ בְּעַד רֵעֵהוּ וַיֹּסֶף ה' אֶת כָּל אֲשֶׁר לְאִיּוֹב לְמִשְׁנֶה, *After [Iyov] had prayed for his friend … Hashem added on to all that Iyov had, until there was double (Iyov 42:10)*. This well may be the source for the well-known Talmudic teaching, כָּל הַמְבַקֵּשׁ רַחֲמִים עַל חֲבֵרוֹ וְהוּא צָרִיךְ לְאוֹתוֹ דָּבָר הוּא נַעֲנֶה תְּחִילָה, *Whoever prays for his friend while he himself needs that thing, he will be answered first (Bava Kamma 92a)*.

In the introduction to the *Nefesh HaChaim*, Rav Yitzchok Volozhiner writes that his father, Rav Chaim Volozhiner, would often say, שֶׁזֶּה כָּל הָאָדָם — לֹא לְעַצְמוֹ נִבְרָא, *This is the essence of man: we were not created for ourselves.*

> "This is the essence of man: we were not created for ourselves."

Every person is created with certain talents. We have to be people of וֶהְיֵה בְּרָכָה! Let us make a commitment as well that from today onward we will become people of סָר לִרְאוֹת. We're going to turn from our own affairs to look after others. May the directive to Avraham and the description of Moshe be guideposts for us for the rest of our lives.

Count Your Blessings

For numerous years, Rebbetzin Zehava Braunstein, ob'm, and Rabbi Paysach Krohn were co-speakers at the Agudah annual Neshei Cares lecture. The following lecture was given just months after the rebbetzin passed away.

Rebbetzin Zehava Braunstein was a special person. Two months before she passed away, I heard that she had stopped accepting visitors, but I asked the family if I could visit anyway. They called back two days later and said I could come.

Although I had known for a year that she was sick, when I saw her, tears came to my eyes. I tried to hide my sorrow, but I couldn't. As the tears rolled down my cheeks, she said something I'll never forget.

She was a millionaire because she had family and she loved family, and they loved her.

"Don't pity me," she said. "I have my wonderful family: my children and grandchildren. I'm a millionaire."

That's the essence of why we are here: to count our blessings. And Rebbetzin Braunstein personified it as well as anyone: a woman who was so sick, who had so much pain — and yet she sat there counting her blessings, telling me not to pity her, because she was a millionaire. She believed it and acted that way throughout the terrible illness.

Count Your Blessings | 129 |

The way you learn to count your blessings is really a question of focus, a question of attitude, a question of perspective.

I remember the rebbetzin once telling me about a *sheva berachos* for one of her children held in the house of Rabbi Shlomo Freifeld, *zt'l*. He, unfortunately, was sick at the time (he passed away in 1990). He quoted *Tehillim* (118:17): לֹא אָמוּת כִּי אֶחְיֶה, *I shall not die* — כִּי *[but rather] I will live, and relate the stories and great deeds of Hashem.* Rabbi Freifeld explained that the word כִּי can also mean "while" or "during." Plugging that back into the *pasuk*, it now reads: *I will not live a life of death* — **while** *I am alive.*

There are certain people who are asleep their entire life. They do not accomplish anything. They waste day after day with things that are not important or significant. Rabbi Freifeld was different — even in his illness, he was a dedicated rebbi and he had a heart for all his *talmidim*, past and present.

Rebbetzin Braunstein knew she was sick for 15 years. It was much worse than she let on. Yet she lived life to the fullest, because she looked at the positive and used *every* ounce of strength she had for *Hashem*. She could have counted the negatives, but instead she counted her blessings.

> **What is the essence of counting our blessings? Always seeking the positive. And if that's hard to find, seek some more.**

It's a matter of focus; it's a matter of attitude; it's a matter of perspective.

The Chozeh's Clock

A story is told about Rav Aaron Kodinover, who was traveling with his *talmidim*. They found an inn to stay in overnight, and the next morning the rebbe asked the innkeeper, "The clock you have that chimes every hour is a special clock. Where did you get it?"

"What do you mean?" the innkeeper replied. "It's just a regular clock."

"I'm telling you, this clock is special."

"I've had it for years. Why do you think it is special?"

"Usually," the rebbe said, "when I hear a clock chime at the start of every hour I get a feeling of sadness, and I think, 'Woe is me, it's one hour closer to death.' (In reality, every hour that passes is indeed an hour closer to our demise.) But this clock, every time I heard it chime, I felt elated, because I felt it was one hour closer to *Mashiach*. Why did the clock make me think that way?"

The intrigued innkeeper did research, and, to his astonishment, found that the clock had once belonged to the Chozeh of Lublin. His family, who had inherited it and then fallen on hard times, sold it.

There are two ways to look at time: as one step closer to death or as one step closer to *Mashiach*. The negative or the positive! That's the way

The way you learn to count your blessings is really a question of focus, a question of attitude, a question of perspective.

to count our blessings. Seek the positive! We're alive! And, hopefully, we will all see *Mashiach*.

It's a question of focus, a question of attitude, a question of perspective.

Opening Your Eyes

A number of years ago on a plane trip to Toronto, I lost my cell phone. I only realized it was missing once I went through customs and wanted to call my host to tell him that I had arrived. I was sure that it was on the plane. However, try as I might, the authorities would not let me get back on to the plane, nor were any airline personnel willing to go back to search for it. It was frustrating and annoying, as I had hundreds of numbers programmed into that phone. I arrived at the home where I would be staying overnight, and one of the children said to me, "Rabbi Krohn, why don't you recite the Rav Binyamin 'thing'? It helps people locate things they've lost."

I knew what the child was referring to. It is the text of the *Midrash* (*Bereishis Rabbah* 21:14), that tells what happened when Avraham sent Hagar and Yishmael away (*Bereishis* 21:19). The child was thirsty and there was no water. The *pasuk* says, וַיִּפְקַח אֱלֹקִים אֶת עֵינֶיהָ וַתֵּרֶא בְּאֵר מָיִם, *Then Hashem opened her eyes and she saw the wellspring of water*. She took her jug and gave water to her son. The *Midrash* comments, "Rabbi Binyamin says, 'Everyone is assumed to be blind until Hashem opens his eyes.'"

Rabbi Mattisyahu Salomon once asked, "Why does the *Midrash* unequivocally state that people are assumed to be blind? It would seem the opposite. Most people in the world do see."

However, said Rav Mattisyahu, it is not really so. The *Midrash* is teaching something profound. In reality, we don't see anything! thing! We are blind. We see only what Hashem wants us to see. Something could be right in front of our eyes and we won't see it if Hashem doesn't want us to see it. It is the same with our understanding and perspective. We simply cannot get to "see" things in perspective unless Hashem, in His kindness, allows us to "see" it and perceive it.

> In reality, we don't see anything! We are blind. We see only what Hashem wants us to see.

What an outlook!

We wake up in the morning and thank Hashem for giving us eyes to see — but it's deeper than that. It refers even to our *perspective* of things. We wouldn't know how to size up *any* event unless Hashem gave us the mind to do so. "Everyone is assumed to be blind." May we be granted the gift to "see" our blessings.

By the way, I don't know if you have the "Rabbi Binyamin" magnet hanging on your fridge, but I have it on mine … when I can find it … and believe me, it works.

Beyond Reference Anxiety

Many people say, "If only we had more money, all our problems would be solved!"

I recently read a study about happiness. A group of secular scientists wanted to find out what makes a person happy.

These were not religious Jews who would know that the study of Torah, the performance of mitzvos, acts of *chessed,* and *ahavas Yisrael* can bring people to ultimate happiness. Nevertheless, in this secular study they came up with fascinating information. They discussed something called "reference anxiety." This means "keeping up with the Joneses." If you have a two-room house and your neighbor has a three-room house, suddenly your nice, comfortable, roomy house is too small. If you have a three-room house and your neighbor has a five-room house, suddenly your very nice, very comfortable, roomy house is too small. That is "reference anxiety."

They claimed that there are six things that make people happy, none of which is sold in stores: love, friendship, family, respect, a place in the community, and the belief that your life has a purpose.

They found that what was most important to many people was family! It is where people get their strength. How many brothers and sisters haven't spoken to each other for years? They don't even remember why they are not talking.

I'm now dealing with a woman who doesn't get along with her daughter-in-law. It's sad, but it happens. I said to her, "Is that a reason not to talk to your grandchildren? They are *your* grandchildren. They are your flesh and blood. Why are you depriving yourself of one of the greatest pleasure in the world: your very own grandchildren?"

I begged the woman to please consider changing. I told her how foolish she was.

I once saw an interesting expression: "Many of us have many acquaintances, but so few friends." How true. If you have good friends (and they can be family members), you're lucky — you're a millionaire. That's what Rebbetzin Braunstein was talking about.

If you're not getting along with your children or grandchildren, your brothers or sisters, you may need a Rav or a professional to intervene, but it's a priority and should be tended to at once.

Making more money is not going to make you happy. If you want to feel fulfilled and happy, then get involved with an organization. There are so many great organizations. If you do something for others, you will feel wonderful about yourself. And if you help those who need help, you will soon realize how fortunate you are, and you will count your blessings. It's a way to focus and count your blessings.

100 Blessings a Day

Rabbi Aaron Kotler, *zt'l* (in *Mishnas Rav Aharon: Tefillah Chelek* 1 page 88 [5742 edition]) asked why we beseech Hashem for things when He already knows exactly what we need. If you need a *refuah*, Hashem knows. If you need children, He knows. If you need a *shid-*

duch, He knows. If you need *parnassah,* He knows. Why, then, do we have to pray if Hashem already knows what we need?

Rav Aaron answered that when you *daven,* the words teach you that everything comes from Hashem. We pray for a *refuah* to remember that Hashem brings the *refuah.* We pray for *parnassah* — a job, income — to remember that it is Hashem Who brings it. That is the purpose of *berachos*: to remind ourselves that everything comes from Hashem.

The *Gemara (Menachos* 43b) says that one is obligated to make 100 *berachos* every day. The *Daas Zekeinim (Devarim* 10:12) explains that there was a terrible plague ravaging the population. A hundred people were dying every day! David HaMelech understood through *ruach hakodesh* that people were dying because they were not focusing on all the good they had from Hashem. Therefore, he made it an obligation to say 100 *berachos* each day. When he did so, the plague stopped.

The *Zohar* explains that when a *neshamah* comes down from the upper world into the body of a human being, Hashem says, לֶךְ לְךָ (a double expression of "going"), which are the exact words He told Avraham, *Get up and go* (לֶךְ לְךָ) *from your land* ... *(Bereishis* 12:1). Hashem tells the *neshamah,* "Get up and go from the upper world down into the world where you should recite 100 *berachos* every day." (The words *lech lecha* equal the *gematria* of 100, which alludes to the obligation to say 100 *berachos* every day.) Indeed, every blessing is a key that opens up a pipeline, a conduit of blessings. That being the case, each of us should make a commitment to be careful to say our 100 *berachos* every day.

A number of years ago, a friend of mine, Reb Shimshon Halpern of Monsey, NY — the man who created the *Asher Yatzar* cards that we all see in shuls, schools, and Jewish homes all over the world — called and told me that he had funding for a project that needed to be done, but he had no idea how to do it. He assured me that were I to be involved in this new project, heavenly reward would surely be great. I agreed to listen.

"There's a fellow who wants a *zechus* for a family member," he said to me, "and was told by two *mekubalim* in *Eretz Yisrael* that he should get people involved in making 100 *berachos* a day. He called me and said, 'Money is no object, but you have to help me produce something that makes everyone aware about making 100 *berachos* a day.'"

I was intrigued by the idea, so I called together a group of renowned Torah educators — the legendary Rabbi Eli Teitelbaum (who has since passed away), Rabbi Avi Pearl from Torah Temimah, Rabbi Binyomin Plotzker from Yeshiva Ketanah of Queens, and my son-in-law Chananya Kramer from Kol Rom Multi-media in Baltimore — and we brainstormed. We came up with an idea to create an interactive CD-ROM, *Meah Berachos* (100 *Berachos*), that would be informative, fun, enlightening (even to adults), and entertaining (even to children). The educators felt strongly that by getting children involved in the program, their parents would follow. Kol Rom produced an incredible interactive CD-ROM that has games, contests, an adorable interview with adults and children outside Madison Square Garden prior to the *Siyum HaShas*, Torah lessons, a large array of foods and their *berachos* presented in an exciting manner, and lectures featuring Rabbi Yisroel Reisman, Rabbi Yissachar Frand, and me.

A new idea for many of us? Perhaps yes, but we can all change. We can all make it a daily habit to say 100 blessings every day. (It's a little more difficult on Shabbos.) In doing so, we'll learn to appreciate Hashem and all the good we have in our lives. We will become aware of everything around us and count our blessings.

Who Should Lead the Birchas HaMazon?

The *Gemara* (*Pesachim* 119b) tells us that Hashem will make a celebration at the end of time when He will ask each of the greatest leaders in Jewish history to lead the *Birchas HaMazon*, the blessing after the meal.

Hashem will begin by asking Avraham Avinu, but he will decline the offer because he had a son like Yishmael. Next, Hashem will ask Yitzchak to lead, but he, too, will decline the offer, saying that he had a son like Esav. Hashem will then ask Yaakov, who will also decline because he married two sisters. (Yaakov married two sisters before *Matan Torah*, when it was permissible; afterward, marrying two sisters was forbidden.) Then Hashem will ask Moshe, but he will say he can't lead the *Birchas HaMazon* because he was never in *Eretz Yisrael*. Hashem will then ask Yehoshua, who also will decline, stating that he never had a son, only a daughter (and thus did not fulfill the first mitzvah in the Torah, פְּרוּ וּרְבוּ [*Bereishis* 1:28]).

However, David HaMelech will get up and announce that he can lead. One wonders: David had three wayward sons, Adoniyahu, Amnon, and Avshalom. How are they different from Yishmael and Esav, who disqualified their fathers?

Nevertheless, David was chosen! Why? I believe the answer is that he had an incredible quality: He was able to cry out to Hashem when things were good just as he did when things were bad! When things were difficult, David cried out, as the *pasuk* tells us, צָרָה וְיָגוֹן אֶמְצָא: וּבְשֵׁם ה׳ אֶקְרָא, *Trouble and sorrow I would find; then I would invoke the Name of Hashem* (*Tehillim* 116:3-4). However, when things were good, the *pasuk* tells us of David, כּוֹס יְשׁוּעוֹת אֶשָּׂא וּבְשֵׁם ה׳ אֶקְרָא, *I will raise the cup of salvations, and I will invoke the Name of Hashem* (ibid. v. 13).

Anyone who *davens* with fervor and intensity to Hashem with thanks, the same way he *davens* to Hashem when he beseeches Him because things are difficult, deserves to lead the *Birchas HaMazon*. David HaMelech counted his blessings and thanked Hashem accordingly.

The Right Perspective

Let me conclude with one more exceptional story about Rebbetzin Zehava Braunstein.

She was the principal in Ateret Torah, a school primarily for girls of the Syrian community in Brooklyn. While there, she taught a class on various Torah topics. There was one girl in the class, a senior, who, with the permission and guidance of her parents, was involved with a *shidduch*. The young lady did not know that Rebbetzin Braunstein knew what was going on.

It was the end of the year and, when it was time to take the final exam, the overwhelmed girl took one look at the test and told the rebbetzin that she did not know a thing, apologizing that she just could not study. Without batting an eyelash, the rebbetzin told her that her final would be to write down three things that are important in marriage.

And that's what the girl did (with a smile). While everyone else was writing, she, too, was writing. When she got back the final, the mark on the paper was, "You're going to make a great wife."

That's who the rebbetzin was. She could have embarrassed the girl. Many teachers would say, "So what if you're involved with a *shidduch*? You still have to know the material." However, the rebbetzin had the right perspective. She knew what was important in life. An impending engagement and marriage take priority. Three days later, the girl became engaged. Of course, when Rebbetzin Braunstein attended the *simchah* they hugged and embraced with a mutual understanding.

It's very painful tonight to realize that we have lost a beloved teacher and role model. However, let's never forget that we had one of the greatest blessings that Hashem could bestow on us, as many of us got to know one of the greatest *mechanchos*/teachers that ever set foot on American soil. We should thank Hashem that we merited to know her, so that we can follow in her ways and count our blessings every day.

Kibud Av V'eim

hen new parents hold a newborn — and as a *mohel* I get to see that quite often — it is one of the most magical moments of life. There are such strong feelings of happiness, excitement, accomplishment, and bonding. When you look at the parents holding the child, you can't imagine that they would ever have an argument with that child or that the child would ever not respect them.

Unfortunately, we know it does not always work that way. As time goes on, parents realize that there is *tzaar gidul banim*, the pangs and pains of raising children. Children eventually realize that there is at times a generation gap and that not all parents are on the same wavelength as their offspring.

> **Parents and children can have the greatest and most exhilarating relationship.**

Despite the minefields in any parent-child relationship, if one nurtures that relationship, building on the love and bonding that is naturally there when the child is born, parents and children can have the greatest and most exhilarating relationship.

A Gadol's Love

Many years ago, I spoke to Rav Reuven Feinstein about a remarkable incident in his life. One of his sons was going to have a bar mitzvah that fell out on the Shabbos of the Agudah convention. Rav Moshe Feinstein, the *Gadol Hador* and Rav Reuven's father, was one of the main speakers at the convention. But how could he miss his grandson's bar mitzvah? On the other hand, how could he miss the convention, where there were close to a thousand people waiting to hear what the *Gadol Hador* had to say about the issues of the day?

Here is how they solved it. On Thursday, in Yeshivah Tiferes Yerushalayim, the boy came and had an *aliyah*. Of course his *zaide* Rav Moshe was there. They had a modest *seudah*. I presume that Rav Moshe spoke, and then for Shabbos he went to the Agudah convention.

And so I asked Rav Reuven, "You didn't mind that your own father wasn't at your son's bar mitzvah?"

No matter where he was going, what was uppermost in his heart was the love he had for his children.

"I know that my father had, and has always had, many responsibilities," he answered me. "But his love for me was never a question. No matter where he was going, what was uppermost in his heart was the love he had for his children. How do I know that my father loved me more than anything else? I'll tell you three ways.

"First, when I was a child, every morning, a half-hour before I got up, my father would come into my room and put my clothes on the radiator. Then a half-hour later, with my clothes and socks warm, he would take the clothes and dress me while I was still under the covers. He did this every morning."

The second way, Rav Reuven explained, was in the summertime, when they went to a bungalow colony in Connecticut. There wasn't much there for children to do. The big event was when the colony owner loaded hay in his pickup truck to let the children sit on the hay as he rode into town to get supplies. Young Reuven would spend a lot of time learning with his father, but whenever his father saw that the owner was getting into his truck to head to town, he would close the *sefer* and say, "Reuven, go get into the truck."

One would think that Rav Moshe valued nothing more important than learning with his son. But he understood that his son was a little boy who loved that pickup truck, and therefore he told him to go; they would learn later.

The third thing, Rav Reuven said, was that he always sat right next to his father at the Shabbos table. No guest (unless it was a *gadol hador*) ever sat next to Rav Moshe instead of his son. Rav Reuven said that his father used to quote *Pirkei Avos* (1:5): וְיִהְיוּ עֲנִיִּים בְּנֵי בֵיתֶךָ, *Aniyim (poor people) should be part of your home,* and then he would add, "but they shouldn't take over. Your children come first."

For those three reasons, he said, he knew that his father loved him. Therefore, even if his father had to be away at the Agudah convention, he still felt secure.

The loving relationship Rav Moshe nurtured with his son allowed Rav Reuven to develop tremendous *kibud av v'eim,* even though, as the *Gadol Hador,* his father had more outside responsibilities than any of us can imagine.

The Bond of Generations

What don't parents do for their children? It is marvelous to watch parents feeding, teaching, learning with, holding, cooing, guiding, or playing with their children.

If that's the case, why does the Torah have to teach us that *kibud av v'eim* is such an important mitzvah, even emphasizing that one who keeps it is *zocheh* to long life? Doesn't it make sense to respect our parents? Isn't it logical? We owe our parents everything. We wouldn't even be here if it weren't for our parents. Why did Hashem stress the magnitude of the mitzvah to the degree that it is even one of the *Aseres Hadibros*?

I'd like to answer that with a question. We know each tablet has five *dibros;* the first five commandments are בֵּין אָדָם לַמָּקוֹם, *between man and G-d,* while the second five are בֵּין אָדָם לַחֲבֵרוֹ, *between man and his fellow man.* One mitzvah, however, doesn't seem to fit the pattern, the fifth one, honoring our parents. Why is it on the first set? How is honoring one's parents a בֵּין אָדָם לַמָּקוֹם mitzvah? It would seem to be better suited to the second set, which include such בֵּין אָדָם לַחֲבֵרוֹ mitzvos as not to steal, not to give false testimony, not to be jealous, etc.

Rabbi Samson Raphael Hirsch explains that there is a special mitzvah of *kibud av v'eim* because parents connect children to the traditions, to the essence of what Torah is all about, to what Hashem wants from us. As Rav Hirsch writes, "Without this bond, the chain of generations is broken. The Jewish past is lost for the future, and the Jewish nation ceases to exist." That is why the commandment of kibud av v'eim is on the side of בֵּין אָדָם לַמָּקוֹם, for parents bring about a child's connection to Hashem.

The *Sefer HaChinuch* writes (Mitzvah 33) that the root of this mitzvah is to teach us *hakaras hatov* (gratitude), because the lowest characteristic is to be ungrateful. When we have gratitude to our parents, we will then come to have gratitude to Hashem; we are going to realize that we owe everything to Him: our lives, health, spouse, children, *parnassah* — everything. Therefore, according to the *Chinuch*, the whole reason that the Torah emphasizes *kibud av v'eim* is so that we will come to understand how much we owe Hashem.

Chutzpah

The greatest thing we can do for our children is to give over the *mesorah* (tradition) to them in a warm, comforting, beautiful, and loving way. But that is not always easy, especially in today's world. The *Gemara* says (*Sotah* 49b): חוּצְפָּא יִסְגֵּא בְּעִקְּבוֹת מְשִׁיחָא, *Before Mashiach comes, chutzpah will increase in the world.*

How true that is in today's world!

I was talking to my grandson when he said to me, "Zaidy, you won't believe the way some kids speak to their parents." Then he told me about a boy in his class who forgot his report at home and was afraid he would be punished. He called his mother and asked if she could bring the report to school. The mother was probably busy, but what doesn't a mother do for her child, so she brought it as soon as she could, which was in the afternoon.

When she walked into the class with the report, what did the boy say? "Ma, you're a little late!" He had wanted it in the morning.

Someone recently told me that they overheard the following conversation between a daughter and her mother in a store. The mother saw something on sale and was considering buying it. The daughter said, "Ma! Do you think I'm going to buy anything that's on sale?" To her, something on sale was an insult; she felt that a sale item is something the store could not get rid of.

How do we as parents deal with such chutzpah? How do we teach our children the value of respect in a society that fosters disrespect?

Invest Time in Your Children

The first way to get your children to have *kibud av v'eim* is to realize that having a child is not only a privilege but a responsibility. You must find time for them. Don't fall asleep Friday night at the table. Come home early Friday afternoon,

> **Having a child is not only a privilege but a responsibility.**

even if it means that you will make one less sale, so that you can rest and be awake at the Shabbos table.

Go on vacations with them. *Baruch Hashem*, my children always looked forward to vacations with my wife and me. It was a lot of fun — we were all in it together. I planned the itinerary, my wife planned the food, and every vacation one of the children could bring one friend who could otherwise not afford a vacation.

One of the greatest ways I was able to bond with my children was that every night we had supper together. Whenever I came home, that's when supper was. If I had an out-of-town *bris* and I didn't get home until later, that's when supper was.

At your supper table, give everyone a chance to talk. That way you get to know what is happening with them, in school and in their lives. When everyone is talking and communicating, you are creating a true family. That's what it's all about.

Sometimes you have to put aside things that may be very important. But the greatest investment you have in your life is your children, and if you don't make time for them they will find other people who will make time for them. And when others validate them they will disregard you. There are no shortcuts; you have to make time for your children.

Parents, Not Pals

Another thing to realize is that parents are not pals. Parents are there to nurture and help, but children should not talk to their parents in the same way that they speak to their friends. Parents have the obligation to teach their children to have respect for them.

One of the things I consider very important in this regard is the *din* in *Shulchan Aruch* that a child should not sit in the father or mother's place at any time. That means even if a child is doing homework, the father's seat at the head of the table is holy. The mother's seat, wherever she sits, is holy. No child should be allowed to sit in that place even if the parent is not home (see *Yoreh Deah* 240:2.)

Rav Elya Lopian writes in *Lev Eliyahu* (Section 3, pp. 337-338; see also p. 276) that children should help in the house. There is nothing wrong with a boy vacuuming on Motza'ei Shabbos. All children should make their own beds. If they don't get accustomed to helping around the house, when they get married their house is going to look like a wreck. And it will be the parents' fault, because they never taught them how to fold laundry or how to clean a house.

In our home, on the refrigerator, was a schedule with the different household chores: one child washed the dishes and another dried them; another set the table; another cleared and cleaned the table; and one child had the night off. There was a rotation. Every night someone had something different to do. I always told them that the word *team* stands for "Together Everyone Accomplishes More." A family is a team and its cohesiveness should be a priority in your and their lives.

Don't be afraid of your children! Don't be afraid to give them chores. And don't be afraid to say no. Children want rules! They want direction!

In *bentching* we ask Hashem to bless אֶת אָבִי מוֹרִי ... וְאֶת אִמִּי מוֹרָתִי..., *My father, my teacher ... and my mother, my teacher.* Rabbi Shmuel Kamenetzky pointed out from this expression in *Birchas HaMazon*, "You are not just the father, but also the rebbi, the one who is passing on the tradition. You are not only a mother; you are a teacher, a role model."

The way you spend your vacations, the way you spend your evenings and free time, the way you talk on the phone, the way you discuss your Rav and the children's teachers are all lessons in *chinuch.*

I once heard a great expression, "The two best things you can give your children are roots and wings." Teach your children to be independent, to spread their wings. But also

Teach your children to be independent …. But also teach your children where they come from.

teach your children where they come from, their roots, their heritage. Think about that: Roots and wings.

David HaMelech says in *Tehillim* (121:1), אֶשָּׂא עֵינַי אֶל הֶהָרִים, *I lift up my eyes to the mountains,* מֵאַיִן יָבֹא עֶזְרִי, *Where is my help going to come from?* The *Midrash* tells us that when Yaakov Avinu was looking for a *shidduch* this is exactly what he said. However, he said the words a bit differently: אֶשָּׂא עֵינַי, *I lift up my eyes,* אֶל הַהוֹרִים, *to my parents,* whom I know were such great people.

When parents are not hypocritical, they will be able to be leaders and teachers to their children, and hopefully, their children will respect and follow them. When we act as loving and responsible parents we give them the greatest gift we can give.

May all our efforts bring about our ultimate desire: that our children be a pride to us and to *Klal Yisrael.* May we always treat our parents with care and dignity so that our children learn from us and treat us with care and dignity. May we and our children merit to the blessing of אֲרִיכַת יָמִים (length of days) as the reward for our and their *kibud av v'eim.*

Making Marriage Special: Part I

This is the first of a two-part series on marriage. This first part focuses mainly on the attitudes needed for a successful marriage. Part II will focus mainly on practical advice.

When the Torah describes how Chavah was created, it says: וַיִּקַּח אַחַת מִצַּלְעֹתָיו וַיִּסְגֹּר בָּשָׂר תַּחְתֶּנָּה, *[Hashem] took one of the sides of Adam and filled in flesh in its place* (*Bereishis* 2:21). The word "filled," וַיִּסְגֹּר, is spelled with a ס. The *Midrash* (*Bereishis Rabbah* 17:6) tells us that the very first time that the letter ס appears in reference to a living creature is in this word, וַיִּסְגֹּר, with the creation of the first woman. Rabbi Yechiel Aryeh Munk, in his wonderful *sefer, The Wisdom in the Hebrew Alphabet,* explains that the reason the ס is first mentioned here is that it represents the idea of marriage.

What is the idea of marriage? Marriage is a protective wall within which a person can feel accomplished and achieve contentment.

This idea is epitomized by the very shape of the ס, which is the only letter of the twenty-two letters in the Jewish alphabet that is completely closed. We know that when the *kallah* comes up to the *chuppah* she walks around the *chassan* numerous times. This tradition is based on a *pasuk* in *Yirmiyah* (31:21), נְקֵבָה תְּסוֹבֵב גָּבֶר, *the woman surrounds the man.* The dominating letter in the word תְּסוֹבֵב is the ס, because the ס is a protective wall. Within the confines of that wall, a couple is supposed to reach new heights, build a family, and feel contentment.

It occurred to me that perhaps that is why after the *kallah* circles the *chassan*, he gives her a perfectly round ring, because just as she is a protective wall to him, he is supposed to be a protective wall for her. Dr. Julius Pfeiffer, *z'l*, father of my *mechutan*, Mr. Fred Pfeiffer of Montreal, once pointed out that the phrase עֵזֶר כְּנֶגְדּוֹ, *a helpmate opposite him* (*Bereishis* 2:18), is 360 in *gematria*, and there are 360 degrees in the perfect circle.

A ס represents the ideal marriage. It is a protective wall within which each partner gives the other the opportunity to achieve what I call the ABC's of married life: (A) to feel a sense of Accomplishment, (B) to Build a family, and (C) to find Contentment.

Tragically, however, all of us know situations where those walls have crumbled and the cracks of rift, conflict, and dissension have crept in. Although the couple went into marriage with the dream of a perfect ס, it was shattered in pursuit of fulfilling that dream.

To improve our own marriages, we are going to first examine marriages in the Torah. However, as we do so, we must never forget that even though in these examples we will also see levels of rift, conflict, and dissension, we are talking about *tzaddikim elyonim*, the absolute paragons of righteousness. Therefore, we cannot compare our petty arguments in any way to the examples the Torah reveals to us. Nevertheless, since the Torah is revealing to us certain things about their marriages, we can and must use them as examples to improve ours.

Rift, Conflict, and Dissension

It is not hard to imagine that if a child living at home is going off the *derech*, *chas v'shalom*, and the father wants to keep him in the home but the mother wants to send him away, there would be a level of rift, conflict, and dissension. That is what happened in the home of Avraham and Sarah. Hashem told Avraham not to be distressed even though he had a different opinion than Sarah about Yishmael. Avraham wanted to keep him in his house, feeling he would be able to influence his son. Sarah wanted Yishmael out, fearing he would influence Yitzchak. Hashem informed Avraham that Sarah was right and that he should listen to her. Among the lessons the Torah is telling us here is that there was a difference of opinion between Avraham and Sarah, yet their marriage was the paragon of harmony. Conflict is not the sign of a bad marriage. But there was conflict.

When Sarah was told she was going to have a child, וַתִּצְחַק שָׂרָה, *and Sarah laughed (Bereishis 18:12). It is impossible*, she thought. There is no way that we can have a child now. Then she added, "וַאדֹנִי זָקֵן, *my husband is old*." When Hashem repeated this story to Avraham, He changed what Sarah said, explaining that Sarah laughed because *she* was old, not *he* (ibid. v. 13). Why did Hashem switch it? Rashi (ibid.) explains that He changed it for the sake of *shalom*. Hashem did not wish Avraham to hear that Sarah may have said something disparaging about him, for that could compromise the *shalom* in the home.

Yitzchak and Rivkah also experienced tension and conflict. Rivkah knew that Yaakov was a *tzaddik* and Esav was a *rasha*, and that Yitzchak loved Esav. Why didn't she say anything to Yitzchak? Why couldn't she tell him something like, "Unfortunately, you don't see [he was blind] the real story, that Yaakov is the *tzaddik*"? Rivkah did not have the relationship that Sarah had with Avraham or Rachel had with Yaakov, the Netziv (*Haamek Davar* to *Bereishis* 24:65) writes. "If Sarah or Rachel had an objection, they could voice it to their husbands. But Rivkah was so in awe of Yitzchak that she simply could not tell him anything that would be different from his opinion." It almost seems from the Netziv that that is why perhaps she was afraid to tell Yitzchak what the truth was. In any case, there was a level of rift, conflict, and dissension and she could not tell him what she felt.

Yaakov and Rachel had the ideal marriage in many ways. Yet, when Rachel did not have children for many years, she said to him, "הָבָה לִי בָנִים, *Please give me children*" (*Bereishis* 30:1). Yaakov responded, "הֲתַחַת ה׳ אָנֹכִי, *Am I in place of Hashem?* " (ibid. v. 2) Yaakov was saying in a sense, "I'm not the one holding back children from you." Hashem became angry at Yaakov and said: כָּךְ עוֹנִים אֶת הַמְעוּקוֹת, *Is that how you talk to people who are unfortunate?* (See *Bereishis Rabbah* 71:7 and *Ramban* to 30:1.)

Again we must stress that although there was some level of conflict in the homes of our *Avos* and *Imahos*, it was on an incomparably more subtle level than ours. Why does the Torah tell it to us? What is the Torah trying to teach us? I believe that the Torah is trying to tell us that conflict and dissension are part of marriage. It's impossible to have a marriage without it.

Hashem said to Adam that it was not good for a person to be alone and therefore He would give him an עֵזֶר כְּנֶגְדּוֹ (*Bereishis* 2:18). עֵזֶר means a "helpmate," while כְּנֶגְדּוֹ means a "counterforce." No two people are alike; a man and woman were not meant to be alike. They have different ideas and ideals. The total picture should be that the wife is an עֵזֶר כְּנֶגְדּוֹ, but there will be both עֵזֶר, *help,* and כְּנֶגְדּוֹ, *opposing views.* That is built into marriage; it cannot be any other way.

There is no question that marriage is a challenge. But there is also no question that the rewards for living up to this challenge are incalculable. Hashem gives every person an opportunity to find a potential best friend, a wonderful companion, a special mate, and, hopefully, a lifetime partner. Why? So that we should be able to fulfill our potential. It is impossible for a man to fulfill his potential without a good wife, or for a woman to fulfill her potential without a good husband. The question is: How are we going to meet this challenge?

Smile!

There is a wonderful book called *Table for Two,* by Rabbi Avraham Peretz (Cary) Friedman, who learned in *Eretz Yisrael* for many years. In his book he makes a magnificent statement that really defines what marriage is all about. He writes that marriage is not a question of *finding* the right partner, but *being* the right partner. If you are the right partner, then your marriage will be successful.

What is the first step to make your marriage successful? The answer is to be *happy.* The *Me'am Loez* (*Devarim* 28:47) writes that if you want to be able to make someone else happy, you must be happy. If you are a negative, despondent person, you will make your spouse feel the same way. The first way to have a happy marriage is to learn how to be a happy person. Then, after you have happiness and feel good about yourself, you can hope to make other people happy about themselves.

One way to do this is to smile. I once heard a great expression: "A smile is a little curve that sets a lot of things straight."

Rav Yisrael Salanter once said that a face is a רְשׁוּת הָרַבִּים, *a public thorough-fare*. How many times a day do you see your own face? Maybe five or six times a day, when you look in the mirror. However, the rest of the world sees your face all the time. If you look like a grouch it affects others. But if you have a happy demeanor, then people feel pleasant around you.

> **A smile is a little curve that sets a lot of things straight.**

Rav Yisrael Salanter was once walking in the street during *chodesh* Elul and saw a person looking downcast and depressed. He went over to him and asked what was the matter.

"What do you mean? It's *chodesh* Elul. I'm doing *teshuvah*," the man replied.

"Just because you are doing *teshuvah*," Rav Yisrael replied, "do I have to suffer?"

Sin Rests at the Door

I spoke about this topic to a wonderful marriage counselor, a friend of mine, Dr. Abba Goldman. He tells husbands that when they walk into the house at the end of the day to think of the words that Hashem said to *Kayin*: לַפֶּתַח חַטָּאת רֹבֵץ, *Sin rests at the door* (*Bereishis* 4:7). You can determine what mood will be set in the home. If you walk in and say something cheerful, it sets a tone of good cheer. But if you say something negative, it will set a bad tone. When a husband walks into the house, the first thing he should say is something positive, "The kitchen smells great." Or he can say, "The *shiur* I heard today was great," or "I made a great deal today."

> **The first thing one says to one's spouse after not seeing him or her for a whole day is something positive.**

The same is true for the woman. When she greets her husband at the end of the day, the first thing she should say is something positive. "One of the kids did something special in school today," or "I baked a special cake," or "I heard some good news today." Something positive.

Of course, she has the right to tell him how crazy the kids were and how difficult her day was, and he has the right to tell her how difficult his job was, or how stressed he became for whatever reason — but do not *start* out that way. לַפֶּתַח חַטָּאת רֹבֵץ. When you walk into the house, know that you can set the tone.

By the way, it is the same thing for children. When they walk into the home, the first comment from the parents should be something positive. Not a critical comment that they forgot their lunch or were not buttoned up properly. Rather a warm hello, a hug, and a kiss, expressing how good it is to see them.

Discovering Differences

When a *chassan* and *kallah* are newly engaged, they are convinced that there was never a *chassan* and *kallah* like them. "Can you imagine," a new *chassan* and *kallah* once told me, "we both want to live in *Eretz Yisrael*! Can you imagine? Unbelievable!"

Another *chassan* once told me, "When I came back from yeshivah, I went to Switzerland because I love the mountains. Then, when I got engaged, I found out that she also went to Switzerland. Can you imagine? We both love the mountains!"

A *chassan* and *kallah* even once told me excitedly that they both used Crest toothpaste with Tartar Protection!

> A *chassan* and *kallah* even once told me excitedly that they both used Crest toothpaste with Tartar Protection!

Another one told me that they both use minted floss! (I have to admit that when I was going out with my wife, I had no idea if she even flossed, to say nothing of what type of floss she used.)

You may find this hard to believe: A *chassan* once said to me, "I knew she was the one when she told me that she loves Rabbi Krohn's tapes!"

That was not all. While they were still dating, he took one of my tapes, erased part of a story that I was telling, and dubbed his voice into that part of the tape. Then, as they were sitting in the car listening to this tape, all of a sudden his voice came on and said, "Devorah, sitting there in the car. Are you going to marry Yehoshua, who is the most special boy and was created just for you?"

She almost fell out of the car, but they did get engaged and married.

It is a wonderful story, of course, but you know what inevitably happens a few weeks after marriage? They find out that Rabbi Frand also has wonderful tapes and only one of them likes them. *Hmm, they think, so we are not as similar as we thought, after all.*

Later, they may find out that he is a night person and she is not, or vice versa. He wants to talk and she wants to retire for the night. There is a level of rift, conflict, and dissension. He is a neatness freak, cleaning the toaster with a toothpick, while she was raised in a home where her mother did not care if the room was messy as long as she closed the door (not realizing that if you do not train a girl when she is young, by the time she gets married, her whole house will look like that). All of a sudden there is rift, conflict, and dissension.

Soon they begin to become frightened and may even panic. They thought they were so similar, but they are not that similar after all.

The *Midrash* (*Bamidbar Rabbah* 21:2) says: "Just as no two faces are alike, so, too, no two minds are alike." If two men do not think alike, then *kal vachomer ben b'no shel kal vachomer* that men and women do not think alike. We do not need a book, *Men Are From Yerushalayim, Women Are From Bnei Brak,* to know that men and women are different. *Chazal* have taught us that.

A young man and woman planning to get married should be excited when they find that they have unique similarities. But no one should fool themselves into believing that over time they will not discover differences, very challenging differences; differences enough to create a level of rift, conflict, and dissension.

What Goes Wrong?

One of my closest friends is Rabbi Yaakov Salomon, a marvelous therapist. He explained something to me that I had not been able to figure out for so many years. Sometimes you hear of a young couple ending the marriage after only three or four months. They were normal. No one was hiding any dark secrets. What went on?

What happened was their first argument. The husband thinks, "Uh oh, my father went through *gehinnom* because of my mother. She was such a nag. She made his life miserable. I'm not going to go through what he went through."

Or sometimes the wife knows that her mother suffered verbal abuse from a non-caring husband, a fellow who did not do anything to enhance the marriage. To the outside world he was terrific, but the kids knew how the mother suffered. Now, she experiences her first argument and thinks, "Uh oh, I'm out of here. I don't want to go through what my mother went through."

They become frightened, they panic — and Rabbi Salomon is the last step before they go to the Rav for a divorce. Many times he is able to stem it, but sometimes he cannot.

He told me that the best *chinuch* for our children's marriage is to have a good marriage ourselves. Dr. Abba Goldman told me that he used to get many calls for speaking engagements, but he stopped accepting them because most of the questions that women asked him were about *chinuch*. He said, "That is not what life is all about. *Chinuch* is important, but marriage is the priority that must be dealt with before *chinuch*."

As parents, we have to be careful. We have to set the example. We have to show our children what it means to have a good, loving, kind, considerate, caring marriage. If we do not, it increases the chances that they won't have it. Most of the time, if parents have been fighting and arguing, their children will think that this is the way it is supposed to be. We have the greatest responsibility to set an example for our children.

Quick Review

Let us briefly review the main points. Let's remember that when the Torah talks about Chavah for the first time it used the letter ס, because that ס symbolizes the idea of a closed, circular wall of protection. That is why the *kallah* walks around the *chassan*: to be a protective wall for him; and that is why he gives her the ring: to offer her that protective wall.

We learned that even in the ideal marriage of Avraham and Sarah there was a level of conflict, albeit on a subtle level that we cannot compare to our own. Similarly, the marriages of Yitzchak and Rivkah and Yaakov and Rachel experienced differences, and the Torah is telling this to us for a reason: so we should know that in *every* marriage there is an עֵזֶר aspect and a כְּנֶגְדּוֹ aspect, yet the total picture should be an עֵזֶר כְּנֶגְדּוֹ.

Marriage is a challenge, and the way we meet that challenge is not so much by *finding* the right partner but by *being* the right partner. The way we will *be* that right partner is by being happy. If you are happy you will be able to make others happy.

Let us remember Dr. Abba Goldman's great advice related to the warning, לַפֶּתַח חַטָּאת רֹבֵץ, *Sin rests at the door.* Even tonight, when you go home, the first thing you say should be a positive remark. Let us remember that every person is different and we cannot expect men and women to have the same mindset. Therefore, if we want to be sure that we have children who will have a good marriage, we have to set the example ourselves, as Yaakov Salomon said. If we indeed set a positive example of what a good marriage is, our children will then hopefully be *zocheh* to have good marriages as well.

Making Marriage Special: Part II

This is the second of a two-part series on marriage.

A young couple once told me how after just a few months of marriage, they began to realize that there were experiencing a certain level of rift, conflict, and dissension — and they were both very frightened about it. The husband then came up with this wonderful idea.

He said to his wife, "I'm going to write down 10 things that are important to me. I'll rate them from 1 to 100. Then you rate them 1 to 100. Then you write down 10 things that are important to you, rate them, and then I'll rate them. Then perhaps we can see if our values are really the same and if we are really on the same page."

Their relationship improved tremendously because of this. And they both thought it was remarkable because they now had a level of communication and way of understanding each other. I'll give you an example. They live in an apartment house and the laundry machines are down in the basement. She wrote: "Taking down the laundry fast when I ask you." She rated that 95; he rated it 30. He did not think it was that important, so it took him 20 minutes to take it down. But now that he saw that it was a 95 to her, he realized why it was such a source of contention.

Another example: She wanted him to look neat. She did not like his shirt sticking out, his hat brim up, and his tie not tightly knotted or straight. She considered that a 97, but he considered it only a 20. He walks in looking like he has just gone through a war, having had a very hard day, but *she* is the one who is upset.

> He walks in looking like he has just gone through a war, having had a very hard day, but *she* is the one who is upset.

Another thing on her list was his not coming home on time and not calling home if he would be late. Like many women, she rated it 100. He rated it 60.

Here is what he wrote: "Friday night the table should be set when I come home from shul." She figured, "What's the big deal? So I'll put out the silverware later. The napkins? What's the big deal?" He rated that 100, whereas she rated that a 65.

He came up with something that I found quite comical. He wanted her to be logical. He rated that 99; she rated it 50.

In any event, they took this chart, slipped it into a clear plastic cover and put it on their kitchen table so they could look at it every day. They told me that it added greatly to their *shalom bayis.*

I know another young couple who did something similar. He is a rebbi who teaches and is home basically only Sunday afternoon. He wanted Sunday to be quiet and peaceful, since it is the only day he has off. He was very upset that the house was upside down on the one day he needed it to be peaceful. She understood why he was upset, but there were 100 different things to do: the laundry, dishes, kids, etc.

What did she do? She gave him a list of 20 things that had to be done on a typical Sunday in the house as the week started. She asked him to rate them in order of importance. "I'll do the first 10," she said. "But I just cannot do all 20." In her mind, the first thing that should be done would be to have lunch ready. She put that at number one, but he put it at 14. Do you know what she put down as the second most important? Wearing a *sheitel* and looking nice when he comes home. He put that at 20! What a husband!

> "I love you the way you are," he said. "You can wear a snood."

"I love you the way you are," he said. "You can wear a snood. You don't have to wear your contacts. You can wear your glasses. That's okay with me."

The thing he wanted more than anything else was that the children should be happy. "If I come in," he said, "and I see that you are playing with the kids and they are content and not fighting with each other, I'm happy." She never thought that was what he really wanted.

But once they had this list, they were able to communicate. They opened up channels toward each other and continued to keep them open. They are today a wonderful happy couple.

The Three Most Important Words

Avraham Peretz Friedman, in his book *Table for Two*, once said that in his marriage–counseling experience, the turning point always comes when the spouse understands, "Maybe there is something that I'm doing that's causing this problem."

Another marriage counselor, Dr. Meir Wikler, once mentioned to me that the three most important words in marriage are not what you think they are. (They are not even, "Yes, my dear.") The three most important words are, "I was wrong."

It is very important for a person to admit that perhaps he or she is the one at fault or that he or she indeed has made a mistake. Many times the problem in marriage may be with you. You have to be honest with yourself and with your spouse. And that is not easy. However, in the long run the advantages outweigh the disadvantages.

Compliments

There is a wonderful piece of advice that I heard from psychotherapist R' Yoel Lipsett. He told me that each partner in a marriage has to know that they have a tremendous power to enhance the relationship simply by giving more compliments.

Many of us make a terrible mistake and think that everything has to be perfect in order to give a compliment. There are many husbands who feel that if the meat is good but the potatoes or other side dishes are not, then the overall meal is not good. Compliment your wife on the meat.

Sometimes a wife who feels that her husband is wearing a tie that will blind someone will say that he looks awful. What about his shoes, his hat, his suit? Compliment that.

A person has to look for the good to compliment. There is no one that a husband wants to compliment more than his wife. Similarly, a wife does not want to compliment anyone else more than her husband. In receiving a compliment, it's the same thing; a husband wants more than anything to get a genuine compliment from his wife and a wife more than anything wants to get a genuine compliment from her husband. But we make this tremendous mistake. We think everything has to be perfect in order to give a compliment. Find the good and then give a compliment.

Rabbi Matis Roberts, who teaches *chassanim* in Yeshivah Shaar HaTorah in Queens, always tells the *chassanim:* "There are four A's to always keep in mind: admiration, attention, appreciation, and affection."

Gratitude

There is another thing. We have to learn how to say thank you. Most of us have forgotten those two words. When was the last time a husband thanked a wife for the meal that she made? When was the last time a wife thanked a husband for the money that he brought home? Men work very hard. It's a tough world out there. I always say that a woman who wants to be thanked for the *challos* she made has to thank her husband for the dough that he brings home!

Rabbi Avigdor Miller has a wonderful tape called *The 10 Commandments of Marriage.* He says that the first *dvar Torah* every Friday night should be that the husband thanks the wife for the meal that she made.

Wives should train the children as my wife trained our children. When she would arrive home with the children from shopping, the children would always come to me and say, "Thank you for the clothes you just bought me."

And now that they are married, *baruch Hashem*, with children of their own, if my wife goes shopping with them or the grandchildren, they always call afterward to thank Zaidy for the clothes he bought. I wasn't even there, but when a wife (or grandmother) trains the children (and grandchildren) to say thank you to the father or grandfather, these children/grandchildren will not take their spouses for granted when they get married.

Never Demean

Never — ever — degrade your spouse in public. Never — ever — degrade your spouse in front of the children.

A husband and a wife are allowed to differ, of course, and they are even allowed to differ in front of their children. In fact, I think it is terrible if a husband and a wife create an aura in their home as though they never have a difference of opinion. Children should know that it is possible that parents have different views and opinions of things. One is more of a spender; one is less. One wants to go on vacation; one does not want to go on vacation. That is not the end of the world. We are different. And if differences are shared and discussed in front of the children with dignity and respect, it prepares children for their own future marriages.

However, in my opinion, we give our children a false sense of security when we never let them know that we have differences of opinion. That is why when children get married and have their first difference of opinion, they panic. You have to know that you are allowed to have differences, but that does mean that you can *ever* — ever — share them in a demeaning or degrading way.

Included in this is demeaning yourself. There are some people that say things like, "Oh, I'm so stupid; I'm so dumb." If you keep saying that, after a while your spouse will believe you are stupid or dumb. Never degrade yourself, especially in front of your spouse.

Being Attractive

Here is something which is embarrassing to talk about in public, but we have to talk about it anyway, because it is an integral part of marriage. Men and women have to continue to be attractive to each other — both physically and mentally. One must be careful about one's weight both for health and appearance reasons.

Men and women have to continue to be attractive to each other — both physically and mentally.

Along these lines, it is important to try to always be neat. Of course, one does not have to look like one is going to a *chasunah* every night, but neatness is at least what every husband or wife expects from each other.

Mentally, you have to be attractive too, of course. When you were going out, there was a whole world to talk about. Did that change? Why does the couple have nothing to talk about after they are husband and wife for a while? The whole world is still out there. There are a million things going on. There is kosher material to read. There are *divrei* Torah to say. There were things that you had as mutual interests. If you want a marriage to grow, you have to make the effort to share with and be interesting to each other.

Another way to be mentally attractive to your spouse — and this is good general advice — is to be a good listener. I know someone who was sitting at the kitchen table, reading something, and his wife began talking to him and suddenly she said, "You are not listening to me."

"What do you mean?" he replied, "Of course I'm listening."

"What did I just say?" she responded agitatedly.

"You said that I was not listening to you."

It is wrong. Put away what you are reading and be a good listener.

How to Criticize

Now we come to a very difficult part of the topic. This is where many marriages begin to unravel. No one is perfect. Therefore, there comes a time when there is a need to point it out. Nevertheless, there is a way to criticize.

There are different types of criticism. Criticism can be specific, global, or demeaning. In cases of specific and global criticism, one can still live with the person. However, there is no place for demeaning criticism. That makes the relationship exceedingly difficult.

Here is an example of a specific complaint: A wife says to her husband, "I'm upset you did not take the cup off the kitchen table. I just cleaned the kitchen. I asked you to put it in the sink." That is specific.

Global begins, "You always ..." or "You never ...." For example, "*You always* leave a mess wherever you go." This type of criticism has nothing to do with this particular cup. This type of criticism is exaggerated and overblown. Although this is worse than specific criticism, it is not necessarily fatal to the marriage.

Demeaning is often fatal. An example of demeaning criticism is, "You are a slob, just like you learned to be in your mother's home."

That is terrible. That is the beginning of the end.

Here is another specific criticism. A husband says to his wife, "I feel bad that you did not pick up my suit from the cleaners like I asked you." That is specific. Everyone can understand and tolerate criticism like that.

Global is, "You never do what I ask you." Or, "You always block me out."

Demeaning is, "You have no brains. That is why you are losing your job. That is why you will probably get fired."

If a couple is engaged in demeaning criticism, they need help *fast*. No one is perfect. We all make mistakes and have faults. A spouse has a right to air complaints (as the Netziv wrote, see Part I). It is acceptable to criticize specifically. Try to avoid criticizing globally. But avoid *at all costs* being demeaning. Never — ever — be demeaning.

Zeh Lo Chashuv

This is a sad but true story. There was a couple with numerous children who had a decent marriage; however, they were quite different from each other. He was more the "on time" type while she always seemed to be a little late. He was more of a "neatness freak" and she did not mind if things were strewn around for a little while. Understandably, there were times that they had words between them, but she would try and defuse their arguments by implying that the matter wasn't really worth arguing about and then say three words in Hebrew: *Zeh lo chashuv*, "It is not that important."

For instance, she might leave the dishes lying around overnight after Shabbos until Sunday morning. He would come into the kitchen Sunday morning and say, "How come you did not clean up the dishes?"

"*Zeh lo chashuv*," she would reply. "I will get to it."

They would be getting ready to go to a wedding. He was ready to get into the car while she was still adjusting her *sheitel*. He would say, "Why can't you be ready on time?" She would smile and say, "*Zeh lo chashuv.*"

She didn't use this quip for the very important things in life; just for small matters that she felt didn't really affect their marriage. And, indeed, many times this saying of hers defused the tense moment.

One summer while she was up in their bungalow in the mountains, she called him in the city and asked him to bring her checkbook as she had important bills to pay. Being the ever-efficient person, he immediately put the checkbook into a shopping bag so that he would not forget to bring it. The first thing he did when he arrived Friday afternoon was to give her the bag with the checkbook in it.

The next day, Shabbos morning, he woke up and noticed the shopping bag hanging on the baby's crib with the checkbook in it. He was very upset. She had made a long–distance call and said how important it was to her to have the checkbook — and yet there it was, still in the bag! She hadn't even taken it out!

However, he did not say anything because he figured he shouldn't make a scene and spoil Shabbos. Besides, if he said anything she would probably reply, *Zeh lo chashuv.* "It's not so important. I'll get to the checks Motza'ei Shabbos."

He went back to the city on Sunday. The next Friday he came back to the bungalow, walked into bedroom, and the bag was still there on the crib with the checkbook in it! He was livid. But, again, he decided not to say anything. What was he going to do? Make a big deal about it and ruin Shabbos? The children were there and he came up only once a week. And besides, you know what she'll say, "*Zeh lo chashuv.*" So he did not say anything about the checkbook throughout the entire Shabbos and went back to the city on Sunday.

On Tuesday he got a frantic call. His wife was expecting a baby and had been rushed to the hospital. He was only told that it was something serious. It took him two and a half hours to drive up from Manhattan to the hospital. When he entered the hospital lobby and saw the numerous relatives and friends, he knew something was terribly wrong. Then they told him. His wife had died of complications during premature childbirth.

Stunned, he went back to the bungalow colony with his friends and relatives. When he went into the bedroom, the first thing that he saw was that bag with the checkbook in it. It was still there hanging on the crib. He took out the checkbook and the first check he wrote was to the *chevrah kadishah*. The second check was used to pay for the funeral. When he came back to his home in Brooklyn to sit *shivah,* he took the bag and hung it up in his closet. On the outside of the bag he wrote three words, *Zeh lo chashuv.* He kept it there for six months.

That lesson, which he learned in death, is what we have to learn in life. Most of the arguments that we get into are really *lo chashuv,* not so important. One negative, nasty comment leads to another until there is this tremendous volcano of emotions bubbling to the surface. Relationships break up, and at the same time innocent children are being destroyed. However, if we would only reason that indeed *zeh lo chashuv,* that most arguments are about things that are really not that important, then that rift and conflict and dissension would not develop.

A petty argument is not worth getting worked up about. You do not have to answer every time your spouse says something. But we want to answer back because we feel it is attacking our honor and pride. Therefore, one side says this and the other side says that, and before you know it, specific criticisms become global criticisms. From global criticisms come demeaning ones and the volcano erupts.

I want to end with this thought. Every home is a miniature *Beis HaMikdash.* If we can only learn to have *ahavah* and *shalom* in our homes, it will set an example for our friends, communities, and business associates. Hopefully, it will spread to all of *Klal Yisrael.* Ultimately, by making sure that our miniature *Beis HaMikdash* is in order and built with *shalom,* hopefully we will be *zocheh* to see the ultimate *Beis HaMikdash* that will be built when, as *Chazal* teach, there will be harmony and unity among us. (See *Medrash Tanchuma Netzavim* 1.)

Caught in the Middle: Helping Children of Divorce

This article is called "Caught in the Middle," because that is the way children from a divorced family often feel. Additionally, many who are going through a divorce, or have gone through a divorce, often feel helpless and abandoned: abandoned by family members who do not agree with their decision and abandoned by society which often does not know the true story of what really went on in the marriage.

My purpose in addressing this topic is to give validation and chizuk to these people who are so vulnerable. I acknowledge and give thanks to Mrs. Faygie Zakheim and Dr. Hindy Klein of the Brooklyn Task Force, and to Dr. Meir Wikler, who together have been advocating for years that this topic be brought to the foreground.

Paining the Vulnerable

The Torah says (*Shemos* 22:21): כָּל אַלְמָנָה וְיָתוֹם לֹא תְעַנּוּן, You are not allowed to cause pain to *every* widow and orphan. Why does it say "*every* widow and orphan"? It could have simply said, "You are not allowed to pain a widow and orphan."

The Rambam is bothered by this question and says "*every*" refers even to a wealthy widow who has many possessions. A widow's pain, anguish, and tears are always there, regardless of how wealthy she is. Therefore, it's not just simply the poor widow who you are not permitted to pain, but even the wealthy one.

Rashi is also apparently bothered by this question. He understands that the extra word "*every*" refers to *any* person in *Klal Yisrael*. The *pasuk* is just telling us what is too often the typical case. However, this prohibition is not limited only to widows and orphans. Since the widow and the orphan are by nature weak and vulnerable, the *pasuk* says not to pain them. However, "*every*" expands the concept to include *anyone* who is weak and vulnerable.

Who is *anyone*? In my opinion, it's the divorcee and the children of divorce. They are just as vulnerable as the widow and the orphan.

Don't Blame; Feel Their Pain

A woman whom I interviewed for this topic said exactly that. "In a way, the widows are better off because nobody blames a widow. In a divorce, there is always somebody to blame, whether it's the husband or the wife. Many people are under the impression that they could have worked it out."

Therefore, the first lesson is that none of us should *ever* blame anyone who got divorced, because you simply don't know the whole story. Additionally, you don't know and really can't imagine how you would have reacted under the same circumstances.

Rather than blaming the parties in a divorce, feel their pain and *daven* for them. Never, ever blame them!

Although the purpose of this article is to help the children caught in the middle, we must think about the parents as well and understand their plight.

Knowing Their Pain

The *Gemara* (*Kiddushin* 30b) tells us there are three partners to a child: the father, the mother, and *Hashem*. When one of the partners is missing, *r'l*, the child feels isolated. He develops a stigma. He's different from his classmates.

Twenty-five years ago there weren't as many people who were divorced as there are today. It is common now for almost every child to have in his class children who come from homes where the parents are divorced. And even so, a child of a divorced family feels different, isolated, alone, and embarrassed.

Hashem says (*Shemos* 3:7), רָאֹה רָאִיתִי אֶת עֳנִי עַמִּי אֲשֶׁר בְּמִצְרָיִם וְאֶת צַעֲקָתָם שָׁמַעְתִּי מִפְּנֵי נֹגְשָׂיו כִּי יָדַעְתִּי אֶת מַכְאֹבָיו, *I saw the affliction of My nation that is in Mitzrayim and I heard their cries because of their taskmasters, for I know their pain.* Three modes of focusing by Hashem are mentioned in the *pasuk*, one higher than the other: seeing, hearing, and knowing. If a person sees or hears something but doesn't focus in on it, it's as if he didn't hear or see it. That's what Hashem is saying to Moshe. "I saw their pain, I heard their cries, and now that I have focused on it, I'm going to do something about it."

Let us, too, now focus on the pain of the children of divorce and do something about it. I have prepared five ways that we can help the children that are "caught in the middle."

AAA

The first thing that we can do is AAA: "Advise Against Anger."

If you have a friend or relative involved in a divorce, the best advice you can give them is "Don't be angry." Tell them, "If in your anger you cause the children to be angry at the other spouse, thereby turning them into pawns in carrying out your anger, you break those same children many times over!"

Chazal teach (*Gittin* 90b): "When a person gets divorced, even the *Mizbe'ach* cries." It doesn't say that if someone eats on Yom Kippur the *Mizbe'ach* cries. It doesn't say that if someone serves *avodah zarah* the *Mizbe'ach* cries. It doesn't even say that if someone kills another person the *Mizbe'ach* cries. Why is the *Mizbe'ach* crying over a divorce?

I believe the answer is that the *Mizbe'ach* is usually consuming animals that are *korbanos*, but during a divorce the children are the *korbanos*. They are being sacrificed on the altar of hatred and anger — and that's something to cry about.

> **During a divorce the children are the *korbanos*.**

The first thing we have to realize in the middle of a divorce is not to make the children into pawns. Sometimes a divorce has to happen. Sometimes it's the best thing for the couple and the children. But even so, you must tell the spouses that they can't continue arguing and arguing.

Rabbi Aryeh Ginzberg told me this story. There was a divorce where the husband and wife were so angry at each other that the husband swore that he would never be in the same room as his wife. At his daughter's wedding, she wanted both her parents there, but the father refused to be in the hall if his ex-wife was going to be there. He didn't even go to the *badekin*, because the ex-wife would be standing right next to the *kallah*! Can you imagine how the daughter felt?

When it came to the *chuppah* he didn't walk her down. Only the mother walked her down. Underneath the *chuppah*, the mother walked around with the *kallah* seven times and then discreetly walked off the platform. Then, through the back door, the father came out. He had two *berachos* under the *chuppah*. When he was done, he went out and the mother came back.

After the *chuppah*, as the *chassan* and *kallah* were in the *yichud* room, Rabbi Ginzberg got a text from the *chassan*. "Rebbi, please come, you have to help."

Rabbi Ginzberg was thinking, "What is going on! They're in the *yichud* room; is there a *shailah*?"

He hurried to the *yichud* room and the *chassan* said, "Rebbi, my wife can't stop crying. From the moment we got to the *yichud* room, all she's doing is crying. What am I supposed to do?!"

To me it seems that the father did a terrible, horrible thing. Can't you give in on the night of your daughter's wedding? Is that what you do to a *kallah*?! It is repulsive and inexcusable!

Hence this is the first bit of advice. This is the first way we can help: AAA. You must advise against anger.

SSS

The second thing is SSS: *Shabbos Seudos* Stabilize.

Invite children with the single mother or the single father for a *Shabbos* meal.

A father told me that after he was divorced, everybody on the block still invited them for *Shabbos* meals, and his children felt stability because they still felt part of the group. A mother told me the opposite, "Once I got divorced, I was so isolated. No one invited me, and my children couldn't go to any of their homes either. They were like outcasts."

Invite these children to your home. Let your children go to their home. When we invite single mothers or single fathers and their children, we are stabilizing that family and making them feel a part of *Klal Yisrael*.

And invite them often. That's how you save these children caught in the middle. One mother told me that for years no one invited her and then one day a new couple moved in down the block and started inviting them. "All of a sudden my children felt like real people," she said.

That is the second thing: SSS. *Shabbos Seudos* Stabilize.

Rei'im Ahuvim

A divorcee told me, "I don't care what seminary a girl went to in *Eretz Yisrael*; we can't learn *Mishnayos* with our boys. We can't learn *Bava Kamma* with them. Who's going to learn with my children?"

She told me of Rabbi Dovid Fishman, Rosh Yeshivah of Yeshivah Gedolah Kesser Torah of Monsey, who allowed two of his *talmidim* to learn with her two sons every night. The young boys would learn the *Gemara* in the daytime and at night they had someone with whom to review it.

I spoke to Rabbi Fishman and asked, "Is this a regular program in the yeshivah?"

"No," he said. "We made this a special case."

"I think *every* yeshivah should do that," I said.

Of course, we have to ask the Roshei Yeshivah. We can't do anything without their permission. But what would be wrong if every yeshivah started an organization — that I would like to call *Rei'im Ahuvim*, which means "Dear Friends" — where boys in the *bais midrash* donate a half-hour of time to either a child of a divorcee, an orphan, or a child of a *ba'al teshuvah* (whose father is not on the learning level yet to learn with his son)? I'm not suggesting that the boys give up their *sedarim* at night, only a half-hour, *bein hasedarim*.

Again, I wish to stress, we have to ask the Roshei Yeshivah, but what a beautiful thing for *talmidim* in a yeshivah to tutor others who are vulnerable: *Toras chessed!* Tutors today can cost $50 to $70 an hour! The vast majority of these mothers can't afford that. Therefore, whether it is formally institutionalized or not, the idea is to help children caught in the middle get the learning support they are missing.

LIP Service

The fourth thing is that we should insist on LIP service. LIP stands for "Life Insurance Policy."

Every mother should have a life insurance policy. And please don't tell me you can't afford it, because you can't afford *not* to have it. And if indeed there are mothers who do not have money for a life insurance policy, we have to either help them find the money or give it to them outright.

Mrs. Gital Kahn works in Bikur Cholim in Mount Sinai Hospital. The doctors in the hospital virtually worship her. They call her the "Angel of Healing." You've never met a woman like Mrs. Kahn. Her dear son, Albert, has devoted his life to helping people obtain life insurance. Do you know that for about $25 a month we can help widows and divorcees? They can get a $150,000 policy. Do you know what that means?

Imagine the anguish of an ill mother who has custody of the children. All she can think of is, "I'm leaving the world and I'm leaving nothing for my children."

Even if a couple is married, when a spouse dies it's a terrible tragedy. However, if a single parent passes away, it's even more devastating!

That's the fourth thing: LIP Service.

RRR

The fifth thing is RRR: Relieve, Request, and Respect.

It is very hard for single mothers to simply get out of the house. Do you know how many *shiurim* there are today in America and how many women go to them? But single mothers can't get out. They have no husband to watch the children and often there are little children at home.

Offer to relieve them. When you hear that a *shiur* is being given in the neighborhood, phone her and say, "You deserve a night out."

And she is also entitled to a night out with her friends. Offer her that opportunity as well.

When a mother is in a good frame of mind, she'll be a better mother. If she can't get out or go shopping at night, it weighs heavily on her. We have to relieve these parents.

A single woman told me that someone on her block called her and told her, "Your car is now my car. If there is any problem with your car, I don't want you to even think about calling a mechanic. I will take care of it. Flat tire, brakes, oil changes, whatever; it's now my responsibility. I will take care of it. That's my service to you."

What a wonderful *chessed*! Who even thinks about that?

It goes beyond cars, of course. Another woman shared with me that someone in her neighborhood told her, "Your kids' *shidduchim* are my responsibility. You just get the names and I'll do the research."

Isn't that a beautiful thing? All she has to do is get the names of potential matches for her child and the neighbor will do all the research. That's called "Relieve."

What is "Request"? Next time you go to the grocery store, call up the divorcee at home and tell her, "I'm in the grocery store, can I bring you anything?"

"Can I take your kids to the park?"

Request, ask, and keep her in mind.

What does "Respect" mean? Respect means don't ask the children questions that are none of your business. Do you know how many amateur guidance counselors ask questions just for the sake of asking? Rather than asking questions that are none of your business, take action to help the family.

The CEO of Ohel, David Mandel, told me that in a shul where he *davens* there are two children from divorced homes. Nobody volunteers to invite these kids to shul for Shabbos, so the mother takes them. She comes early but doesn't *daven* a word because she's standing behind the *mechitzah*, looking at the kids, seeing if they're *davening*. That's not a mother's job. That's the job of someone else in the community.

Each of us should look around in our neighborhood. I'm talking to the men specifically. If you see a child from a divorced home (or single-parent home) who has no one to walk to shul with, no one to take him to a Little League game, invite him to join you. If you're going on a picnic or outing, see how many kids you can take who are not your own children, and make your own children feel special for bringing them. When the child finally does come to shul, make sure that you sit next to him, or that he sits next to you and he feels part of your family.

"Deep Down, I Knew That You Cared"

Let me end with a heartwarming story.

A man and a woman went through a terrible divorce. The father would poison the mind of his son against the mother every day, to the point that the boy wanted nothing to do with the mother at all. His mother would come to the yeshivah and bring her son food, but he would say, "Ma, get away from here."

She would bring him money or presents, but he would always say, "Ma, please, you're embarrassing me. I don't want your food or your money. I don't want to have anything to do with you."

She was devastated. As often as she came, he rejected her. Finally, she stopped coming. She remarried and went on to live a life of her own. Eight years later, she got a call from her son one day.

"Ma, do you think we can go out for coffee?"

"Do you really want to go out for coffee?"

"Yes."

They came to a café and sat at a table. He took his mother's hand and said, "Ma, I'm a *chassan*."

She said, "I know, but I just didn't want to call you because I didn't think you would want my call."

They both started crying and he said, "Ma, now I realize I was on the wrong side." Then he added, "Ma, all those times that I rejected you, all those times that you came and I turned you away, I appreciated that you came. Deep down, I knew that you cared. I never forgot that. Ma, I realize now,

> "Ma, all those times that I rejected you ... deep down, I knew that you cared. I never forgot that. ... I was on the wrong side."

I was on the wrong side. Please, Ma, would you walk me down to my *chuppah*?"

She did indeed walk him down to his *chuppah*. And today, they have a wonderful relationship.

Psychologists and *Rabbanim* say the same thing. The spouse who berates the other spouse will eventually lose the child 95 percent of the time. The spouse who was victimized will usually develop a real relationship with the child when he or she eventually comes to his or her senses.

And in most cases the children of divorce *will* come to their senses. It might take until they're 20 or 25 years old, but when a mother or a father is decent to the child and gives that child unconditional love, eventually it's going to be repaid.

Caring for Our Elders

I wish to introduce our topic with a most incredible comment Rashi has in *Chumash*. It's tucked away in the last *pasuk* of *Parashas Noach,* which states: וַיִּהְיוּ יְמֵי תֶרַח חָמֵשׁ שָׁנִים וּמָאתַיִם שָׁנָה וַיָּמָת תֶּרַח בְּחָרָן, *Terach lived 205 years; and Terach died in Charan* (*Bereishis* 11:32). Prior to hearing Rashi's comment, let's set the scene. The next *parashah, Lech Lecha,* begins with Hashem telling Avraham to leave his father's house. It sounds as if Avraham left his father's house *after* Terach died. However, that's not what happened. Terach lived many years after Avraham left his house. If so, why does the Torah say at the end of *Parashas Noach* that Terach died?

The answer, Rashi says, is so that people should not say that Avraham did not honor his father; that he left an old man at home.

Practically speaking, Avraham had no choice, of course. Hashem told him "*Lech lecha,*" so he had to go. Nevertheless, the Torah didn't want to say that Avraham left while his father was still alive, because each of us has that tremendous obligation to honor our parents, and the Torah didn't want anyone to get the wrong impression about Avraham.

A Nation of Caregivers

The Wall Street Journal recently devoted an entire section to care for the elderly. "We have become a nation of caregivers," the paper declared. Then it listed statistics: one in five adults in America — that's 44 million Americans — provides unpaid care to another adult. An organization called the NAC (National Alliance for Caregiving) did a study and found that in 22 million homes people are being cared for when they are over 50. Incredible!

> **One in five adults in America — that's 44 million Americans — provides unpaid care to another adult.**

Interestingly, three out of four informal caregivers are women. Two million women are now not only caring for children, but parents as well. We know the famous expression "the sandwich generation." What should our attitude be in caring for our elders?

The Right Attitude

I believe the attitude has to be what the *Sefer HaChinuch* writes (Mitzvah 33). How do you approach the mitzvah of *kibud av v'eim* (honoring your father and mother)? It is worthwhile to recognize that when somebody does you a favor, you have to do them a favor in return. Denying the good that someone did to you is *middah ra'ah* (a terrible characteristic). We exist only because of our parents. When a person realizes how much he owes his parents, how they took care of him and worried about him, he should be filled with gratitude. Even more so, the purpose of *kibud av v'eim* is to realize that not only did our parents do great things for us, but Hashem Himself bestowed so many favors upon us.

Taking care of elderly parents is not only a mitzvah and the right thing to do: it's the logical thing to do. Therefore, when we talk about the care we need to give to elders, especially parents, we have to realize that they are the conduit not only to our existence but, for the most part, to our *Yiddishkeit*.

Caring for Our Elders
the Way They Cared for Us

The other day I was speaking with a wonderful person from Baltimore, a geriatrician named Dr. Menachem Cooper. He told me that a few weeks earlier he was very busy planning his daughter's upcoming wedding. Two weeks before the wedding, his mother collapsed and went into a coma.

"On one hand," he told me, "I had to plan my daughter's wedding. And on the other hand, my mother was in a coma; she didn't recognize me anymore. I was running back and forth between the plans for the *simchah* and taking care of my mother. How much time could I spend with my mother? Besides everything, I also had a job — a very demanding job!

"Then," he added, "I reminded myself that when I was 11 months old I was deathly ill. They told me that my mother would sit by my bed day and night until she was so exhausted that she lost her voice. She couldn't even talk. When I remembered this, I immediately decided that I'm going to take care of my mother the way she took care of me. I sat there at the foot of her bed and took out a *Gemara* and learned so it would be a *zechus* that she should have a *refuah sheleimah*."

Some Practical Ideas

How do you make elders feel special? One answer is staying with them for Shabbos. If you have brothers and sisters, take turns. For my mother, one of her most delightful *Shabbosim* was when she had a number of her grandchildren come for Shabbos, all sitting with her at the Shabbos table.

The idea is try to get elderly parents stimulated. There are men and women who would go to *shiurim* if they knew about them. It's your job as the child to find out about available *shiurim*.

Another idea: Get a group of women together and invite your elderly mother to go out once a week or once a month for lunch or dinner. It makes a huge difference. She has to get dressed for the occasion and it will make her feel special.

Sometimes, an elderly parent doesn't like to go out of the house. What do you do then? There are visiting services. We have an outstanding high school in the neighborhood, Shevach High School. Many years ago, my wife ran the *chessed* program there and among the activities was a program called "Visit a Bubby." If one had an elderly mother in Queens, with just a call to the school, a girl or two in the *chessed* program would visit. This type of program can be started in many schools throughout the metropolitan area.

You could even encourage elderly parents to take a summer tour to a foreign country. Over the last number of years I have led tours to places such as Lithuania (Vilna, Kelm, Radin, etc.), Czechoslovakia (Prague), Poland, Morocco, Gibraltar, Spain, etc. The trips have usually had about 120 people and a number of them were indeed elderly people, either married or now single, and their lives were enhanced and changed by these experiences.

My daughter, Chaviva Pfeiffer, would phone my mother and say, "Bubby, I love how you make mac-n'-cheese. Nobody makes it like you. We would love it if every Wednesday night, if it isn't too much trouble, if you could make us that for supper. I'll come pick it up."

It made my mother feel so special. She looked forward every week to making supper for her oldest granddaughter's family. She was proud that she was helping the "new" generation.

Let me share a personal incident. I believe we can all do things to make our elderly parents feel special; we just have to spend some time in creative thinking. The stories that I write in the Maggid Series of books are edited by ArtScroll's primary editor, Rabbi Nosson Scherman. To me he is among the finest writers and editors in the Jewish world. (My stories read smoothly because of him.) However, I learned writing from my mother and she took great pride in her writing and editing. I always had her edit the stories as well. I would tell her, "Ma, I need your input. Tell me how I'm doing." She edited them meticulously and returned them within days of my giving them to her. It made her feel special. We always discussed beautiful expressions and poetic phrases. It made her feel important.

When my mother had to quit the job she had because the company moved out of state, I contacted a dear friend of mine, a *tzaddik* named Dovid Schild who now lives in Bergenfield, New Jersey. He had a somewhat similar company and I knew he did not need any more employees. I called him anyway and said, "I know you don't need my mother to work for you, but I'll pay you her 'salary' and you give it to her at the end of the week. Call her up, tell her you need her in the office, and she'll come in a few hours every day."

And that's what happened. For a while, I paid her salary. She had no idea, but she was thrilled that she had a job and felt important. After five or six months Dovid called me and said, "I love having your mother in the office. She's a good-luck charm. My business has increased ever since she arrived, so I'm taking over the salary."

It was wonderful. She worked there a few years until he moved. Why can't everyone do that? What do you have money for? You have money to make your mother or father feel special. Buy them a trip to *Eretz Yisrael*. How many times will they get to go there? Let them go away for a Chanukah or a Shabbos. Get them a hotel room (in an off–season, if need be). Do something special for them. You won't always have that opportunity.

> **Another thing you can do is call them every day, especially Motza'ei Shabbos. Stay in contact.**

Another thing you can do is call them every day, especially Motza'ei Shabbos. Stay in contact. That's how you make them feel special. Don't forget about them.

Getting the Right Care

Many times, r'l, when an elderly parent is ill, we feel guilty. How can we put them in an assisted–living place? Why can't we take care of our parents?

However, you have to do what is best for them. If parents need a ventilator or skilled personnel, they don't belong at home. If the parents really need that facility, that's where to place them.

Nevertheless, you have to go and find out what kind of place it is. Seek out someone who works in these places. Don't just go to the office, get a tour, and let them tell you all the good things. Instead, walk around the rooms and speak to the children of the residents. Ask them what happens when their parent rings the bell, how fast is the response, etc. What is the food really like? How clean are the rooms? Is there an odor? What about bedsores? Do they turn the patients often?

Insurance for the Perplexed

Let me mention something that is so confusing and difficult to manage for elders, and even for ourselves: insurance.

Here's a guide for the confused (in other words, just about everybody). I'll give just a brief overview. We all know that Medicaid is for low-income people, but did you know that each of us, as an American citizen, is entitled to Medicare? All you have to do is make it to 65 (or to 62, if disabled).

However, Medicare isn't so simple. There are things called HMOs and PPOs. HMO means "health maintenance organization." It's much cheaper to get an HMO with Medicare. But the problem is you have to use their doctors and facilities. You can't switch out of it. What happens if you are stuck? I know someone who was terribly stuck in Florida using doctors she didn't want. She couldn't get to the ones she wanted because she had an HMO policy! The family wrote letters, and were denied. She never got to the doctors she wanted. The PPO costs more, but you can get any doctors you want (usually within a preferred network of providers).

Since Medicare doesn't pay for everything, there is something called Medigap, which fills the "gap" left over from what Medicare does not pay. If you are not confused enough, there are 10 levels of Medigap plans. Some will pay for drugs, some for pills, some won't pay for a long hospital stay, etc. And heaven help if you live half the year in Florida. The New York policy doesn't pay for the doctors in Florida.

It can be so confusing to elderly parents. We have to guide them through it. If you can't figure it out yourself, find someone who can. Call an insurance agent you trust and try to work it out so that the elderly will get the best care if they become ill.

A Mammeh's Question

I would like to end with a beautiful story. In 1980 Rabbi Moshe Faskowitz, Rabbi Boruch Graydin, and Rabbi Avrohom Marmorstein of the Lakewood Kollel started the Jewish Learning Experience Outreach Program. They decided to give *shiurim* on various levels in nearby communities and so Rabbi Faskowitz called Rabbi Berel Rothman of Cherry Hill, New Jersey to ask if his congregation would be interested in *shiurim*. He answered yes and provided Rabbi Faskowitz with a list of people who might be interested. The list was not long and so Rabbi Faskowitz asked if there were any Yiddish-speaking men in town. Rabbi Faskowitz thought such a person might be interested in a *Gemara shiur*, having come from Europe. Rabbi Rothman said there was an older person whom everyone knew as Harvey. He spoke Yiddish but was not a member of any shul. "I could call him if you wish," said Rabbi Rothman, "but I can't promise you he'll show up."

Harvey was called and told that Rabbi Faskowitz of Lakewood would like to speak to him. He never called back, but on the first night of the classes, as people were gathering in their respective groups, Harvey approached Rabbi Faskowitz.

"You wanted me?" he said in Yiddish.

"Yes," said Rabbi Faskowitz. "We are starting a *Gemara shiur* and I thought that you might be interested in joining us."

"*Dee mechutzef* (You ill-mannered person)!" he stormed. "How dare you call me here to learn *Gemara*? Since Auschwitz, I hate *Yiddishkeit*, I never *daven*, I never make

> "Since Auschwitz, I hate *Yiddishkeit*, I never *daven*, I never make *berachos*, I don't do mitzvos. Leave me alone and don't call me again!"

berachos, I don't do mitzvos. Leave me alone and don't call me again! You have a chutzpah calling me here for this!"

Rabbi Faskowitz was taken aback by this explosive tirade.

"My mother was killed in the ghetto right before my eyes. Not only my mother, but the mothers of all my friends were killed. I don't want any connection to your God and your type," Harvey spat out his words with vehemence and disdain.

Rabbi Faskowitz was now standing. "Look," he said softly to Harvey, "just give me a bit of respect. Don't walk out on me before I start. The others here will get a terrible impression. Just stay for a few minutes and then you can leave. I won't say anything."

Harvey thought for a moment and looking down to avoid Rabbi Faskowitz's gaze and said, "All right. Just a few minutes." Rabbi Faskowitz began teaching *Mesechta Pesachim*, and after 15 minutes, Harvey got up and left.

The next week as the small group sat down to learn again, Harvey walked in. He did not take a *Gemara*, but he sat at the table. Rabbi Faskowitz knew to leave well enough alone. This time Harvey sat through the entire *shiur* but did not participate. He listened and observed without making a comment.

The third week, Harvey had with him a *Mesechta Pesachim*. It looked brand new and Rabbi Faskowitz assumed that Harvey had gone to the effort and expense of buying it. After the *shiur* Harvey approached Rabbi Faskowitz and asked, "Did you ever hear of the town Pruzhin?"

"Of course," said Rabbi Faskowitz. "Reb Elya [Feinstein] Pruzhiner was from there." (Reb Elya was Rabbi Moshe Feinstein's uncle.)

Harvey's face lit up. "Rav Elya was a great *tzaddik* and *talmid chacham*," he said softly and with reverence. "Everyone loved him."

"He wrote a *sefer, Halichos Eliyahu*," said Rabbi Faskowitz.

"Do you have it?" asked Harvey.

"No, but I can borrow it from the yeshivah library. I'll bring it next week."

"I would appreciate that," said Harvey. "Thank you."

It was obvious to Rabbi Faskowitz that over the three weeks since the first *shiur,* Harvey's demeanor had changed dramatically. He wasn't angry any more. Something had softened him. Was it the Talmudic give-and-take that brought him back to his youth? Was it the familiar feel of the sacred pages of the *Gemara* and its distinctive layout that he had not seen in years?

The next week Rabbi Faskowitz showed the *sefer Halichos Eliyahu* to Harvey. Harvey took the *sefer* in his hands and went off to the side. He sat down at a table. He opened it to the title page and stared at the Hebrew word Pruzhin. He began stroking the word. Softly and gently, over and over, he ran his cupped fingers over the word Pruzhin, as tears welled in his eyes. Then his hands moved over the name of Rabbi Elya Pruzhiner. Harvey began crying. Soon he was weeping uncontrollably. Memories of the youth he no longer had, but subconsciously craved, washed over him. The simple purity of those long-gone days stirred his essence.

He became a regular at the *shiur*: He asked Rabbi Faskowitz to call him Yankel, "*Mein mammeh flegt mir roofin Yankele* (my mother would call me Yankele)," he said with a pained smile.

After the seventh weekly *shiur*, Rabbi Faskowitz announced that after the next week's *shiur*, which would be on the third night of Chanukah, there would be a festive *mesibah* (gathering) for all the attendees and the teachers.

The next week, during the *mesibah*, Yankel asked Rabbi Faskowitz if he could speak to him privately. The two went off to a side. "Rebbi," Yankel began, "I lied to you that first night that I met you. I said that I never go to shul and that I never *daven*. It's not true; I have been going once a year. I don't even go on Yom Kippur but I do go on my mother's *yahrtzeit* to say *Kaddish*.

"I never told you this," he continued, "but I am very sick. I am dying. I will soon meet my mother in Heaven. And I know that she will ask me, '*Nu, Yankele, vus hust du getun far mir*? (So, Yankele, what have you done for me?)'

"I was going to tell her, '*Mammeh, ich hub gezugt Kaddish far dir.* (Mother, I said *Kaddish* for you).' "But I know," he said, "she would tell me, '*Dos is gurnisht* (that is nothing).' But now after these eight weeks I will tell her, *Mammeh, fahr acht vuchen hub ich gelerent far dir a blatt Gemara* (Mother, for eight weeks I learned a page of *Gemara* for you),' and I know she will smile and be happy."

A few weeks later, Yankel passed away.

In Conclusion

Harvey, Yankele, knew as we all do what our parents want more than anything else: that we be *ehrliche Yidden* and follow the ways of the *Ribono Shel Olam* with His Torah and mitzvos and *ahavas Yisrael*. May we indeed follow these ways and merit that we have the *zechus* to be reunited with them at *techias hameisim*.

Forgiveness: Part I

We have all said the words שְׁמַע יִשְׂרָאֵל, ה׳ אֱלֹקֵינוּ, ה׳ אֶחָד thousands of times in our lives. However, the Maharal (*Ner Mitzvah*, p. 12 n. 60) offers a profound explanation of the word אֶחָד that is sure to change the way we say them.

The word אֶחָד is spelled, ח, א, and ד. Numerically, א equals one, which represents Yaakov Avinu, who was considered the בְּחִיר שֶׁבְּאָבוֹת, the "most prominent of the forefathers." Why? Because Avraham had a son like Yishmael and Yitzchak had a son like Eisav, but all of Yaakov's children were perfect. Therefore, א represents Yaakov Avinu.

The ח represents the eight children that he had with his two wives, Leah and Rachel: Reuvein, Shimon, Levi, Yehudah, Yissachar, Zevulon, Yosef, and Binyamin. The ד represents the four children— Dan, Naftali, Gad, and Asher — that he had with the maidservants, Bilhah and Zilpah.

Therefore, *every* Jew in the world is rooted in this word אֶחָד. We all come from Yaakov Avinu and we all come from one of the 12 *Shevatim*. If so, it behooves us all to feel "the three Cs": concern, consideration, and connection. We have to be concerned for each other, considerate of each other, and connected to each other — because we are all אֶחָד.

Let me share with you now a few stories about what it means when somebody shows concern, consideration, and connection for others.

Going the Extra (Six) Miles

Rabbi Dr. Phillip Zimmerman was the founder of Freeda vitamins. In 1953, he was a chaplain in the United States Army and stationed in Georgia. One Friday night a serviceman from New York came in and said, "Chaplain, I need help. I have

> My parents and I went through the Holocaust and I am their only child. If they find out that I was transferred to Korea, they will die ....

three letters here. The first says that I'm supposed to be transferred to Korea on Sunday morning. The second and third letters are from my parents' cardiologist. My parents and I went through the Holocaust and I am their only child. If they find out that I was transferred to Korea, they will die from the trauma of it, the cardiologist writes."

He showed the chaplain the letters. "Please," the soldier pleaded, "please try to help me!"

Rabbi Zimmerman had no idea how he could help the young man; chaplains had very little say in such matters. But he did not let that stop him. The next morning, which was Shabbos, he walked six miles to the military commander on the base.

"Chaplain, what are you doing here so early?" the commander asked.

"I need a favor. A serviceman came to me last night and told me he's supposed to be transferred to Korea, but his parents, who are Holocaust survivors, are so frail that they will literally die of fright if he is transferred. I have letters from cardiologists attesting to this."

"What are you talking about?" the commander snapped angrily without even looking at the letters. "The United States is at war!"

Then he grabbed the lapel of the chaplain's jacket. (The official jacket of the chaplaincy had the *Aseres HaDibros*, the Ten Commandments, on its lapel.) "You see your tablets? They're made out of stone. Do you know why they're made out of stone? Because stone can't be broken. Well, my laws are like stone: they can't be broken. There are no exceptions and no transfer."

The chaplain felt terrible. It was obvious there was nothing he could do, so he turned around and left.

He hadn't gone far outside when, all of a sudden, the military commander called out, "Chaplain, where's your jeep?"

"I have no jeep, sir."

"What do you mean, you have no jeep? How did you get here?"

"I walked, sir."

"You walked six miles from your camp to here?"

"Yes, sir."

"How are you getting back?"

"I'm going to walk the six miles again."

"Why didn't you take a jeep or have someone drive you?"

"Because it's my Sabbath and I can't drive a car or be driven in one."

"You walked six miles for that serviceman and you're going to walk another six miles for him?"

"Yes, sir."

The commander said, "Come back into the office."

The commander looked over the letters, picked up a phone, called his second-in-command, and ordered that the serviceman be transferred to Governor's Island in New York ... with a direct command and explicit instructions to visit his parents every night.

When the commander saw *echad*, when he saw the concern, consideration, and connection one Jew has for another, he was so inspired that he changed his original command.

Rav Moshe and the Shabbos Kallah

Michoel Sorotzkin was a youngster when his father passed away. He was living in Israel and his mother contacted her brother-in-law, Rav Boruch Sorotzkin, who was at the time one of the Roshei Yeshivah of the great Telshe Yeshivah in Cleveland, Ohio. Rav Boruch agreed to take care of young Michoel, and indeed "Mickey," as he was known then, was there for numerous years. He learned in other yeshivos as well, but eventually Rav Boruch suggested a Cleveland girl as a *shid-*

duch for Michoel and they became engaged. The wedding was to take place in Cleveland.

At this time, his mother, still living in Israel, was quite ill. However, she wanted very much to attend her son's wedding and so she made plans to come to America. The wedding was to be on a Sunday night and she would fly in a few days earlier. The Sunday before the wedding Michoel called his mother to wish her a safe flight. A few hours later he got a frantic call from Israel that his mother had suddenly passed away.

The question became: Should he go to Israel for the funeral? If he did go, the *shivah*, which would start after the burial, would extend past the night he was to be married. Rav Moshe Feinstein was consulted. The *Gadol Hador* ruled that Michoel should not go to his mother's funeral in Israel; rather, he should stay in America and start sitting *shivah* right away. The *shivah* would be over before next Sunday night and he would be able to be married as planned.

The Friday afternoon of *shivah*, Michoel was told that he had a person-to-person call from Rav Moshe. Most people today don't know what a person-to-person call is. But it was a special, direct call made specifically to one person and no one else. This was done so one did not have to pay for a long-distance call if the party was not there. When Mickey heard that there was a person-to-person call from the *Gadol Hador*, Rav Moshe Feinstein, he almost fainted. He thought that perhaps Rav Moshe had had a change of heart and decided that he shouldn't be married that Sunday.

However, that was not Rav Moshe's intention.

"You are an *avel*," he said, "and tomorrow is going to be the *Shabbos Kallah*. All your future wife's friends are going to be there. The *minhag* in America is that the *chassan* gives the *kallah* a beautiful bouquet of flowers and everybody admires it. But an *avel* is not allowed to give a gift. So you can't buy these flowers for her. Nevertheless, I want you to tell one of your friends to buy her a beautiful bouquet of flowers in your name and give it to her before Shabbos. Tomorrow, when all the friends come, she'll have the same bouquet of flowers that every *kallah* has."

That's a *Gadol Hador*. What is on his mind on Erev Shabbos? That a *kallah* in Cleveland should have flowers no less than any other *kallah*!

That's אֶחָד. That's concern. That's consideration. That's connection. That's what we're talking about.

Being a Vatran

Achdus is a lofty ideal. Even as we succeed many times in demonstrating "the three Cs" — concern, consideration, and connection — we also often fail. Life's challenges are daunting. There may be many reasons that we fail to follow through on ideals we know to be true. That is why we need to constantly work on our *middos*. Of all the *middos* we need to work on, there is one I want to focus on now — one which is particularly important in achieving forgiveness, and that is *vatranus* — yielding. I would like to introduce it with the following *Gemara*.

Chazal (*Taanis* 25b) teach that a drought was taking place in Israel and the people were frightened that no crops would grow. They beseeched Rabbi Eliezer to *daven*. He did, but it didn't rain. Then they asked Rabbi Akiva to *daven*. He did and it rained.

As a result, everybody thought that Rabbi Akiva was a greater *tzaddik* than Rabbi Eliezer. However, a voice was heard from *Shamayim* saying it wasn't because Rabbi Akiva was greater than Rabbi Eliezer; rather, it was because Rabbi Akiva had a certain *middah* that caused the rain to fall in his merit. The *middah* was that he was מַעֲבִיר עַל מִדּוֹתָיו: he was able to look away when somebody hurt him. He was yielding.

We all have done things that we're not proud of and that we want Hashem to look away from. What can make Hashem overlook our faults and answer our *tefillos*? We need to overlook the faults of others.

There are certain people who are *vatranim*, meaning that they're able to yield, to look away from a wrong done to them. Rabbi Akiva was a *vatran*; he was able to look away if somebody said something painful to him. Since he was able to look away, Hashem also looked away from *Klal Yisrael*'s faults and caused it to rain in the merit of Rabbi Akiva's *tefillos*.

So many of us spend so much time in *davening* and saying *Tehillim*, yet we want to know why Hashem is not answering our *tefillos*. Maybe this is the reason: Hashem is judging us by the strict letter of the law in the same way we are judging others. If we would but look away and be *mevatair*, then Hashem would also look away, so to speak.

The essence of being a *vatran* is the negation of self. It doesn't mean that you're supposed to let yourself be stepped all over, to be a *shmatte, chas v'shalom*. In fact, Rav Tzadok HaKohen in *Tzidkas HaTzadik* writes, כְּשֵׁם שֶׁצָּרִיךְ אָדָם לְהַאֲמִין בַּה' יִתְבָּרַךְ כַּךְ צָרִיךְ אַחַר כַּךְ לְהַאֲמִין בְּעַצְמוֹ, *Just as you've got to believe in Hashem, you've got to believe in yourself.* You have to have self-esteem. But though one must have self-esteem, one must also realize that another person is also something of value. Sometimes we feel so haughty or superior about ourselves that we can't give in; we can't be a *vatran*. A *vatran* is somebody who thinks about somebody else. That's what Rabbi Akiva was able to do and that's why Hashem answered his *tefillah*.

Let me share with you a few stories about *vatranus*.

The Soul of a Name

We know that naming a child after someone is very special. When I was writing the book *Bris Milah* for ArtScroll, I researched the importance of naming a child. I saw that the Rebbe Reb Elimelech says that when you name a child after someone, there is a connection between the *neshamah* (soul) of the child and the person for whom the child is named. It was then that I realized that the two middle letters of the word נְשָׁמָה — שׁ and מ — spell שֵׁם, *name*. The very word *neshamah*, "soul," has at its core the idea of a name being connected to the person who had the name before. That's why we name people after *tzadikkim* and other righteous people.

Rav Michel Birnbaum was a great *tzaddik* and *Mashgiach* of Rav Moshe Feinstein's yeshivah, Tiferes Yerushalayim. When he was dying he said, "I know that my grandchildren are having children and are going to want to name them after me. However, if at the time of the *bris* there's a widow from the other side of the family present, name the child after her husband." [In this way the *almanah*, the widow, would feel less pain.]

Everybody wants to have a great-grandson named after him. But Rav Michel was a *vatran*. He was willing to give up his right and privilege so that a widow, whom he didn't even know if she existed yet, would have the *nachas ruach* of having a grandchild named after her husband.

That's greatness. That's what being a *vatran* is all about.

Framing the First Wife

A widower who had been living alone for a while decided to remarry. In the beginning of the new marriage he said to his wife, "I don't have anything in the house left from my first marriage ... except for one picture of my first wife. I put it in my shirt drawer at the bottom beneath all my shirts. I just can't throw it out. If you don't want it in the house, I understand. Take it and do whatever you want with it."

The next afternoon after he came home from work, he went to his room and quietly opened up the drawer. He saw the picture was gone! His heart skipped a beat — and then he looked up and saw that his new wife had framed the picture and hung it up on the wall!

Can you imagine? There are simply no words to explain her sensitivity and willingness to think of others first.

The Shtreimel Story

Avraham Peretz Friedman, an experienced marriage counselor, told me that the turning point in a troubled marriage invariably comes when one of the partners is able to say, "Maybe it was my fault; maybe I made a mistake."

When a person is able to negate the self and admit that he made a mistake, the relationship can build.

One of my favorite stories that Rav Sholom Schwadron, the Maggid of Yerushalayim, used to tell was about a chassidishe young man in Yerushalayim who was married right before Pesach. The *minhag* (custom) is for a newly married couple to spend the first Pesach at the *kallah*'s parents' house. And that is what happened. The morning after the *Seder*, however, the *chassan* looked terribly distressed. In shul, Rav Shmuel Salant said to the father-in-law, "Why is he so upset?"

The father-in-law was embarrassed and said, "Something terrible happened at the *Seder* last night. It was during the meal. We were eating and suddenly the *chassan* noticed some wheat kernels in his soup. He got very angry as if to say, 'This is the family that I married into?' It was very uncomfortable."

Rav Shmuel Salant did not delay. "Quick, come outside right now: you, the *chassan,* and the *shamesh.*"

They came into the courtyard of the shul and the Rav said to the *shamesh*, "Bring me a rag."

He brought the rag and then Rav Shmuel Salant said to the *chassan*, "Give me your *shtreimel.*"

He took off his *shtreimel* and gave it to him. The Rav then took the rag and rubbed the top of the *shtreimel* vigorously. He rubbed it firmly until three wheat kernels came out of the *shtreimel!* The *chassan* stood there open-mouthed! He couldn't believe it!

The *minhag* is that the Shabbos before the wedding there is an *aufruf* for the *chassan,* and as part of the celebration everyone throws candies at him. However, in *Eretz Yisrael* they throw wheat kernels instead of candies. This fellow was wearing his *shtreimel* during his *aufruf*, and when the people threw wheat kernels at him, some of the kernels became stuck in his *shtreimel.* When he was bending over as he ate the soup at the *Seder,* it was some of those wheat kernels that fell out of his *shtreimel* and into the soup. In short, it was his own fault.

When Rav Sholom would tell this story he would smile and say, "Before you accuse somebody else, check your own *shtreimel.*"

Asking Forgiveness

I have a very close friend named Harry Ashkenazi. He told me the following story.

Years ago, he was driving to a wedding and as he approached the hall, he saw that there was a long line of cars waiting for valet parking. It was a bitterly cold night and the line was moving very slowly. He was getting impatient; the cars were barely inching forward.

He noticed that the woman driving the car in front of him was talking with a friend rather than moving forward. He became impatient and drove around her. As it turned out, he got the last spot available for valet parking that night. This woman had to now find parking on one of the small side streets in Brooklyn. As you can imagine, she was very upset. When she arrived at the wedding, she had some choice words for Mr. Ashkenazi.

He told me that he avoided her for the rest of the night. This was in February. Several months later, in October, before Yom Kippur, Harry was thinking about whom he had to ask forgiveness from. Not from his wife nor his co-workers — he had been fine with them. But suddenly he remembered that woman at the wedding hall.

It took some research but he found her number, called her up, and said, "Listen, my name is Harry Ashkenazi. I don't know if you remember me, but last February I did something that I shouldn't have done. I took your spot in the line as we were driving up to the wedding. I know you were very upset. I was impatient and I'm sorry. Please forgive me. I'm really sorry."

"You remembered?" she said surprised. "I forgot about it a long time ago. Of course I forgive you. I can't believe you remembered."

"Are you sure that you forgive me, because I feel terrible about it?"

"Yes, of course I forgive you."

Then he explained to her the importance of getting a *kaparah*, having a clean slate, before Yom Kippur. She was so moved that after she got off the phone, she decided to go through her phonebook to ask forgiveness from people she may have slighted throughout the previous year. She called a whole list of people, her rabbi, a schoolteacher, the principal .... She was on the phone half the night!

Now, listen to this! Three years later, Harry Ashkenazi's daughter was suggested as a *shidduch* to this woman's son! When she heard the name, she said, "Harry Ashkenazi! Such a wonderful man who can admit that he made a mistake even months after it happened! That's a family that I want my son to marry into."

Sure enough they met, dated, and were married. Now Harry Ashkenazi and this woman share the same grandchildren. Why? Because somebody was able to say, "I was wrong." Somebody was able to negate himself.

This leads to a point with which I want to conclude Part I of this article. It is a statement written by a certain physician named Dr. David Mullen:

> **Forgiving people report less depression, less anxiety, and less hostility than their non-forgiving counterparts.**

"People who are forgiving report less depression, less anxiety, and less hostility than their non-forgiving counterparts. When people feel less hostile, they tend to have fewer cardiovascular problems and fewer heart attacks." He adds, "I've worked with people who have held onto resentments and grievances toward family members for so long that they became emotionally and physically ill."

When people feel less hostile, they tend to have fewer cardiovascular problems and fewer heart attacks.

Vatranus, then, not only provides spiritual health. It provides physical health as well.

Forgiveness:
Part II

In Part I we discussed achdus, stressing the "three Cs": showing consideration, concern, and connection to others. We then spoke about one of the most important middos for achieving forgiveness: being a vatran, someone who looks away from the faults of others.

In Part II, as we approach the Yamim Nora'im and the Y'mai HaDin, we will discuss more examples of the principle of forgiveness.

W hen we talk about forgiveness we have to know that forgiving benefits not only the person who is receiving the forgiveness, but the one giving it as well.

As noted in the previous article, Dr. David Mullen wrote, "People who are forgiving report less depression, less anxiety, and less hostility than their non-forgiving counterparts. When people feel less hostile, they tend to have fewer cardiovascular problems and fewer heart attacks."

Forgiving makes you not only a better person, but also a healthier person. People who are always angry and upset at others are quite often going to become emotionally sick *and* physically sick as well.

I recently heard a story that is worth consideration and thought. I know that not everyone will agree with the ideas brought forth in this episode, but I believe it has value and merit.

A divorced woman whose former husband had abandoned her came to her rabbi angry and bitter because the rabbi had told her to forgive him.

"Forgive him?! What do you mean forgive him?!" she said. "He deserted me and our kids. We have no money. Every month the bills are so difficult to pay. I can't give my children any money. I have to tell them that we can't afford the toys that other kids in their class can afford — and I should forgive him? Why should I forgive him?"

"I'm not suggesting that you forgive him because of what he did," the rabbi replied.

> **I'm asking you to forgive him because he does not deserve the power to live in your head and turn you into a bitter, angry person.**

"What he did is not acceptable and reprehensible. He was cruel and selfish. I'm asking you to forgive him because he does not deserve the power to live in your head and turn you into a bitter, angry person. I'd like to see him get out of your life, emotionally, just like he's out of your life physically. But you keep holding onto him. You're not hurting him by holding on. Just the opposite, you're hurting yourself."

Not forgiving creates that resentment that makes us a victim. Forgiving frees us from the role of the victim — a victim of anger that can cause ill health and depression.

Forgiveness does not necessarily mean admitting that the other person was right. But it helps us to remove self-destructive anger from our system. Forgiveness is not pretending everything is fine; it is the decision to look beyond the limits of another personality.

Two Weddings, Unequal

In Yerushalayim there is a wedding hall called Wolf Hall. It actually has two halls, one known as Ulam Aleph (Hall Number One) and another alongside it known as Ulam Beit (Hall Number Two). It is run by Yad Eliezer, a wonderful *tzedakah* organization. Ulam Aleph happens to be a little bit nicer and a little bigger than Ulam Beit, but we are talking about two modest halls.

Once, two families called the same day: the Goldbergs and Silverbergs (both names are fictional). The Goldbergs called in the morning and the Silverbergs in the afternoon. The Goldbergs asked if they could have Ulam Aleph and were told they could.

A couple of hours later the Silverbergs called and also requested Ulam Aleph, but were told it had just been taken.

A few days later the Silverberg *kallah* called the Goldberg *kallah* and asked, "I know you called first, but would you mind if we switched, because our family's coming from America, and I know Ulam Aleph is a little bigger and a bit nicer."

"I have to discuss the matter with my parents," the Goldberg *kallah* said.

They discussed it and after a few days the Goldberg *kallah* called back the Silverberg *kallah*, "I'm sorry, but we can't give up Ulam Aleph. We also have people coming from America and we need the space."

The Silverberg *kallah* was disappointed, but politely said she understood and wished her well.

A couple of weeks later, during *Parashas Vayeitzei*, the Goldberg *kallah* was listening to *kriyas haTorah* about how Rachel was *mevater*; how she gave the *simanim* to Leah. She thought about how Rachel is always referred to as Mamma Rachel and how many thousands *daven* at her *kever*. Additionally, Rachel was Binyamin's mother and Binyamin had the *Beis HaMikdash* in his *cheilek* (section) of Israel.

The Goldberg *kallah* said to herself, "I've got to be like Rachel." She went home after *davening* and discussed it with her parents. Her parents said, "This is your wedding. If you would rather take the smaller hall for yourself, it will be a bit more crowded. But if that's what you want, it is okay with us."

That night, Motza'ei Shabbos, she called the Silverberg *kallah* and said, "I was thinking about it. You can have Ulam Aleph."

The Silverberg *kallah* was ecstatic and thanked her profusely.

Listen to what happened next ....

The night of the wedding the caterer got a call from someone in New York: "Tonight I'm marrying off my daughter," he began.

"*Baruch Hashem*, I'm able to do it in a comfortable manner. I'm so grateful to Hashem that I want to pay for a wedding in Yerushalayim. I know you've got two wedding halls, Aleph and Beit, and Ulam Beit is a little bit more modest. The people making the wedding in that hall probably need the money more than the people in Ulam Aleph do. So I'd like to pay for the entire wedding for the people in Ulam Beit."

And that is what he did. He paid for the whole wedding: the photography, the flowers, catering — everything.

The Goldberg *kallah* was a *vatran*. She wasn't thinking only about herself. And as a result, Hashem took care of her. He orchestrated it so that the whole wedding was paid for.

Do You Have to Forgive Lashon Hara?

The *Shulchan Aruch* (*Orach Chaim* 606:1) cites a halachah that comes as a surprise to many: One is *not* obligated to forgive a person who speaks *lashon hara* against him.

This is surprising, because at night, before saying *Shema*, we say, "I am *mochel* [I forgive] anybody who said anything against me." Why should we say that if the halachah is that there is no obligation?

The answer is that it is *lifnim mishuras hadin* — going beyond the letter of the law — to forgive in such a case. Technically, you don't have to. As the *Mishnah Berurah* (note 11) says, forgiving in such a case is an expression of the *middah* of *anavah* (humility). But, technically, if somebody hurts you by spreading *lashon hara* against you, you don't have to be *mochel*.

On this topic, the Rambam offers a suggestion: If your friend does not want to be *mochel* you, bring three of his friends to him and plead that he should forgive you. Try this three times. If he does not want to forgive you after three times, and you are sincerely asking for forgiveness, then "he is the sinner."

He is the sinner?! The victim is the sinner? Suddenly he is the one who did something wrong to you!

Rav Dovid Cohen explained that "he is the sinner" because he is not a *ma'amin*, he does not believe. Everything that happens to us happens because Hashem wills it. Perhaps we are permitted to be upset at that person, but nonetheless it was supposed to happen, and if something was supposed to happen then the person who caused it to happen was Hashem's *shaliach* (messenger).

A person has to know that anything that happened to him happened for a reason. Hashem wants to test him. Hashem wants to improve him. But if that offending person comes three times and the one who was hurt does not want to be *mochel*, he then becomes the "sinner" — not so much because he's not *mochel* but because he does not realize and accept that everything that happened is only because Hashem wills it.

"I Am Mochel"

Rav Meir Zlotowitz, the founder of ArtScroll, learned in Tiferes Yerushalayim and was very close with Rav Moshe Feinstein, *zt'l*. One day, he came to Rav Moshe's house and was waiting in the living room when he heard Rav Moshe speaking with two people for whom he had resolved a *din Torah*.

Rav Moshe said to one of the people (both fictional names): "Reuven, ask Shimon for *mechilah*. And Shimon, you give him *mechilah*."

Reuven said to Shimon, "I'm sorry for what I did. Please forgive me."

Shimon said, "It is fine. It is not a problem."

Rav Moshe said to Shimon, "No. Tell him that you are *mochel* him."

Shimon said, "I'm not angry. The Rosh Yeshivah worked it out. Everything is fine. It was supposed to happen *min haShamayim*. I understand."

Rav Moshe looked squarely at Shimon and said, "No. Tell him *b'feirush* [explicitly] that you are *mochel* him."

Shimon said, "Reuven, I am *mochel* you." Then they shook hands and left.

When Rabbi Zlotowitz came in, he said to Rav Moshe, "Rosh Yeshivah, I hope you don't mind, but I overheard that you were insisting that that person say *b'feirush* that he was *mochel*. Why did the Rosh Yeshivah insist he do so?"

Rav Moshe showed him a Rabbeinu Bachaya in *Parashas Vayechi* (*Bereishis* 50:17). After Yaakov passed away, the brothers thought that now Yosef was going to get even with them, so they asked him for *mechilah*. How did Yosef respond?

"Don't be so distressed and don't be angry at yourselves that you sold me. Hashem sent me as a provider; that is why you had to sell me. It was all *min haShamayim* so that I should be able to feed you" (ibid. v. 20).

He then added (ibid. v. 21): "Don't worry. I'm going to take care of you and your children." And the Torah tells us that he comforted them and spoke to them soothingly.

However, he never said outright, "I forgive you."

Rabbeinu Bachaya writes that that was why the *asarah harugei malchus* (Ten Martyrs) were killed by the Romans! Centuries later, 10 *tzaddikim* were killed because 10 brothers never achieved forgiveness. Because Yosef never said, "I am *mochel.*"

> Centuries later, 10 *tzaddikim* were killed by the Romans because 10 brothers did not get forgiveness.

When you are *mochel,* you have to say the words explicitly, "I am *mochel.*"

Ticket to Gan Eden

Rav Chanoch Ehrentreu, the Dayan in London, who now lives in *Eretz Yisrael*, told the following story:

The town of Telz was looking for a Rav. Rav Yehoshua Heller had been the Rav in Telz but had left, so they had various candidates applying for his position.

The *Av Beis Din* of Telz was a *talmid chacham* named Rav Abba Werner. He thought that they were going to appoint him as the Rav. However, they ended up taking an outsider, someone from a different city, and made him not only the Rav, but the Rosh Yeshivah as well. His name was Rav Lazer Gordon, whose name from then on became synonymous with Telz.

Rav Abba Werner left the town not telling anyone how disappointed he felt. He went to Helsinki, then came to London and became the head of the prestigious Machzikei Hada'as shul. Rav Lazer Gordon, of course, did not know how Rav Abba Werner felt. He just heard that the *Av Beis Din* left to Helsinki.

When Rav Lazer Gordon became the Rav he had to test all the *shochtim* to see if they were truly qualified. There was a man named Rav Mendel Rappaport, who had been a *shochet* for many years.

Rav Lazer Gordon started asking him very basic questions and Rav Mendel Rappaport felt insulted. *This young Rav is asking me these questions? I'm a shochet here 20 years! Who does he think I am, a little boy who is first starting?*

He felt so bad that he decided to leave. And he, too, ended up in London.

Twenty years later, in 1910, there was a great fire in Telz. Most of the buildings in town were made out of wood and were destroyed, including its famous yeshivah.

Rav Lazer Gordon now had to raise money. Everybody thought that he would go to Poland or the Ukraine, where many *talmidim* came from. Nevertheless, for a reason no one could fathom at the time, he went to London.

He arrived one afternoon and went to the Machzikei Hada'as shul. Rav Mendel Rappaport, the *shochet*, who was now very wealthy, recognized him even though he had not seen him for 20 years.

Rav Rappaport invited Rav Lazer Gordon into his palatial home for dinner. As they were talking, he said, "Rosh Yeshivah, I don't know if you remember, but I was also in Telz. I was a *shochet*. Do you remember that you came in and started asking me questions? I felt very bad because I had been a *shochet* for many years."

"*Oy vey*, you felt bad?" Rav Lazer Gordon said. "I'm sorry. I didn't realize that I hurt you. Please forgive me."

"Don't worry," the *shochet* said. "I forgive you. It's no problem. You see, Hashem sent me here and I became

> "You felt bad?" Rav Lazer Gordon said. "I'm sorry. I didn't realize that I hurt you. Please forgive me."

very successful. I forgive you. But I think we should go visit Rav Abba Werner. He is now the head of Machzikei Hada'as."

They went to visit Rav Abba Werner. After talking in learning for a while, Rav Abba Werner said to Rav Gordon, "Rosh Yeshivah, I want to tell you something. You know, *baruch Hashem*, that I have a wonderful position here today. But I must tell you I felt a little bad when you took the position as the Rav in Telz."

"I am sorry to hear that," said Rav Gordon, "Why did you feel bad?"

"Because I was the *Av Beis Din* and I thought that they were going to give the position of Rav to me. But they brought in an outsider. You, as a young man, should have asked me if you could take the position. I felt that it wasn't *kavod* that you didn't ask."

"I feel so bad," Rav Gordon said. "I had no idea you felt this way. Please forgive me."

"I surely forgive you. You see, Hashem sent me here and everything is wonderful."

Motza'ei Shabbos at a huge *melaveh malkah*, Rav Lazer Gordon gave a very memorable passionate speech about the yeshivah. Shortly after, he had a heart attack and died. He was buried in London … and eventually Rav Mendel Rappaport was buried right next to him.

Rav Chanoch Ehrentreu made an amazing comment on the whole incident. He said that the *pasuk* in (*Mishlei* 20:24) tells us, מֵה׳ מִצְעֲדֵי גֶבֶר, *All the footsteps of man are only from Hashem*. Hashem directs us. Why did Rav Lazer Gordon go to London? Nobody could understand it. There were no supporters of Telz in London at the time nor were there *talmidim* from England at the time in the yeshivah.

Rav Lazer Gordon was such a *tzaddik* that he had a ticket straight to the *Olam HaEmes*. However, there were two people who were upset with him. Hashem wanted him to go directly to Gan Eden. That is why he went to London: he had to get *mechilah* from those people and then he had no impediments preventing him from going directly to Gan Eden.

Beyond the Letter of the Law

We say at night, before going to sleep, before saying the *Shema*: "I am *mochel* anybody who said anything against me."

We say it because we should be above the letter of the law. We have to be able to forgive *even when it is difficult*, because it is not only good for that person but it is good for ourselves as well.

During this time of year, as we approach the *Yamim Nora'im* and the *Yemai HaDin*, when we are especially encouraged to seek forgiveness from Hashem and people, may we be big enough to grant forgiveness to others.

Bitachon in Difficult Times

e live in times of great fear the world over. So many people have questions, and so many people have experienced tragedy. We hear of sickness, death, challenges to families, challenges in *parnassah*, and challenges with children at risk. People in those situations need *chizuk*, but in reality we all need *chizuk*.

I'd like to share with you a letter that the *Imrei Emes*, the Gerrer Rebbe, Rav Avraham Mordechai Alter (1866–1948) wrote right after the terrible years of the Holocaust:

> *To my brothers in Klal Yisrael who have been spared from the horrible sword. Wherever you may be, the Ribono Shel Olam should be with you. We have to remain strong. Right in the beginning of the Torah (Bereishis 1:5) the pasuk says,* וַיְהִי עֶרֶב וַיְהִי בֹקֶר יוֹם אֶחָד *[And it was evening, and it was morning, day one]. Klal Yisrael at times goes through periods of* עֶרֶב *— evening, darkness — and Klal Yisrael goes through periods of* בֹקֶר *— morning, loving kindness — but it is all* אֶחָד. *The goal is*

Klal Yisrael ... goes through periods of עֶרֶב **— evening, darkness — and** בֹקֶר **— morning, loving kindness — but it is all** אֶחָד.

---

always one, to get that illumination, to get insight into the ways of Hashem Who is Echad — the One and Only.

Every day, we hear of people who go through עֶרֶב. Every day we see people who go through בֹּקֶר. But it's all יוֹם אֶחָד. It's all from that One Source of illumination: the *Ribono Shel Olam*.

We all need that יוֹם, that illumination, that strength. Perhaps, more than anything else, we need to acquire armor to face the fear, to face the questions, and to face the tragedy.

The Master Tailor

I want to tell a very painful story. In 1996, in my neighborhood of Kew Gardens, New York, on a Shabbos morning, there was a terrible fire in a private home, and a little girl, Chana Baila, passed away together with her grandmother. Chana Baila had an older sister, Masha Miriam, who was severely burned, and she was taken to the Cornell burn unit in Manhattan. *Nebach*, she suffered terribly. I went to see her. It was frightening. Tragically, a little more than two months

> **All one had to do was see that little coffin and it broke everyone's heart.**

later, on Succos, she passed away. On Succos, because it is a Yom Tov, one is not allowed to say a *hesped*, but everyone was crying anyway. All one had to do was see that little coffin and it broke everyone's heart.

A rav in the community, Rabbi Aryeh Ginzberg, who had a daughter in Masha Miriam's class and knew Masha Miriam well because she used to come to his house, spoke *divrei chizuk* as he related a remarkable insight from the Vilna Gaon.

During the recitation of the Mussaf *Shemoneh Esrei* of Yom Kippur we read about the terrible tortures that the *Asarah Harugei Malchus* (Ten Martyrs) went through. When R' Yishmael was being tortured, the *malachim* (angels) cried out with bitterness to Hashem, "זוֹ תוֹרָה וְזוֹ שְׂכָרָהּ, *This is the Torah and this is the reward?*"

Hashem responded, "If I hear one more sound from you, I'm going to destroy the whole world and bring it back to תֹּהוּ וָבֹהוּ [*emptiness*]!"

How do we understand Hashem's answer? It was a logical question by the *malachim*. Indeed, how can a great *tzaddik* be tortured?

The Gaon explained this with a parable about a tailor who was asked by a king to make a special suit. The king hated Jews, but the tailor, a Jew, was the best tailor in his kingdom. Having no choice, the king had to use him. He gave the tailor a significant amount of material and asked him to make a beautiful suit.

After a few weeks, the tailor brought back the suit — and it was truly magnificent. All who saw the king in this suit remarked on its elegance and style. However, the queen, who was a worse anti-Semite than her husband, told the king, "It's nice … but the tailor robbed you. You gave him a great amount of the most expensive material, and even though he made a beautiful suit out of it, it does not contain all the material you gave him. He cut away half the material and kept it for himself."

The king thought for a moment, looked at his suit and decided she was right. He became so angry that he called the tailor in immediately and accused him of stealing half the material.

"I didn't steal it," the puzzled tailor replied. "It's all right there in the suit."

"What are you talking about?" the king replied. "It's not all the material. I gave you yards and yards."

"Okay," the tailor said, "let me show you where it went."

He had the king change into his usual clothing and then took the suit he had made, placed it on a table, and began taking it apart. He showed the king how the lapels were double-lined and reinforced, how the cuffs were triple-stitched and how the pockets were padded and how the reinforced waistline seamlessly blended with the rest of the suit. He took apart each section and laid out the material so that it could be measured. The king screamed at the tailor, claiming that he was ruining the suit, but the tailor calmly replied, "But, Your Majesty, now you understand where all the material is."

The Gaon explained that Hashem said to the *malachim*: "If you go back with Me to the beginning of the world, to when it was emptiness and void [תֹהוּ וָבֹהוּ], then you will see the whole plan (similar to the tailor who brought the material back to its original state). But you only came in the middle. You can't ask why things happen. You aren't aware of the whole master plan. You haven't been around long enough to know what is going on."

"It is the same with all of us," explained Rabbi Ginzberg. "We only live a certain number of years and we have not been here since the beginning of history. Hence we cannot know Hashem's master plan."

Indeed, if a boy comes late to a *shiur* and the rebbi has been lecturing for a half hour, it makes no sense for the boy to ask a question. He wasn't there from the beginning. Had he been there from the start, he would have understood what the *rebbi* was driving at.

And we all left that funeral bewildered and saddened, but strengthened.

Rav Simcha Wasserman on Suffering

I had the great *zechus* to get to know Rav Simcha Wasserman, son of the great Reb Elchonon, *hy'd*. Rav Simcha once told me that ever since he was a little boy and realized what his name "Simcha" meant, he decided he would always be happy. And he was — despite having a lot to be sad about.

Rav Simcha's father was murdered by the Nazis, *y'shm*. (I had the opportunity on a trip to Lithuania to be in the house and in the hallway in Kovno where Rav Elchonon was taken.) Rav Simcha went to Strasbourg, France, and built a yeshivah there, but it did not last. He relocated to Los Angeles and built a yeshivah there, but there, too, the yeshivah did not grow as he would have wanted. Tragically, he never had children. Toward the end of his life, he joined Rav Moshe Mordechai Chodosh in Jerusalem in building Yeshivas Ohr Elchonon. However, life was never easy for him.

I remember him telling me that when he was in Los Angeles, his wife had to stay behind in Detroit, where she was a teacher in the Bais Yaakov. In the early 1950's, Los Angeles was not what it is today, a city with *yeshivos*, Bais Yaakovs, and *kollelim*. In the 1950's, few were interested in building a yeshivah. However, Rav Simcha was there with a few very special *talmidim*, some of whom became *gedolei hador*. Despite all his efforts, the community was just not receptive. He felt especially guilty that he had left his wife back in Detroit, and yet was not accomplishing what he sought in Los Angeles.

He wrote his wife a letter telling her that he was considering leaving Los Angeles. She replied in a letter:

You are the only one who can stay there, because we don't have children. You can try and build Torah in a place where nobody else can. If someone else who has children tried to do what you are doing, they would have to leave because there would be no yeshivah for their children. But you don't have to leave. You can stick it out.

Imagine! How much pain they must have felt not having children; yet the rebbetzin turned it around and used it to tell her husband that specifically because of that, he can build Torah in a place that nobody else could.

The *navi* Yechezkel (11:19) tells us that in the times of *Mashiach*, Hashem will give every Jew a רוּחַ חֲדָשָׁה, *a new spirit*. Furthermore, Hashem says, וַהֲסִרֹתִי לֵב הָאֶבֶן מִבְּשָׂרָם וְנָתַתִּי לָהֶם לֵב בָּשָׂר, *I will remove their heart of stone, and give them a [soft, compassionate] heart of flesh*. Rav Simcha explained that many people think the *pasuk* is saying that the "heart of stone" is a terrible thing. But it is just the opposite, he said. In this world, before *Mashiach*, we have to have a "heart of stone" to withstand disappointments and tragedies. Otherwise, we would be broken by events. A "heart of stone" can't be broken easily. Yes, we have to be sensitive, caring, and compassionate, but not to the point where we are broken.

At the time of *Mashiach*, however, we will receive "a heart of flesh" and we will then be able to feel in the deepest sense the pain of other people. "But until that time," said Rav Simcha, "a person cannot afford to be broken in this world. Everything we hear is a test to see how we can survive: a test of our *emunah* and *bitachon*. At the end of time, then Hashem will be able to give us that לֵב בָּשָׂר [*heart of flesh*] and we will really be able to feel for everyone else."

Irwin and the Sefer Torah

A number of years ago, a young man, Rabbi Chaim Silver, went to Phoenix, Arizona, to become the rabbi of the shul. Rabbi Silver told me that when he came to the shul, he wanted to check all the *Sifrei Torah* to make sure they were perfect. Some of the *Sifrei Torah* were old and he knew he'd have to spend a lot of money to repair them. As he was going through them, there was a knock on the door.

"Hello, Rabbi," the fellow said when Rabbi Silver opened the door. "My name is Irwin Pasternack and I'd like to have a *Sefer Torah* written for this shul."

Rabbi Silver couldn't believe it. He was literally just looking through the *Sifrei Torah* and now this stranger walked in and announced that he wanted to write a *Sefer Torah*!

"Irwin," he said, "why do you want to have a *Sefer Torah* written?"

Irwin explained. He was in his 40's and had finally become a *chassan*. Thirty days before the wedding, he, his mother, and his *kallah*, Daina, had just finished discussing arrangements with the caterer. He and his mother left in one car while Daina took another car — and, r'l, was killed in a terrible accident.

Less than a month before her wedding!

Irwin paused for a moment and then continued. "I grew up in Wyoming," he said to Rabbi Silver. "I remember when I was 7 years old that a *sofer* came to our town as our shul was having a *Sefer Torah* written. They were selling the letters of the *Sefer Torah*. My father bought for me the last word in the Torah. You know what the last word in the Torah is? Yisrael. My Hebrew name is Yisrael. I remember sitting in my father's lap and holding his hand as he was holding the *sofer's* hand and they filled in the last letters of the word of the Torah. All the years that I was a businessman, I always went back to that shul. I would open up the *aron kodesh* and look at that *Sefer Torah*, which had the word that my father had bought me. It gave me such strength. I thought to myself after this accident, if one word in the Torah could give me such strength, imagine what a whole *Sefer Torah* could do."

This is why Mr. Pasternack wanted to have the *Sefer Torah* written.

Rabbi Silver sent him to Rabbi Heshy Pincus, a *sofer* in Brooklyn. R' Heshy showed him the *ksav* (script) of various *sofrim*. Irwin is an architect and an artist, who demands the best for himself and his clients. So he picked out the most expensive and beautiful *ksav*, even though he didn't understand the nuances of all the letters. All he knew is that he wanted the best.

The *Sefer Torah* was written and today it is in that same shul in Phoenix, Arizona. If one word can give so much *chizuk*, perhaps we must rededicate ourselves to the study of *Chumash*. How many of us really know the *parshiyos* and their full meaning, especially in the *Chumashim* of *Vayikra, Bamidbar,* and *Devarim.* It all starts with the words of the Torah, which are our ingredients for life. It behooves us to know *every pasuk* and to understand what Hashem wants from us. It is from these words that we can reinforce our *emunah* and *bitachon* in difficult times.

The Buried Shofar

In *Eretz Yisrael,* there is a wonderful organization dedicated to learning *mishnayos.* A number of years ago 20,000 children who had learned *mishnayos* gathered together in a huge arena. They each were given a name of a child who died in the Holocaust. More than a million children perished in the Holocaust. Each child who attended the *mishnayos* gathering received a membership card stating that he was learning *l'zecher nishmas* a particular child who had perished in the Holocaust.

After special prizes were given to the boys who had learned 3,000 *mishnayos,* R' Yitzchok Aron Shapiro, the founder of the organization, rose to speak. He told the boys why he had founded his organization. He told how he had gone to Europe to one of the concentration camps, Theresienstadt. He stood in areas where so many had perished and realized that there was no remembrance for the children whose lives ended there. He decided that one day he would have Jewish children learn *mishnayos* for those children.

As he was speaking, he told the children that in Lodz, Poland, during the war, there was a group of Jews who wanted to blow *shofar* on Rosh Hashanah. However, they knew the Nazis were watching, so a few people at a time sneaked out to a cemetery on the outskirts of town where they had hidden a little *shofar.* They blew it softly and then buried it, expecting it never to be found again.

However, recently somebody had gone back and found that *shofar.* Now, this Rabbi Shapiro, in front of 20,000 children, took out that little, brown, cracked *shofar,* and said, "I want to blow *shofar.* I want to do an act that those *heilege Yidden*

> Now, this Rabbi Shapiro, in front of 20,000 children, took out that little, brown, cracked *shofar* ....

did with this small *shofar*. We remember their *mesirus nefesh* and I want to do something *l'zecher nishmasam*."

He blew the *shofar* as hard as he could.

When I heard that story, I was thinking: He blew a small *shofar*, but one day in the future, the *pasuk* in *Yeshayahu* (27:13) tells us: וְהָיָה בַּיּוֹם הַהוּא יִתָּקַע בְּשׁוֹפָר גָּדוֹל, *It shall be on that great day, a great shofar will be blown*, and that will herald the *geulah*. Then we will recognize the יוֹם אֶחָד — that One Source of illumination — Hashem.

From Nowhere Comes My Help

I want to finish with this thought. We have all recited this *pasuk* many times. שִׁיר לַמַּעֲלוֹת אֶשָּׂא עֵינַי אֶל הֶהָרִים מֵאַיִן יָבֹא עֶזְרִי, *I lift my eyes to the mountains, from where will my help come?* (*Tehillim* 121:1).

A great *tzaddik* once said, "מֵאַיִן, *from nothing*" — "יָבֹא עֶזְרִי, *my help comes*." Our help is going to arrive so quickly that people will turn around and say, "Where did it come from? We weren't even expecting it." It will be as if it came out of nowhere.

We should have that confidence that just as Hashem built the world יֵשׁ מֵאַיִן — "from nothing" – so, too, the *geulah* will come from nothing, out of nowhere. We don't know the whole story. We can't know the whole story because we are not around in this world long enough. But, if we keep hanging in there, we'll hopefully be *zocheh* to see that מֵאַיִן יָבֹא עֶזְרִי.

Timely
Topics

Shabbos

uring the 16th-century in Tzfas, there were three renowned *tzaddikim* who not only made their mark on Tzfas, but on all *Yiddishkeit* until this very day. The first was the Arizal, the second was Rav Yosef Karo (who wrote the *Shulchan Aruch*), and the third — although he is not as widely known — was Rav Shlomo HaLevi Alkabetz.

Rav Alkabetz wrote many beautiful *tefillos*, but the most famous is the לְכָה דוֹדִי, which we sing every Friday night. The *siddur Otzar HaTefillos* tells us something about the famous line: לִקְרַאת שַׁבָּת לְכוּ וְנֵלְכָה, *Let us go out and welcome the Shabbos*. It states that originally the minhag Tzfas was to literally go out to the fields and say לְכָה דוֹדִי. Close

> **Close your eyes and picture this beautiful scene: All these holy men, leaving the *beis haknesses*, going out into the fields saying together, לִקְרַאת שַׁבָּת לְכוּ וְנֵלְכָה, *Let's go out and greet Shabbos*.**

your eyes and picture this beautiful scene: All these holy men leaving the *beis haknesses*, going out into the courtyard and into the fields saying together, לִקְרַאת שַׁבָּת לְכוּ וְנֵלְכָה, *Let's go out and greet Shabbos*.

What a beautiful sight that must have been. Let's study this wonderful gift called *Shabbos* and learn to bask in the beautiful blessings it brings to our lives.

Why Is Shabbos so Special?

Shabbos is a special gift. As it says in כִּי הִיא מְקוֹר הַבְּרָכָה :לְכָה דוֹדִי, *[Shabbos] is the source of all blessing.* That's based on a *Gemara* (*Shabbos* 118b): כָּל הַמְעַנֵּג אֶת הַשַּׁבָּת נוֹתְנִין לוֹ מִשְׁאֲלוֹת לִבּוֹ, *Whatever your heart desires, Hashem will give you if only you can learn to delight in Shabbos.*

What makes it so special?

It says in *Midrash Rabbah* (*Bereishis* 22:13) that after Adam was banished from Gan Eden he was very depressed. Then, he saw his son Kayin, who had himself done a terrible thing: he had murdered Hevel. But for some reason Kayin was not so depressed. Adam went over to Kayin and asked, "I thought Hashem was angry with you."

"But then I did *teshuvah*," Kayin answered, "and my punishment became lighter. Hashem accepted my *teshuvah*."

The *Midrash* teaches that Adam put his hands to his head and said, "I did not even realize there was such a thing as *teshuvah*. מִזְמוֹר שִׁיר לְיוֹם הַשַּׁבָּת! *A song for the Shabbos day,* and he was *mekabeil Shabbos.*

What's the connection? Why did he sing the *shir* (song) of Shabbos immediately after he found out about *teshuvah*? What does Shabbos have to do with this discussion?

Mefarshim explain that Shabbos doesn't only mean "rest." Shabbos has in it the word שָׁב, "to return," to do *teshuvah*, to return to that state of closeness we had with Hashem before we sullied ourselves with *aveiros*. The essence of Shabbos is that it's a day to return, to come close to *Hakadosh Baruch Hu*. It's a day when a person can *daven* slower, learn more; it's a day when a person can have peace and serenity and ponder his purpose in this world.

That's why, I believe, Yom Kippur is called *Shabbas Shabbason*, because it's שָׁב שָׁב; it's the ultimate day of return. Every week we have a mini-Yom Kippur — it's called Shabbos. But Yom Kippur itself is called שַׁבָּת שַׁבָּתָן, because that's the ultimate day of returning, the ultimate day of *teshuvah*.

Of Glue and Labels

In his wonderful *sefer Nesivos Shalom*, the Slonimer Rebbe explains in the name of the Chida what Moshe meant when he was giving *mussar* to *Klal Yisrael* (*Devarim* 30:2), "There will come a time, וְשַׁבְתָּ עַד ה׳ אֱלֹקֶיךָ, *when you will return to Hashem*, וְשָׁמַעְתָּ בְּקֹלוֹ, *and you are going to listen to His voice.*" The Chida wrote that וְשַׁבְתָּ is spelled: ת, ב, שׁ, וּ — which contains the letters of the word Shabbos, and thus alludes to the fact that Shabbos is integral to the *teshuvah* process!

The Chida explains that if a person does an *aveirah* he can do *teshuvah*, but the total *teshuvah* doesn't come until he is מִתְעַנֵּג (delights in), מְקַבֵּל (accepts), and מְכַבֵּד (honors) Shabbos.

The reason is that every *aveirah* has with it an outer part (*chitzonius*) and an inner part (*pnimius*). The outer part of *teshuvah* is if you decide that you are not going to do the *aveirah*; if you have *charatah* (regret). If you do that, then the outer part of the *aveirah* goes away. However, the *pnimius* part of the *aveirah* only goes away when וְשַׁבְתָּ עַד ה׳ אֱלֹקֶיךָ, which alludes to Shabbos. Let me try to explain his words with a beautiful story.

A young man who had recently become a *baal teshuvah* bought a new set of pots and pans before Rosh Hashanah. People told him that he had to take the pots and pans to the *mikveh* to ritually immerse them, but he had not been told to remove the labels before the immersion. When he was told afterward that the labels had to be removed and that the pots and pans had to be re-immersed, he did so with great enthusiasm, as he wanted to perform the mitzvah properly. However, in the process he came up with an intriguing and inspiring insight that is remarkable.

When he was taking off the labels, he realized that the labels were the easy part. The glue underneath the labels — that was difficult to take off. It then occurred to him that every *aveirah* has an outer part and an inner part. There's the label and there's the glue. Once a person says he's not going to eat *treif* anymore, that's the *chitzonius*. But there's the glue of the *aveirah*: that means the effect the *aveirah* has on a person. *Chas v'shalom*, when a person does an *aveirah* it makes him more susceptible to do another *aveirah*. That's the "glue" of the *aveirah*, the thing that's going to cause him to do another *aveirah*.

This *baal teshuvah* said, "It's one thing to take off these labels. But it's another thing to take off the glue. The labels are the *chitzonius*, but the glue is the *pnimius* of the *aveirah*."

It occurred to me that that is what the Chida is telling us. When a person does *teshuvah*, he gets rid of the *chitzonius* of the *aveirah*; from now on you are not going to do something you were doing until now, whether it's getting angry, speaking *lashon hara*, eating before *davening*, or eating something that doesn't have the best *hashgachah*. But what about the *pnimius* of the *aveirah*, the glue that makes you want to do another *aveirah* or do the same one over again? That only comes וְשַׁבְתָּ עַד ה׳ אֱלֹקֶיךָ, when we take delight in Shabbos. Shabbos helps remove the *pnimius* of the *aveirah*.

(And that's why, I think, on Yom Kippur we mention two concepts: כִּי בַיּוֹם הַזֶּה יְכַפֵּר עֲלֵיכֶם לְטַהֵר אֶתְכֶם, *For on this day you will be forgiven, so that you are purified* (Vayikra 16:30). יְכַפֵּר (the forgiveness) is for the outside *aveirah*, the *chitzonius*; but the טָהֳרָה (the purity) is what comes when you get rid of the "glue" of the *aveirah*.)

If we make a commitment that from now on we are going to be careful about Shabbos — to be מִתְעַנֵּג (delight in), מְקַבֵּל (accept), and מְכַבֵּד (honor) it — then we peel away the "glue" and come closer to Hashem than we ever thought possible.

The Road Back

There was a teenage boy, not *frum*, whose greatest pleasure was riding his motorcycle. He lived in the northern part of *Eretz Yisrael* and whenever he had time off he would go riding in the Galil, up and down its gorgeous hills with the wind flying in his face. Riding his motorcycle was the most exhilarating experience for him.

One day he was riding his motorcycle and passed through a certain town. As he sped down a small street — *Hashem yeracheim*, it should never happen — a little girl ran out across the street and he crashed right into her. Everyone who saw it was stunned. People were yelling and screaming as the girl lay there motionless. The cyclist was terribly shaken; he certainly didn't mean to hurt that child.

The little girl was in a coma for days. Every day the cyclist would go to the hospital and ask how she was doing. It was almost as if he were a victim as well. After a few days he heard that the little girl was beginning to come out of the coma and was slowly getting back her memory. After about a week and a half she was ready to go home. It was a nothing short of a miracle!

The day that the mother was to go home with the child, this cyclist went to the hospital and said to the mother, "I feel so terrible about what I did. I can't express my grief enough. I wish there was something that I could do to make it up to you. I'm not wealthy, but please tell me what I could do for you and for your daughter to show you how sincerely sorry I am."

This mother said, "You know, the day that you hit my daughter was Shabbos. Promise me that you will never ride your motorcycle again on Shabbos."

The boy was stunned. Of all the things that he had thought that this woman might say, it never occurred to him that she would say something like that. He never thought about it being Shabbos. Shabbos was just like any other day to him.

But he had said he would do whatever she wanted. So the next Shabbos he was getting ready to ride on his motorcycle — a natural inclination because he was off from work — but then he remembered that he had promised not to ride it. He was a little bit upset with himself, but he stuck to his word and went back to his apartment.

On the way, he told himself that he would walk through the town, and, he would knock on the door of the first house that had a *mezuzah* on the doorpost, and ask them about Shabbos. Sure enough, he knocked on the door that had a *mezuzah* and a man opened it and greeted him; he and his family were sitting around the table.

"Can I help you?" the father asked.

"Can I talk to you for a minute?" the boy asked.

"Sure."

They sat down and the boy got right to the point, "Why can't I ride my motorcycle on Shabbos?"

The father was taken aback, so the boy told him the whole story. The father then told the boy that Shabbos is a day of rest. The boy responded by saying that riding a motorcycle was his way of resting. Riding along the fields and up and down the hills on his motorcycle was how he relaxed.

This father was a very sincere fellow but didn't know what to say, so he told the boy that down the block lived a Rav, a very smart man, who could answer his questions. The boy went to the Rav and over the next few weeks they had several friendly chats. However, the boy felt that the townspeople still looked at him as "the kid who almost killed that little girl." One day he said to the Rav, "Rabbi, I can't be in this town anymore. I'm going to take a backpack and travel."

"Where are you going?"

"I don't know. I'm just leaving this town."

The rabbi had to think fast. Finally, he said, "It's Thursday. Do me a favor. This Shabbos, why don't you go to Yerushalayim, to a place called Ohr Somayach? If you go for just one Shabbos, you'll understand the importance of Shabbos for the rest of your life."

He went to Ohr Somayach that Shabbos. Three weeks later he returned to the Rav and said, "The people at Ohr Somayach were so wonderful. I'm going back to study and stay there." With time, this fellow became a *baal teshuvah* and a *talmid chacham*.

Why did he take his bike and drive through that particular town on that Shabbos? Hashem wanted him to take the road home, and through Shabbos he returned to his people.

Anticipation

The *Torah Temimah* (in *Tosefos Berachah*) comments on two *pesukim* that appear in *Parashas Ki Sisa* which talk about Shabbos. One *pasuk* says (*Shemos* 31:14), וּשְׁמַרְתֶּם אֶת הַשַּׁבָּת, *You shall observe the Shabbos …*, yet two *pesukim* later the Torah writes, וְשָׁמְרוּ בְנֵי יִשְׂרָאֵל אֶת הַשַּׁבָּת, *The children of Israel shall observe the Shabbos*. He asks: Why does it have to say twice that we "observe" Shabbos?

He points out that the word שָׁמַר actually has two meanings. One is "to observe," but it is used in another way as well. When Yaakov Avinu heard about the dreams that Yosef was having, it says (*Bereishis* 37:11), וַיְקַנְאוּ בוֹ אֶחָיו, *His brothers were jealous of him*, however, וְאָבִיו שָׁמַר אֶת הַדָּבָר, *but his father was waiting*. שָׁמַר in this case means "waiting with anticipation." Yaakov was anticipating that his son's dreams would come true.

The *Torah Temimah* says, in the same way, there are two important things to know about Shabbos: We have to "watch and observe" Shabbos by keeping its *halachos*. But there is a second element as well; we must "anticipate" and be excited about the forthcoming Shabbos.

My favorite bumper sticker reads, "Hang in there, Shabbos is coming!"

The *Gemara* (*Avodah Zarah* 3a) tells us: מִי שֶׁטָרַח בְּעֶרֶב שַׁבָּת יֹאכַל בְּשַׁבָּת, *Those who toil on Erev Shabbos will eat on Shabbos.* Rav Yaakov Kaminetzky said, "In America we have gained Shabbos but we have lost Erev Shabbos." What the Rosh Yeshivah meant was that we have made political strides so that observant Jews do not have to work on Shabbos, but because we rush at such a frantic pace every Friday until the moment Shabbos arrives, we have lost Erev Shabbos, the tranquility and anticipation with which Shabbos should be welcomed.

> **Rav Yaakov Kaminetzky said, "In America we have gained Shabbos but we have lost Erev Shabbos."**

We must know that it is not how late you can stay in the office on Friday afternoon that is important, but how early you can leave the office to get home in the proper frame of mind in order to welcome the Shabbos.

In our home, my wife usually sets out the Shabbos tablecloth on Thursday night so that when the children come down the next morning, they realize it's not simply Friday morning, it's Erev Shabbos. Why should anyone wait until just a few minutes before Shabbos to whip out the tablecloth and set the table? Is there any reason that children can't take showers or baths on Thursday night? Why does everyone in the household have to argue for the shower or bath 20 minutes before Shabbos? Does it say anywhere that you have to go to the cleaners or the grocery an hour before Shabbos? Does it not make sense to do these things Thursday afternoon or Thursday night?

This is all so that one can calmly anticipate Shabbos and welcome it with serenity. (It also helps in getting one to the Erev Shabbos Minchah on time).

A Chanukah Minhag

There is an old *minhag* in *Eretz Yisrael* to give Chanukah *gelt* on the fifth night of Chanukah. Many are not familiar with the reason. However, recently Rabbi Eliyahu Weisfish, a great *talmid chacham* and author of the popular *sefer Arba Minim*, told me that indeed when the Steipler Goan, Rav Yaakov Yisrael Kanievsky, gave his son, Rav Chaim, Chanukah *gelt,* it was on the fifth night. When Rav Chaim inquired specifically as to why that night, his father's answer was fascinating.

The fifth night of Chanukah can never be a Friday night! That is because Chanukah can never begin on a Monday night. It can start any other night but not Monday. Thus, if one always gives Chanukah *gelt* on the fifth night, he will *never* even inadvertently violate the Shabbos, because it always comes out on a weekday or Motza'ei Shabbos!

Hence we have a *minhag* on Chanukah, no less, that anticipates Shabbos. No wonder that it is imperative to maintain the *minhagim* of *Klal Yisrael*.

Some Advice

So how can we anticipate Shabbos? And once Shabbos arrives, what can we do to make the Shabbos table special? Here are some practical bits of advice.

At my son-in-law's Friday-night table, he calls out with great enthusiasm the "miztvah note" that every child has won throughout the past week. A child is awarded a "mitzvah note" if he or she did something positive in the previous week. Thus, after the fish, my son-in-law calls out, "Nechama watched the baby so that Mommy could get some rest!" And everybody cheers, "Nechama got a mitzvah note!"

Thus, throughout the week when she watches the baby, she wants to know, "Mommy, did you write a mitzvah note so Tatty can read it Friday night?"

Here is another one, "Rochel cleaned the kitchen so that Mommy could do something else meanwhile!"

When Rochel cleans the kitchen, she wants to know, "Mommy, did you write a mitzvah note so Tatty can read it Friday night?"

"Avraham shared his new toy with the other children!" When Avraham shares his new toy he wants to know, "Mommy, did you write a mitzvah note so Tatty can read it Friday night?"

And even Tatty gets a mitzvah note … when he goes shopping Thursday night. (The note is written, like most of the others, by my daughter.) And when my wife and I are there for a Shabbos meal, they somehow find out something good that she or I did during the week and announce it with flair, all so that we should not feel left out!

Of course, that is more for younger children. Nevertheless, today there are so many *shiurim* and *divrei Torah* available in all sorts of media that both a father and mother can prepare spiritual food for the Shabbos table. Indeed, if you hear an inspirational story or Torah thought, write it down and bring it up Friday night at the table. Tell it to your children. Let them discuss it. You'll see how it enlightens those present.

Another son-in-law of mine presents a halachic question in dramatized form so that the children and guests get to debate what the *psak halachah* would be. After an enlivened debate with *svaros* (reasons) offered around the table, my son-in-law quotes the source and the halachic ruling. Today, books and Torah sheets are available for these types of table discussions.

You have to make sure that the table is vibrant. When you prepare these things, the table is *geshmak*!

The Shabbos table talk need not only be about Torah topics. Don't make that mistake. Rav Mattisyahu Salomon says it all the time: The Shabbos table is the place to bond with the family. Don't make it a classroom. Rav Mattisyahu says that women who are teachers commonly make a grievous mistake in that they come home and treat their children as if they were still in the classroom. A home is supposed to be a place where children feel secure and safe, a place where they should be able to express their feelings openly but respectfully.

"The home should be an עִיר מִקְלָט (a city of shelter)," says Rav Mattisyahu. Children have to be able to relax at a Shabbos table; they should be able to talk about anything. If they are taught the value and reverence of *zemiros* at an early age, there is nothing as beautiful as a family singing together on Shabbos.

We must be role models at the Shabbos table because children pick up on everything. The great *askan* (community activist) in Antwerp, Rav Pinchus Kornfeld, told me this delightful story. In Antwerp, there is a wonderful *cheder* for very little children. One week the teacher wanted to teach the class about Shabbos, so she told them that they were going to make a Friday-night Shabbos-seudah party on Wednesday. Wednesday

> Little Chaim confidently walked up to the front, sat down at the head of the table, leaned back and said, *"Oy, hub ich gehat a shverer voch!* (*Oy,* did I have a hard week!)"

came and they set the table as they do on a Friday night. Then the teacher said, "Chaim, you be the Tatty." Little Chaim confidently walked up to the front, sat down at the head of the table, leaned back and said, *"Oy, hub ich gehat a shverer voch! (Oy,* did I have a hard week!)"

There is more to being a good Shabbos Jew that not being *mechaleil Shabbos.* Of course one must avoid being מְחַלֵּל שַׁבָּת (desecrating the Shabbos), but there is more; we have to be מְקַדֵּשׁ שַׁבָּת, we have to sanctify it. We must honor it and take pleasure in it. We do so by anticipating it, by making the table lively and relaxed; by singing *zemiros* and exuding warmth. That's what Shabbos is all about.

Let us hope that we should all be *zocheh* לְיוֹם שֶׁכֻּלּוֹ שַׁבָּת וּמְנוּחָה , to *the day that will be completely a Shabbos* (an allusion to the World to Come after the final redemption). May we see it in our day!

A Living *Beis HaMikdash*

In 1967, the year that *Klal Yisrael* once again took control of the *Kosel* during the Six Day War, many soldiers came up to the Wall for the first time. They were so moved that they started crying and kissing the old stones as they poured out their hearts with *tefillos*.

Among them were non-religious soldiers who didn't understand the significance of the Wall. Yet, all of a sudden, one of the non-religious men began crying. A second soldier whispered to him, "*Lamah atah bocheh*, Why are you crying?"

The answer was both poignant and illuminating. "*Ani bocheh al mah she'ani lo bocheh*, I'm crying because I don't understand what there is to cry about."

This year on Tishah B'Av, thousands of Jews throughout the world will shed tears over the loss of both *Batei Mikdash*. Sadly, perhaps even more will have no idea of what there is to cry about. Indeed, what is it exactly that we cry about? Is it the structure of that great complex that we mourn? Is it the service that took place there that we lack? Is it the closeness that we felt to Hashem that is missing?

A Dwelling Place in the Heart

The *Gemara* (*Bava Basra* 25a) discusses a famous *pasuk* in *Yeshayahu* (2:3): כִּי מִצִּיּוֹן תֵּצֵא תוֹרָה, *For from Zion will come forth*

Torah. *Tosafos* asks, "What is it about Tzion (i.e., Yerushalayim) that makes Torah emanate from there?"

Tosafos answers that it's not the city itself that fosters inspiration, but rather the holy Jews of the city. Specifically, when the people would come to the *Beis HaMikdash* and see how the *Kohanim* performed the *avodah*, it would inspire them to *yiras Shamayim, limud haTorah,* and the doing of mitzvos. That's what the *Beis HaMikdash* was all about: observing the *Kohanim* and becoming inspired by those great people as they did their holy work.

Rav Aharon Kotler in *Mishnas Rav Aharon* (Vol. 3 p. 54) cites this *Tosafos* and derives an interesting lesson. He says that each man, woman, and child has to look at himself/herself as a living *Beis HaMikdash*. Just as the *Kohanim* inspired others and embodied the essence of the *Beis HaMikdash*, so too should we become people of inspiration and embody the essence of the *Beis HaMikdash*.

In the beginning of *Parashas Terumah*, the *Malbim* has an interesting insight on the *pasuk*, וְעָשׂוּ לִי מִקְדָּשׁ וְשָׁכַנְתִּי בְּתוֹכָם, *Make for Me a sanctuary and I will rest in them* (Shemos 25:8). To whom does "in them" (the plural form) refer? Some say that Hashem will rest in *Klal Yisrael*. Others say it refers to both of the *Batei Mikdash*. However there are additional words in the following *pasuk*. It

> Every individual should build a *Beis HaMikdash* in his or her own heart. Our heart has to be a dwelling place for Hashem's presence.

states, וְכֵן תַּעֲשׂוּ — *And so shall you do it*, on which the *Malbim* comments, "This means that every individual should build a *Beis HaMikdash* in his or her own heart." Our heart has to be a dwelling place for Hashem's presence.

A Living Beis HaMikdash

How does one become a living *Beis HaMikdash*? Let me give you some examples.

R' Dov Lesser from Lakewood told me the following story. Over the years he has been involved in starting many yeshivos throughout America. In 1977 he was traveling with R' Shneur Kotler, Rosh Yeshivah of Beth Medrash Gevohah, to Buenos Aires to start a yeshivah there. R' Shneur ordered a kosher meal for the flight. After the stewardess brought the meal, he turned to R' Lesser and said, "You know, I won't eat that meal. I never eat the meals on a plane."

"Why then did the Rosh Yeshivah order the meal?" he asked.

"Whenever I travel I order a kosher meal," said Rav Shneur, "because often somebody will come over to me, take a look, see that I'm a rabbi, and say, 'Oy, Rabbi, I remember when my grandmother used to eat kosher. I remember as a child I used to eat kosher.'

"Then I say to the person, 'I'm not going to eat the meal today. Do you want it?' Sometimes he will take it, and then you have a Jew eating kosher. Or when he gets off the plane he will remember that holy-looking Jew who ate kosher and he will then say to himself, 'I'm also going to start eating kosher once in a while.'"

R' Shneur realized that he was a source of inspiration, a living *Beis HaMikdash*, and hence he acted accordingly.

Even After Death

Many years ago in a neighborhood not far from Kew Gardens, there was a *tzaddik* named R' Menachem Perr. He had a shul in South Ozone Park. However, many people in the shul were not observant. Every Friday he'd go to the local stores and tell people about Shabbos, *kashrus,* and learning Torah. He literally gave his whole heart and soul for those people.

When he was getting older, he said to his son, R' Yechiel, "I would like to be buried in the Beth David Cemetery in Elmont. That's where the people in our shul are buried and we have a plot there."

R' Yechiel protested, "But we have a very special place, Rayim Ahuvim, where all the *chashuvah* people are buried. Why would you want to be buried in Elmont?"

"I know the people in my shul, their children, do not keep mitzvos. But the one thing they will do is come to the cemetery on the *yahrtzeit* of their parents. They will walk around the cemetery and see the monuments and maybe they will see my monument and maybe they will remember something that I taught them about Shabbos or *kashrus,* and maybe it will awaken the *pintele Yid* in them."

Rabbi Perr looked at himself as a living *Beis HaMikdash*. Incredibly he felt this opportunity to be so strong that he applied it to himself even after his passing. Hence he wanted to be buried by "his people," so that perhaps someday, someone would be inspired.

The Office Planner

Mr. Jack Braunstein was driving through the Brooklyn Battery Tunnel to Manhattan when he realized he had to make a business call, but didn't have a car phone. (This was years before cell phones.) When he exited the tunnel he saw a telephone booth and got out of his car to make his call. As he was about to take the phone off the hook, he noticed that right on top of the booth was someone's office-planner book filled with appointments, names, addresses, and phone numbers.

"Maybe someone lost it and I can do the mitzvah of *hashaves aveidah* [returning a lost object]," he thought. But then he thought, "I am in the city of Manhattan. Here, halachah doesn't require me to trouble myself with this. Maybe I will just leave it." (See *Bava Metzia* 24a and *Choshen Mishpat* 259:3.)

However, he happened to be a *baal korei* and it was Erev Shabbos of *Parashas Ki Seitzei*. He thought, "How can I hide myself from an *aveidah* [lost object] when tomorrow I'm going to read, לֹא תוּכַל לְהִתְעַלֵּם, *You are not allowed to hide yourself from a lost object* [*Devarim* 22:3]. I just can't be a hypocrite. I'll pick it up."

He opened it up, but there was no name. Now what? He turned to that day's appointments. One was on Wall Street and another on Madison Avenue. Go try to find someone who has an appointment on one of those streets. He started looking through the telephone listings in the book. He saw the names of Rav Dovid Cohen and Rabbi Moshe Zwick in Brooklyn. But what was he going to do? Call one of them and ask, "Excuse me, do you know anyone who lost a planner with your name in it?"

Fine, he thought to himself, *I'll take it home and see if my wife comes up with any ideas*. Motza'ei Shabbos she opened to the back of the planner and saw the word "MOM" with a 305 area code alongside it. 305 is the area code of Miami. *Maybe this Mom has a child living in New York who lost the planner*, she thought.

Mrs. Braunstein called the number and said to the woman on the other end, "We are Orthodox Jews trying to perform a religious commandment. My husband found an office planner and we would like to return it to the proper owner. We don't know to whom it belongs, but it has your number in the back. Did perhaps one of your children lose it?"

"Yes, yes," the woman said. "My daughter works in Manhattan. She'd be so happy if you returned it."

She gave Mrs. Braunstein her daughter's number and Mrs. Braunstein called her at once. The young woman was ecstatic! The next morning, she came to Brooklyn to retrieve it. She explained that she had been on her way to the mountains for Shabbos and didn't even know she had lost it. She thanked Mrs. Braunstein for her kindness.

The next Friday, *Parashas Ki Savo*, she stopped by the Braunsteins with a huge bouquet of flowers and a thank-you note. And then she said the following incredible words:

> There is no way I can thank you. Let me tell you what happened last Saturday night. You see, five years ago I became a baalas teshuvah and
>
> **My mother kept telling me, "What's wrong with the way we live? Why do you have to change?"**
>
> my mother stopped talking to me. We have had a very strained relationship. My mother kept telling me, "What's wrong with the way we live? Why do you have to change?" And it's been very difficult these last five years.
>
> But last Saturday night, my mother called me after you called her and she said, "If you are trying to be like those people I just got off the phone with, then I now understand what you are doing." The whole week she's been telling all her friends in Miami about the long-distance telephone conversation you had with her and all about the mitzvah you people were going to do. This week, my mother has called me more often and has been warmer to me than she has been in the last five years.

How does such a beautiful thing happen? It happens because a person feels an *achrayus* to be a living *Beis HaMikdash*. The Braunsteins acted in an inspirational manner as they were simply trying to perform a mitzvah. How wondrous their deeds and how special was the effect of their actions.

Answering Bruno

R' Yosef Friedenson, editor of the *Yiddishe Vort*, the Yiddish magazine that Agudath Yisrael publishes, lived through the *gehinnom* of numerous concentration camps. One of them was the labor camp, Starachowice. It was a terrible place where men, women, and children were murdered without compunction.

They worried for their lives every day. Most of the men there, like R' Yosef, were about 20 years old. In the camp, there was a German officer, Bruno, who, much to their surprise, had a kind streak. When the other Nazis weren't looking, he'd do favors for Jews. He had a soul somehow. Nevertheless, they feared him because he was still a Nazi and you never knew what such a person was capable of.

In Starachowice there was a 40-year old Gerrer *chassid*, Akiva Goldstadt. He had been a wine merchant in Krakow before being sent to this concentration camp. He and Yosef Friedenson became very close friends. As Pesach was nearing, Akiva said, "Why don't we ask Bruno if he'll let us have some flour to bake matzah?"

"Are you crazy?" R' Yosef replied. "The guy will do us a favor here and there, but giving us flour? He'll never do that."

"Maybe I'm crazy, but let's ask him anyway."

They came to Bruno and asked. Bruno couldn't believe it. "That's what's on your mind? Flour and matzos? Here in the labor camp?"

"Yes," Akiva answered, "that's what's on our minds."

He thought a moment. "If it means that much to you, I will try to get it."

And, indeed, he got them flour. Secretly, arrangements were made so that R' Yosef's wife, Gittel, who had access to the kitchen, baked the matzah. The oven was 2000 degrees! Can you imagine? She put the flour in and a second later it became matzah.

On the morning of Pesach, the Jews in the barracks were eating the matzah when Bruno walked in. The way it worked in the camp was that there were little buckets in which rolls or pieces of bread were stacked for all the people. Everyone would come and take his bread. As Bruno walked in he saw that all the bread was right outside the door. No one had taken it. Instead they were all sitting and eating matzah.

He became furious and started yelling, "Your G-d has forsaken you and this is how you react? You fools! Why do you still act as if He has not forsaken you?"

Everybody froze. They were terrified what he might do. Then, he walked over to Akiva and repeated himself, "Don't you know that your G-d has forsaken you?"

"No," Akiva replied bravely, "not totally and not forever."

"Not totally?" Bruno yelled back

"Not totally," Akiva said softly. "You let us bake the matzah, didn't you? No, He has not forsaken us."

Imagine being a *Beis HaMikdash* in Starachowice!

Yirmiyahu HaNavi told us (*Eichah* 3:31-32): כִּי לֹא יִזְנַח לְעוֹלָם ה': כִּי אִם הוֹגָה וְרִחַם כְּרֹב חֲסָדָיו, *Hashem does not reject us forever. He does afflict us, but in the end He pities us.* Despite our failures, in the end He has *rachmanus* on *Klal Yisrael*. The afflictions are not total and are not forever.

Yet we have to know, in our hearts at least, that we have not done the job completely. *Klal Yisrael* has achieved much in Torah and *chessed*. But it's not enough.

Each of us has to become a living *Beis HaMikdash*. We have to improve ourselves and improve others. If we do that, hopefully we will be *zocheh* that Hashem will rebuild Yerushalayim and the *Beis HaMikdash* so that we can witness once again the great *Kohanim* doing their *avodah* as they inspire all who come to see it up close.

From Generation to Generation

I want to end with this personal note.

Many years ago, my eldest daughter, who was in first grade at the time, came home from Bais Yaakov and said, "I learned a new song today in school."

I stopped everything and told her that I wanted to hear the song. She started singing a song about *galus*, about how Yerushalayim was destroyed. As I was listening to the song, tears came to my eyes. I turned to my wife and said, "I can't believe a new generation is singing about *galus*."

> As I was listening to the song, tears came to my eyes.

Now that daughter is married, *baruch Hashem*, and has daughters of her own. My granddaughter will soon start school. Let us hope that that little girl, together with all the little girls and boys who will go to school this September, will no longer have to sing songs of *galus*. They should only sing songs of *geulah*.

How will they end up singing songs of *geulah*? Only if we make it happen. Each of us has to become a living *Beis HaMikdash*. We have to remember that great *tzaddikim* realize that they are each a moving, talking *Beis HaMikdash*. We each have the capacity to inspire others. People are constantly watching and judging us. They want to see: How do the Orthodox behave? What are they doing differently than we? Do they stand up for other people on the bus? Do they give other people the right of way when they drive? Are they honest in business? Do they treat people with respect and kindness?

They can tell an Orthodox Jew from a distance. Thus, if we act properly, then people will point at us with pride and say, "There goes an *erliche Yid*. There goes someone I am proud to be identified with, someone I want to emulate."

Then we will sing songs of *geulah*. May *Hashem* bring it about, speedily in our days.

Elul:
Pounding on the Door

In 1924, the Chofetz Chaim decided that the yeshivah in Radin needed a new and different type of Rosh Yeshivah. Since the beginning of the Yeshivah Movement — with the founding of the Volozhin Yeshivah in 1803 — *yeshivos* would start learning from *Masechta Berachos* all the way to the end of *Masechta Niddah*. It was *bekiyus* in style; they covered a great deal of ground. Then R' Chaim Solovetchik instituted the idea of learning one *masechta* with tremendous depth. This became the norm in all the *yeshivos*.

The Chofetz Chaim decided to bring in a Rosh Yeshivah who was only 30 years old. His *chiddushim* had been published in pamphlets and many people already knew his name, R' Naftali Tropp. Not only was he a great Rosh Yeshivah, but he was a great *baal mussar* as well. The Chofetz Chaim would ask R' Naftali to give *shmuessen* in the yeshivah during the *Yemei HaSelichos*, Rosh Hashanah, and Yom Kippur. This was unheard of because it was always the Mashgiach who gave the *shmuessen,* not the Rosh Yeshivah.

The great Rosh Yeshivah, R' Shlomo Heiman, always used to talk about one particular *shmuess* that R' Naftali Tropp gave. It was on the *pasuk* that we all say in *Selichos:* כְּדַלִּים וּכְרָשִׁים דָּפַקְנוּ דְלָתֶיךָ, *Like paupers and beggars we knock on Your door.* We also say: דְּלָתֶיךָ דָּפַקְנוּ רַחוּם וְחַנוּן, *We knock on Your doors, Compassionate and Merciful One.* "What is the meaning of knocking on the door?" R' Naftali asked.

דָּפַקְנוּ means to knock *very hard.* If a pauper comes to your house, he will knock softly because he is embarrassed or because he does not want the man at home to get angry or frightened and send him away empty-handed. Why then does it say דָּפַקְנוּ? Why are we knocking so hard? Shouldn't we come to Hashem as paupers with *aidelkeit*, in a quiet, dignified way?

The answer is that when a pauper knocks softly, with *aidelkeit*, he indeed wants something. However, if *chas v'shalom*, it's a matter of life and death — he has nothing to eat, his children are

> **It's a matter of life and death spiritually.**

starving, and if he doesn't get money it's all over — then he pounds on the door *hard*, in desperation, דָּפַקְנוּ!

R' Naftali Tropp said that starting in the month of Elul and through Rosh Hashanah until Yom Kippur we make a *cheshbon hanefesh*. We don't look at ourselves as others look at us, but we look in the mirror and see ourselves for what we really are — not what other people think we are. We know what we are. We know how far we are from where we should be in *ruchniyus* and how far we are from Hashem. It's a matter of life and death spiritually. That's why we are in a state of דָּפַקְנוּ, knocking hard and begging Hashem to bring us closer.

Climb Aboard

Rav Yehudah Zev Segal, the Manchester Rosh Yeshivah, commented on the famous passage in *Eliyahu Rabbah* (Chapter 25) which says: שֶׁכָּל אֶחָד וְאֶחָד מִיִּשְׂרָאֵל חַיָּב לוֹמַר, "מָתַי יַגִּיעוּ מַעֲשַׂי לְמַעֲשֵׂי אֲבוֹתַי אַבְרָהָם יִצְחָק וְיַעֲקֹב", *Every Jew is obligated to ask, "When will my ma'asim (actions) reach the ma'asim of my fathers — Avraham, Yitzchak, and Yaakov?"* R' Segal explained it with an interesting *mashal* (parable).

Imagine someone taking a trip from Manchester to London. He gets on the train, turns to his partner, and says, "When will we be in London?" That's an acceptable question. You're on the train, so you're entitled to know. However, if you are still home and haven't even gotten on the train, then the question doesn't make sense.

When *Eliyahu Rabbah* tells us that each of us is supposed to say, "When will our *ma'asim* reach those of Avraham, Yitzchak, and Yaakov — you can't just sit home and do nothing. If you haven't started the journey you can't begin to ask this question!"

All of us, hopefully, are already on this trip. All of us, hopefully, are on our way with Torah and *ma'asim tovim*. But, if not, now – during Elul and through the next 40 days until after Yom Kippur – is the time to begin this trip.

Do as I Do

R' Shimon Shkop comments on the *pasuk*, וְשִׁנַּנְתָּם לְבָנֶיךָ, *And you shall teach your children* ... בְּשִׁבְתְּךָ בְּבֵיתֶךָ וּבְלֶכְתְּךָ בַדֶּרֶךְ, *when you are sitting in your house, and in your travels on the way* (*Devarim* 6:7). R' Shimon asks, since we are talking about teaching our children, shouldn't it have said, וּבְלֶכְתָּם ... בְּשִׁבְתָּם — *when **they** are sitting in your house and when **they** are going on the way?* However, it says you should teach your children when *you* are sitting.

R' Shimon offers an amazing answer. What it really means is בְּשִׁבְתְּךָ, *when you are sitting in **your** house —* וּבְלֶכְתְּךָ בַדֶּרֶךְ, *and when **you** travel*, that's how your children will learn the lesson. They will learn it not by what you tell them, but by how you act.

If *bentching* at *Shalosh Seudos* in shul takes seven minutes and *bentching* at home takes a minute and a half, the children see that. They won't listen when you tell them that they have to take their time *bentching* and to say every word clearly and with the proper *kavanah*. בְּשִׁבְתְּךָ — teach your children *when you are sitting at home*. That is where they will really absorb who you are.

The same thing with וּבְלֶכְתְּךָ בַדֶּרֶךְ, when you are away from home, traveling. When you drive, do you listen to a Torah tape or to a secular talk show? Children learn a set of values when driving with you in the car.

What do you read at night? Do you ever open a *sefer*? Someone once called me and asked how I could say that people should learn at home; shouldn't they be learning in a *beis medrash*? Certainly, people should go to a *beis medrash*, but you have to open up a *Gemara* or *Chumash* at home as well. Otherwise your children will never see you learning.

Children know the way you talk on the telephone — even when they are in the other room and you think they don't hear. When you criticize the Rav or say something nasty that could harm a potential *shidduch* — you may think they don't hear. But they do.

Perhaps the most important thing we can do for a successful Elul is to remember that we set an example for our children. As Rav Shmuel Kaminetzky teaches, "In *Birchas HaMazon* we say, הָרַחֲמָן הוּא יְבָרֵךְ אֶת אָבִי מוֹרִי וְאֶת אִמִּי מוֹרָתִי, *May the Compassionate One bless my father, my teacher, and my mother, my teacher.* Not every father is a teacher nor is every mother a teacher in the conventional sense. However, in reality, says Rav Shmuel, parents are teachers even if they are not in the classroom. They teach their children about daily life and how an *ehrliche Yid* is supposed to conduct himself.

The Time Is Now

Let me tell you a story that R' Yaakov Galinsky told me. He is a great, energetic *baal mussar* from the Navardok school of *mussar*.

In the Slobodka school they emphasized *gadlus*: If a person knew how "great" he was, he would never come to sin. In Navardok they emphasized just the opposite: If a human being understood how insignificant he was compared to Hashem, he would never have the audacity to sin.

The Navardok approach was to do things to break one's arrogance. In Elul, for instance, the *talmidim* were told to go to a drugstore and ask for a salami sandwich. The man behind the counter would say, "Huh? Are you are out of your mind?" Or they would go into a restaurant and ask for a hammer. The fellow at the cash register would say, "Are you crazy?" The *talmidim* were supposed to be quiet and not respond, accepting the humiliation in stride. That was one way the Navardok *talmidim* would work on breaking their bad *middos*.

Shortly after his bar mitzvah, R' Yaakov's father sent him to Navardok. He came into the yeshivah and the *Mashgiach* took one look at this little child and told him that if he had any chance of getting into the yeshivah, he first had to go down the block to a shul and learn some *mussar*. R' Yaakov, who didn't know the area, left the yeshivah into the dark of night and saw a building that looked like a shul. He went inside.

It was dark, as few places had electricity in those days. People learned by candlelight. He walked into this large shul. Apparently, no one was there. It was pitch black … except for a *yungerman* learning. R' Yaakov only saw his back and didn't know who he was. There was a candle burning, casting light on the open *sefer* on the table. The *yungerman* was saying the *Gemara* (*Eruvin* 54a) over and over, "תַּלְמִיד אֶחָד הָיָה לְרַבִּי אֱלִיעֶזֶר שֶׁהָיָה שׁוֹנֶה בְּלַחַשׁ — לְאַחַר ג' שָׁנִים שָׁכַח תַּלְמוּדוֹ, *Rabbi Eliezar had a student who used to learn quietly after three years he forgot it all.*"

In other words, when you learn you have to learn aloud; you can't learn quietly. People say that today you can go to *Eretz Yisrael* and hear Rav Elyashiv, *shlita*, learning in his same, regular, sweet voice he learned with 60 to 70 years ago. He always learns vocally. It's not good enough to just see the words; you will forget them. You must enunciate them.

In any event, R' Yaakov Galinsky watched this *yungerman* from the back as he continued along in the same *Gemara*. However, now he was singing the words: חֲטוֹף וֶאֱכֹל … חֲטוֹף וֶאֱכֹל … חֲטוֹף חֲטוֹף וְאִישְׁתֵּי …, *Grab and eat … grab and eat … grab… grab… grab and drink.*

> **Grab and eat … grab and drink.**

And then with a melodious tone he continued, "כִּי הַאי עָלְמָא דְּאָזְלִינַן מִינֵּהּ, *because this world that we are leaving* — כְּהִלּוּלָא דָמֵי, *is like a wedding.*"

The simple meaning of the *Gemara* is that even if you go to a beautiful wedding, it's only five or six hours and then it's over. So grab and eat and drink, because it won't last forever. However, the *baalei mussar* understood this *Gemara* on a deeper level. This world is like a festive wedding. As glorious as it is, the festivities do not last forever. It's the same with humanity. No one lives forever. Therefore, grab all the Torah and mitzvos and *chessed* that you can do. … חֲטוֹף וֶאֱכֹל חֲטוֹף וְאִישְׁתֵּי.

R' Yaakov heard the *yungerman* saying it over and over until it went straight into his *neshamah*. He then went back to the yeshivah with a newfound humility. He approached the *Mashgiach* and said, "Rebbe, I heard what I had to hear and I'm ready." Of course the rest is history and he became the great *baal mussar* that we know him to be.

As an aside, do you know who that *yungerman* singing the *Gemara* was? R' Yaakov Galinsky told over the story at that person's funeral. It was none other than the *Gadol Hador*, the Steipler Gaon, R' Yaakov Yisroel Kanievsky, *zt'l*. As a young man he was singing out loud, "... חֲטוֹף וֶאֱכוֹל ... חֲטוֹף וְאִישְׁתֵּי".

The First Step

Many times you will hear somebody *daven* in such a way that's memorable. I always felt nobody could say Chapter 142 in *Tehillim* the way Rav Sholom Schwadron said it. He had a certain *nusach* that was so beautiful. I remember the way Rav Yaakov Teitelbaum would say the *pesukim* before *tekiyas shofar*. No one could say it that way. Not that it was such an unusual *nusach*, but there was a certain *hargashah*, a certain feeling to it.

Every Erev Rosh Chodesh, Sarah Schenirer would take the girls in her seminary in Cracow to *daven* at the *Rema's kever* and say *Yom Kippur Katan* together with them. The graduates of that seminary always said that there was one *pasuk* that Sarah Schenirer would lead the girls in that was so memorable: הֲשִׁיבֵנוּ ה' אֵלֶיךָ וְנָשׁוּבָ חַדֵּשׁ יָמֵינוּ כְּקֶדֶם, *Return to us, Hashem, and we will return to You. Renew our days as of old* (Eichah 5:21). That *pasuk* is the last one we read in *Eichah*. The intensity and sincerity with which she uttered those words made a lifelong impression on her *talmidos*. (I heard this from two of them, Rebbetzin Chana Rotenberg of Williamsburg and Mrs. Pearl Benisch, author of *Carry Me in Your Heart*, a book about Sarah Schenirer.)

There's something unusual you probably never noticed before. The word וְנָשׁוּבָ ("And we will return") is missing a ה. Normally it ends in a ה, but here it just has a *kamatz* under the ב. Thus the word can be read וְנָשׁוּבָ even without the ה. Why is the ה missing?

Chazal (*Menachos* 29b) tell us that the world was created with the letter ה. What they mean is that the bottom of the letter ה is open, a bottomless floor. This teaches that if a person is not careful and commits *aveiros,* he can fall into a bottomless abyss. However, *every person* must know that on the side toward the top of the letter there is a little opening. It is a doorway that is always open. It is the doorway of returning — through *teshuvah*! That is why the world was created with the letter ה. It may be easy to fall, but it is always possible to pick oneself up and return — to come back and live within the confines of Hashem's ideal plan for man and His world.

It is a doorway that is always open. It is the doorway of returning — through *teshuvah*!

Chazal tell us that Hashem (*k'viyachol*) has a *machlokes* with *Klal Yisrael.* We say, "הֲשִׁיבֵנוּ ... *Bring us back to You, Hashem, and we shall return, (Eichah ibid.).*" However, Hashem says the opposite in *Malachi* (3:7), שׁוּבוּ אֵלַי וְאָשׁוּבָה אֲלֵיכֶם, *You return to Me ....* You take the first step, and *then I'll return to you.* We want Hashem to make the first move, but He wants us to take that first step! That is the *machlokes.*

In my opinion, the ה is missing in the *pasuk* in *Eichah* because there we are asking Hashem to take the first step. And if indeed Hashem will take the first step, in a sense our *teshuvah* will not have been complete, for the ideal way would have been that we, His nation, take the first step. That is what the missing ה in וְנָשׁוּב represents. It is *teshuvah* after Hashem takes the first step. That's not complete *teshuvah*. Real *teshuvah* is when we take the first step. Hashem wants us to take that first step, as the *pasuk* in *Malachi* encourages us.

That is why the *berachah* of הֲשִׁיבֵנוּ — the *berachah* of *teshuvah* — is the fifth *berachah* in the *Shemoneh Esrei.* (The letter ה is numerically equal to five.) It begins with the letter ה — הֲשִׁיבֵנוּ — and ends with a ה — הָרוֹצֶה בִּתְשׁוּבָה. The *Tur* (*Orach Chaim* 115) says that represents the ten days of *Aseres Yemei Teshuvah.*

Perhaps this is why Sarah Schenirer said הֲשִׁיבֵנוּ ה' אֵלֶיךָ וְנָשׁוּב with such feeling. It had deep meaning to her. Standing there with her students saying *Yom Kippur Katan,* she was keenly aware how vitally important it was for us to take that first step toward Hashem, to be aware of our own shortcomings and to voluntarily seek growth and wholeness.

So let's review some of the things that we said and see what steps we can take in Elul now — and for the rest of our lives.

R' Naftali Tropp taught us about דָּפַקְנוּ: We have to realize that we have to knock so hard on the doors of *Shamayim* because we are so far away.

מָתַי יַגִּיעוּ מַעֲשַׂי — when will our actions reach to the actions of the *Avos*: Avraham, Yitzchak, and Yaakov? We have to start the trip; otherwise, how can we even begin to ask how we'll be like the *Avos*? We have to set the examples, בְּשִׁבְתְּךָ בְּבֵיתֶךָ. Our children have to see the way we act and speak.

No one lives forever. Therefore, grab all the Torah and mitzvos and *chessed* that you can do. חֲטוֹף וֶאֱכוֹל חֲטוֹף וְאִישְׁתֵּי.

Finally, don't wait for Hashem to bring something in your life that causes you to take the first step toward Him. Take that first step yourself. Be a complete person. Be a whole person. And may this Elul be the year all *Klal Yisrael* takes that first step: שׁוּבוּ אֵלַי וְאָשׁוּבָה אֲלֵיכֶם — *You return to Me... and then I'll return to you.*

Refining Our Character

All of us know that during these awesome and holy days, the *Sefer HaChaim* (book of the living) and *Sefer HaMeisim* (book of the dead) are open. The conventional understanding of that is that we are all being judged as to which of those two books we will be inscribed in.

However, I once heard a beautiful interpretation: The *Sefer HaChaim* refers to the book of all of us who are alive today, whereas the *Sefer HaMeisim* refers to the book of all those who have already passed away. We can easily understand why our book — the book of the living — is open, but why should their book, the book of those who have already passed away, be open?

The answer is that even people who are no longer with us nevertheless live on through their influence on our lives. Their book, the book of *meisim,* is open, because the good (and heaven forbid, the evil) they did is still being judged. The deeds they did that have had long-term ramifications are once again re-judged at this time of year.

> People who are no longer with us nevertheless live on through their influence on our lives.

People learn from what we do: either for the good or, *chas v'shalom,* the bad. And these lessons last for generations. Hence, if we have acted in a favorable manner because of the lessons that we learned from those who came before us, it is an *aliyah* once again for their *neshamos* as they are judged on Rosh Hashanah for the good that they perpetrated.

May Hashem help that the *neshamos* of those who passed away have an *aliyah*, as they are judged in their *Sefer HaMeisim* favorably for the good they have done. And may Hashem help as well that we, too, be judged favorably in our *Sefer HaChaim* for the good we have done.

L'zecher Nishmas

Let me tell you a little story that I heard from a *Bluzhever chassid* in Brooklyn, R' Mordechai Leiner. He told me that shortly after he became a disciple of the Rebbe, the Rebbe started a *minyan*. One Friday night, R' Mordechai was asked to *daven* at the *amud*. There was a large *chazzan's siddur* that everyone used at the *amud*; however, as he approached the *amud,* he closed it because he had his own little *siddur* that he was used to, that he always *davened* from.

When the Rebbe saw what R' Mordechai had done, he called him over, and asked, "Why did you close the *siddur*?"

"I want to use my own *siddur*," R' Mordechai replied.

"Did you know," the Rebbe said, "that a man donated this *chazzan's siddur* in someone's memory? When you use this *siddur* it's a *zechus* not only for the man who donated it, but it's an *aliyah* for the *neshamah* of the person for whom it was donated."

What a beautiful thought! Who thinks like that? Only a person with refined *middos*, a *tzaddik* who is so sensitive that he not thinks only about people who are living but even about the *neshamos* of those who are no longer among us.

Wake Up!

When the Torah (*Bereishis* 2:21) describes Hashem putting Adam to sleep (in order to create his partner in life), there is an unusual description regarding the sleeping process. The Torah says, וַיַּפֵּל..., תַּרְדֵּמָה עַל הָאָדָם, [*Hashem*] *made a sleep descend on the man.* The *Midrash* comments: תְּחִלַּת מַפָּלָה שֵׁינָה, *The beginning of a downfall is falling asleep* (*Bereishis Rabbah* 17:5). A lack of awareness can be the downfall of man; a person can be considered asleep even with his eyes open!

We all know that if we are not aware of what our children are doing at night — where they are and with whom they are hanging out — that's the beginning of the downfall of our *chinuch* for them. If a businessman is not aware of new developments in his business, thinking he will get away with the old system, that's the beginning of the end of his business. Every person has to be awake, aware, and attentive to everything that is going on around him.

The Rambam (*Hilchos Teshuvah* 7:3) warns us not to think that *teshuvah* is only for substantial *aveiros* such as outright *geneivah* (robbery). Rather, we all have to look into our hearts and examine our character and inner-thought processes to understand what leads us to the traits of anger, hatred, or jealousy. What causes us to ridicule others or to pursue endless financial gain or immoral pleasures? These attitudes need *teshuvah* as well. There is something wrong when a person is always angry and frustrated, always wants to have what somebody else has, socially or financially. What he really needs is a wake-up call.

How are we going to wake up to these inner shortcomings? How are we going to really change, to finally break the cycle of concepts and attitudes that are poison to us?

The Way You Judge Others ...

The *Gemara* (*Sotah* 8b) says these short but vitally important words: בְּמִדָּה שֶׁאָדָם מוֹדֵד בָּה מוֹדְדִין לוֹ, *In the way that a person measures other people, that's how they will measure him.* The way you act toward others, that's how others — and how Hashem — will act toward you.

If a person has anger toward others or embarrasses others or hates others or causes damage, Hashem will, *chas v'shalom*, cause all those things to come back to him. However, if a person strengthens others or looks for the good in others or does *chessed* for others, Hashem will pay him back with the same.

I'd like to share with you a remarkable story. In the 1800's in the city of Pressburg, which was then part of Hungary, there lived a saintly couple: Reb Yosef Yisroel and Faigy Reichner. They had eight boys and sent them to a local yeshivah. In this yeshivah, there was a tremendous *tzaddik*, R' Lazar HaKohen Katz. He was known as the *tzaddik* of Pressburg. He was a *melamed* who instilled the children with tremendous *yiras Shamayim*, *ahavas Torah,* and *kavod* for *bnei Torah.*

R' Lazar grew older and eventually had to stop teaching. He was poor and lived alone. However, Mrs. Faigy Reichner never forgot what a wonderful *tzaddik* he was and she'd send him lunch every day. Before *yamim tovim* she would also send him a substantial amount of money. This was how he sustained himself for years and years until he passed away.

A number of years after he was *niftar*, Mrs. Reichner and her husband also passed away. In 1944 her eight sons still lived in Pressburg. That year the Nazis, realizing that they were going to lose the war, tried to quickly capture and send as many Jews as they could to the concentration camps. The day after Yom Kippur, they broke into homes in Pressburg looking for Jews and ransacking everything in sight. In one of the houses there lived one of the Reichner sons, Ashi, with his wife, and a little girl named Miriam.

"What do you want from me?" he told the Nazis. "I'm an old man."

Nevertheless, they dragged him, his wife, and his daughter outside and told them to wait. Somehow, for some reason, the Nazis disappeared. Nobody could figure out why. Maybe they went into a different house to look for other people and figured that these people were so terrified that there was no way they were going to run away.

Either way, the Reichners had a moment to make a decision. Should they run away? If so, where would they run?

"I know a place in the west side of the city where they are hiding Jews," the husband said. "Let's run there. It's safe."

"No, it is on the east side of the city," the wife said. "Let's go there."

Can you imagine their fear? They had maybe 10 seconds to make a life-or-death decision. They argued back and forth, until finally the husband decided to listen to his wife. He remembered the *Gemara* (*Niddah* 45b) that says that שֶׁנָּתַן הקב״ה בִּינָה יְתֵירָה בָּאִשָּׁה, *Hashem gave women an extra sense of insight.*

They went east and found an elderly frail, non-Jewish woman named Anna Nanie. She had a closet that led to two rooms hidden behind it. This man, his wife, and their little girl — as well as about a dozen other Jews — were saved by hiding in those rooms.

Anna Nanie used to go to the grocer to get food three times a day. The grocer was also in on it. They'd cover the food with coals and wood, so that no one else would know. They were risking their lives to save Jews.

Do you know whose apartment Anna Nanie lived in? That was the apartment of the *melamed*, R' Lazar HaKohen Katz! She moved in after he passed away.

Isn't that unbelievable? For years, Mrs. Faigy Reichner sustained a *talmid chacham* who lived in that apartment. Years later, her children and grandchildren were saved in that apartment!

We see בְּמִדָּה שֶׁאָדָם מוֹדֵד בָּהּ מוֹדְדִין לוֹ, *In the way that a person measures other people, that's how they will measure him.* Sometimes we may not be paid back for the good that we do. Maybe not even our children. However, our grandchildren will be paid back. Human beings forget, but Hashem never forgets. (See *Ohr HaChaim Shemos* 20:6.)

Mi Hikdimani Va'ashalem

There is a *Midrash* that quotes a *pasuk* in *Iyov* (41:3): מִי הִקְדִּימַנִי וַאֲשַׁלֵּם, *Whoever precedes me, I'll have to pay him back.* (See *Bamidbar Rabbah* 14:2 and *Vayikra Rabbah* 27:2.) What does that mean? Consider these examples:

If a *bachur* is looking for a *shidduch*, and he's looking and looking without any success, he should pay *s'char limud* for someone else's child. Hashem will see this act and say, "Look, he doesn't have children or a family, but he pays tuition for a child. Therefore, I have to find him a wife and give him a child."

There is a *minhag* at a *bris* that if a person doesn't have children yet, he pays for a *bris*. Hashem says, מִי הִקְדִּימַנִי וַאֲשַׁלֵּם, *Whoever precedes me, I have to pay him back*; I didn't even give him the opportunity, but since he is doing it anyway, *I have to give it to him.*" I believe this is the source for a couple who want to have a child being honored at a *bris* with being "*kvater.*"

If a person doesn't have much money, but gives *tzedakah*, Hashem says, "Look, he's giving *tzedakah* even though he doesn't have much money." מִי הִקְדִּימַנִי וַאֲשַׁלֵּם, *Whoever precedes me, I have to pay him back.*

If you know of a sick person in the family, get involved in *bikur cholim*. If you want someone in your family to find a *shidduch*, get involved in *hachnasas kallah* or *shidduch* organizations. When you do for others you will be blessed in the field of your endeavors. This goes for *limud haTorah, shidduchim*, finances — literally anything.

The Reluctant Ba'al Bris

A doctor once called me on a Thursday night to do a *bris* on Shabbos at the West Point Military Academy. "Why are you first calling me now on Thursday night?" I asked the doctor. "The child must have been born a week ago, last Shabbos."

"I'll tell you," he said. "This is not my baby, but the child of a non-religious dentist and his wife. They had refused to have a *bris* done for their child under any circumstances. But my wife and I have been talking with them all week. Finally, tonight, we convinced them. That's why I'm first calling you only now to make the arrangements for them."

"That is so special of both of you," I said to the doctor who called. He was an ophthalmologist serving in the United States Army, and as an Orthodox Jew he had requested to be stationed near a Jewish community. Therefore, he was at West Point, which was within driving distance of Monsey, New York. After making the arrangements for the *bris*, he assured me that my wife and I could be his guests for Shabbos. On Friday afternoon, my wife and I, along with one of our children, went to spend the Shabbos at West Point.

When I arrived at the home of the dentist to leave my instruments there before Shabbos, the mother of the child so despised Orthodox Jews that she wouldn't even let me into the house. "Rabbi," she said, "I don't want you to take one step into my house earlier than you have to. Tomorrow is the *bris* and not today."

"But I have to bring my instruments into your home before Shabbos," I said.

"Then leave them outside."

"I can't leave *bris* instruments lying outside, even if they are in a medical bag," I insisted.

"Fine," she said. Reluctantly she let me open the door so that I could reach in and put my instruments at arm's length from the door. She wouldn't even let me take one step into her home. That's how negative she was.

As if that wasn't enough, she added, "Rabbi, a doctor will watch you tomorrow to make sure you are doing a good job."

We stayed with our wonderful hosts, and I once again thanked them for being involved to make sure the mitzvah would happen. The ophthalmologist and his wife had one child, a little boy, and had been told that medically they couldn't have any more children. West Point is a difficult place for an Orthodox Jewish couple to live, but this couple did everything they could to show their child, during their stay at West Point, what *davening* at a shul on Shabbos was all about. They set up their living room as a shul, with a small *Aron Kodesh* up front and a *mechitzah* across the center of the room, so that any men who were there for Shabbos would *daven* up front and the women would be *davening* in the back.

Baruch Hashem the *bris* went smoothly. (The doctor who was called to observe me was so impressed that he gave me a book on aerobics as a token of recognition.) As we left on Motza'ei Shabbos I was thinking, "Imagine what a *berachah* it would be if this couple, who arranged the *bris*, would have a baby of their own!" As we said our goodbyes I wished them *hatzlachah* with the silent prayer that one day they would merit making a *simchah*.

A year later, the ophthalmologist phoned me and said, "I have another *bris* for you at West Point."

"I hope it's not that same dentist again," I said.

"No, no, no," he said, laughing. "It's me."

"You?" I said. "I can't believe it."

"You are not the only one," he said. "The doctors didn't believe it either."

I performed that *bris* in the lieutenant's quarters as many cadets and officers up and down the military scale attended with reverence and dignity. It was a tremendous *kiddush Hashem*.

> We made a *bris* in the lieutenant's quarters along with many soldiers and officers.

How did it come about? מִי הִקְדִּימַנִי וַאֲשַׁלֵּם.

The ophthalmologist and his wife became involved in making sure that someone else had a *bris* and Hashem saw to it that they made one of their own.

Yad Avshalom

During the *yemei hadin*, Rav Chaim Shmulevitz used to be *mispallel* at Yad Avshalom, the grave of Avshalom, the son of David HaMelech. Avshalom was a *rasha* who rebelled against his father, David and wanted to take his throne. Why would Rav Chaim go to Yad Avshalom of all places?

"Why don't you go to the *Kosel* or *Kever Rachel*?" people would ask him.

Listen to his answer.

When Avshalom was fleeing for his life, his long hair was caught in a tree and while he was hanging by his hair, David's soldiers — against David's explicit command — killed him (*II Shmuel* 19:1). When David asked the messenger what happened to his son, the messenger was afraid to tell him. But David pressured him to answer. The messenger finally told him that what happened to his son should happen to his worst enemies. David got the message. He knew Avshalom was dead.

It then says, וַיִּרְגַּז הַמֶּלֶךְ ... וַיֵּבְךְּ, *The king trembled ... and cried* (ibid.). He cried continuously, saying one word over and over again: בְּנִי, *My dear son.* He cried out the word בְּנִי eight times! (See also verse 5.)

R' Chaim explained, "Look at this rebellious son — and yet look at the love that the father had for him. I've been a rebellious son to Hashem," Rav Chaim said. "I go to Yad Avshalom because just like David loved his son, I want Hashem to love me, His son."

That should be our attitude. Yes, we have sinned, but we are coming to Hashem on this Yom Kippur in the hope that He should love us no less than David loved Avshalom.

Should we be frightened during these days of awe? Certainly. However, we don't have to be afraid that we will lose the battle. As long as we have breath in our lungs we have hope.

If we come to Yom Kippur with a broken heart we have great hope. The Gerrer Rebbe said that there's no more complete thing than a broken heart. We have to come with hearts filled with remorse. Yet, at the same time, we have to come with resolve that we can improve and grow and thus merit Hashem's blessing.

We have it within our own hands to look for the good in one another. The way we look at others is the way Hashem will look at us. We all have *aveiros* on our ledgers. But that shouldn't destroy us, because when we look for the good in one another, Hashem will look at the good in us. When we go out of our way to do good to others, Hashem will be inclined to treat us the same way.

> **The way we look at others is the way Hashem will look at us.**

May we all be inscribed for a great year that is filled with the bounty of *berachah, nachas,* and *mazal* and with all that is good for us.

A Life, Some Shoes, and an Old Baby Bottle

As we move away from the festive Yom Tov of Succos and head toward the celebration of Chanukah, I would like to share some personal, seasonal thoughts that come to mind every year at this time.

Celebrating the Life

When my mother, Mrs. Hindy Krohn, passed away on Chol HaMoed Succos in 2006, I realized that my siblings and I would be sitting *shivah* the same way we did 40 years earlier, when my father, Rav Avrohom Zelig Krohn, passed away on Shemini Atzeres, 1966. The *shivah* would begin right after Yom Tov, at the close of Simchas Torah. Thus, for the remaining days of Chol HaMoed and the subsequent days of Yom Tov, I had some time to collect my thoughts before the *shivah* began.

I knew that when people would come to be *menachem avel*, many would ask how old my mother was. She was an extremely private person and never told anyone, including her children, her age. I went to Rav Zelik Epstein on Yom Tov and asked what I should say when people would inevitably ask me her age. He said that after her death I could tell them her age because the reason she didn't want anyone to know during her lifetime was not to cause an *ayin hara.*

It was a very interesting insight, because I hadn't told Rav Zelik how sensitive she was in matters regarding *ayin hara,* yet he picked that up immediately. In fact, I remember taking her once to Rav Yaakov Kamenetzky (we had a family *sheilah* [religious question]) and when Rav Yaakov asked my mother how many grandchildren she had, she didn't answer. Rav Yaakov told her that not only was she allowed to count her grandchildren (he also understood that she was hesitant to give a number because of *ayin hara*), but that in his opinion people should count their grandchildren to be *makir tov* (express gratitude) to Hashem. However, despite the assurance of a *gadol hador,* she was still hesitant to say a number.

Therefore, out of deference to my mother, as I was positive she would not want her age discussed, I decided to not tell anyone her actual age. I would just say that I believed she was born in 1919. "If it means that much to you, you do the calculations. I won't," I would say. And that's how the discussion went with those who came to be *menachem avel,* at least for the first two days.

Then I got a call from a cousin in *Eretz Yisrael.*

"You are mistaken," he said to me. "I know positively that she was not born in 1919" (he proved it, by the way), and later that day another cousin confirmed that my date was wrong. I smiled and was thrilled. רְצוֹן יְרֵאָיו יַעֲשֶׂה, *Hashem* does the will of those who fear Him (*Tehillim* 145:19). And so indeed, Hashem kept my mother's secret. I still have no idea if she was born in 1919 or some other year. (And, frankly, I am not interested.)

> It really makes no difference when a person was born or died. What matters is what he does with his life.

What do we do with our lives is really what is most important. And to all who came to be *menachem avel,* I spoke of my mother's accomplished life.

Why We Say Kaddish

As the days, weeks, and months of saying *Kaddish* went on, I wondered why we do not even mention the name of the person for whom we are saying *Kaddish*. Is *Kaddish* not a prayer for the departed, and if it is, why not mention the name?

It occurred to me that *Kaddish* is not only for the *niftar*. It's for the person who is still in this world, because each of us, in our lives, has the opportunity to be *mekadesh Shem Shamayim*, to make a *kiddush Hashem*. However, once a person leaves this world — that's it. He can no longer be *mekadesh Shem Shamayim*. When a person leaves this world, there's a vacuum, a void. Who is going to fill that vacuum? Who will fill that void?

The answer, of course, is the *avel*. That's why the *avel* says, יִתְגַּדַּל וְיִתְקַדַּשׁ שְׁמֵהּ רַבָּא, *May His great Name be exalted and sanctified*, over and over and over: to make sure that he remembers that it is up to him to fill that vacuum, that void, that empty pair of shoes once filled by a loved one who can no longer be *mekadesh Shem Shamayim*.

When an *avel* says, יִתְגַּדַּל וְיִתְקַדַּשׁ, he is saying in effect, I make a commitment to living a life of *kiddush Shem Shamayim*. That's what I'm going to do with my life. Filling the void that is now left by the departed one: that is the commitment of the person saying *Kaddish*.

The Red Danube

Whenever I talk of filling a void, I am reminded of an incredible trip I once led to Budapest. In preparation for this trip, I visited Reb Avrohom Schonberger of Borough Park, who lived in Budapest during the war. He told me how along the Danube River, the German and Hungarian Nazis lined up Jews and literally shot them into the water. It was even more horrible, because to save bullets, they would sometimes tie three Jews together and only shoot the middle one, forcing the other two to be dragged into the water to die by drowning.

The famous Swedish diplomat Raoul Wallenberg did whatever he could to save Jewish lives and our people will always be grateful to him. When Wallenberg found out about this newest atrocity, he placed divers nearby and had them try to rescue those underwater who were still alive. My *mechutan*, Alex Kramer, told me that his mother and an older sister of his (he hadn't been born yet) were once on one of those lines. As they were being lined up, Wallenberg arrived and waved 10 visas at the Nazis. The Germans were mass murderers, but they took

A Life, Some Shoes, and an Old Baby Bottle | 253 |

pride in their exactitude. If someone had a visa, they would honor it. In this way, Wallenberg was able to save 10 women and the children they had with them. Among them were Alex's mother and older sister.

Alex had gone to stand along the Danube River the afternoon before I arrived there. At dinner, he showed me pictures of a stunning new memorial that had been placed along the Danube River to commemorate the death of the innocent Jews who were murdered there. The memorial consists of empty shoes. Shoes of parents. Shoes of grandparents. Shoes of children. All stark empty! (They were bronzed and nailed into the boardwalk so they could not be removed.)

When I saw those pictures, I knew I had to take my group there the next day. When we arrived, I told them, "Look at the Danube River. The water looks blue ... but it's deep red with Jewish blood."

> "Look at the Danube River. The water looks blue ... but it's deep red with Jewish blood."

I told them the story of the senior Mrs. Kramer and how she and her daughter were saved. It was indescribably moving. We started singing the stirring melody of עַל נַהֲרוֹת בָּבֶל שָׁם יָשַׁבְנוּ גַּם בָּכִינוּ בְּזָכְרֵנוּ אֶת צִיּוֹן, *By the rivers of Babylon, there we sat and also wept when we remembered Zion* (*Tehillim* 137:1). We *davened*, cried, and resolved to fill those shoes by living lives of *kiddush Hashem*. It was an unbelievably powerful moment, absolutely incredible!

I returned to New York and shared this experience with many people. At *Yizkor* on Yom Kippur, I addressed our shul and told them that something incredible had happened in our shul on the first day of Rosh Hashanah. No one understood what I meant. Then I told them the story of the Danube River and I explained that at the end of Mussaf on Rosh Hashanah, the *Kohanim* approached the front of the shul to *duchen*. After *Birchas Kohanim*, I removed the *tallis* from over my head and saw a sight that penetrated deep into my heart. Next to the *aron kodesh* there were shoes, empty shoes. Shoes of parents. Shoes of grandparents. Shoes of children. Stark empty shoes — and they reminded me of those shoes on the Danube River!

I just looked at the shoes ... especially those of the children. I couldn't get over it. I thought to myself, "What is the difference between these shoes of the *Kohanim* and those shoes at the Danube

River?" The answer, of course, was that in a few moments these shoes would be filled with living people. And they could eventually go and do mitzvos, learn Torah, visit the sick, etc. But those shoes on the Danube River would always remain empty.

The past is gone, but we have a tremendous responsibility to those who are no longer here. We have a tremendous responsibility to *our-selves* as well to appreciate the gift of life and make the most of it. That's why we came into this world, to fill those shoes that can never be filled again. That's our mission.

Chanukah Insights

The *Midrash* (*Bereishis Rabbah* 2:4) notes that one of the *gezeiros* (decrees) that the Greeks made against *Klal Yisrael* was that Jews were forced to take the horn of an ox and write on it, אֵין לָנוּ חֵלֶק בֵּאלֹקֵי יִשְׂרָאֵל, *We have no portion in the G-d of Israel*. What was this *gezeirah* all about? What was the point of it?

Some connect it to the חֵטְא הָעֵגֶל, *the sin of the Golden Calf*, which was always a source of embarrassment to the Jewish people. Imagine taking your ox, which is like an עֵגֶל, and having to write on it that you have no חֵלֶק in Hashem. It was a humbling reminder to *Klal Yisrael* that just a few weeks after they had been given the Torah, they sinned with the Golden Calf. The underlying message of this *gezeirah* was that Jews should feel ashamed of themselves. In essence, by sinning, they were not so great or so special.

Another explanation is that many Jews were farmers in those days. To them, owning oxen was like owning a car is for us, and, in essence, the Greeks were telling all the Jews to put a kind of a "bumper sticker" on their oxen and write that they had no connection to Hashem.

Rav Avrohom Gurwicz, the Rosh Yeshivah in the Gateshead Yeshivah, told me that his father was once learning with a man in England, R' Hirsch Bendes, a very great *talmid chacham*. They were learning *Mesechta Keilim*, which is one of the most difficult *Mishnayos* to learn, as it deals with *tumah* and *taharah* and vessels that we don't even have today. When R' Bendes was learning this *mesechta,* he decided to go to the British Museum, because they had some ancient *keilim* from the *Beis HaMikdash* and he wanted to see the *keilim* that the Mishnah was discussing.

When he saw the display in the museum he joyfully exclaimed, "Now I understand the *Midrash*."

The museum displayed a baby bottle from the era of the *Beis HaMikdash*. It looked like a small *shofar*. People at the time would take the horn of an ox, hollow it out, make a little hole on the bottom, and pour the milk or the water in from the top. The baby would then suck from the little *shofar*. (See Rashi to *Shabbos* 35b, who writes that that they used to put water into a *shofar* and use it as a drinking cup.)

Rav Bendes explained, "Why did the Greeks make Jews write that on the horn of the ox? So that when these little babies were sucking the water or milk they would already see with their eyes, אֵין לָנוּ חֵלֶק בֵּאלֹקֵי יִשְׂרָאֵל." By osmosis, they would be getting a terrible message.

Now, all of a sudden, we have a different understanding of what that *gezeirah* was all about. The Greeks understood that *chinuch* starts from the time a child is in the cradle. That was why they made that *gezeirah*.

Mechitzos

Let me share with you a remarkable insight from the Ponevezher Rav, Rav Yosef Kahaneman *z'l*.

David HaMelech writes in *Tehillim* (144:7), שְׁלַח יָדֶיךָ מִמָּרוֹם פְּצֵנִי וְהַצִּילֵנִי מִמַּיִם רַבִּים מִיַּד בְּנֵי נֵכָר, *Hashem, stretch Your hand out from above; please release me and save me from the great waters, from the hands of the nations*. The nations are compared to "great waters," to a raging storm. However, asked the Rav, there is a famous *pasuk* in *Ovadiah* (1:18) that compares *Klal Yisrael* to a fire: וְהָיָה בֵית יַעֲקֹב אֵשׁ וּבֵית יוֹסֵף לֶהָבָה, *The house of Jacob will be fire, the house of Joseph a flame*. In other words, the nations are great, raging waters, whereas the Jewish people are like fire. Since water puts out fire, what is David teaching us? That the stormy, raging nations will, *chas v'shalom*, extinguish the Jews?

However, the Ponevezher Rav derived a tremendous lesson from this. When does water put out fire? It is when they touch each other, when they are connected. However, if you have a *mechitzah*, a pot, between the fire and the water, then fire controls the water. The *mechitzah* controls how hot or cold the water will be. With its intensity the fire can even dry up the water.

That is what David HaMelech is teaching us, the Ponevezher Rav said. A Jew has to have *mechitzos* (barriers).

Chanukah is a time to remember this lesson of fire. Every night we increase the fire. The fire not only represents the physical fire, but the fire that is within us. Chanukah is a time to strengthen the fire within us, but to do that we need *mechitzos*.

> The fire does not only represent the physical fire, but the fire that is within us.

We who live in *galus* must be attentive to make self-imposed barriers. If a person has no *mechitzos*, he starts to think, act, talk, and behave like the non-Jews. The water extinguishes the fire, *chas v'shalom*. When there is a *mechitzah,* however, when there is a barrier between them, then we are in control.

Everything you do in life leaves an impression forever. Impressions stay even after a person is gone. Living one's life in accordance with Torah values is imperative for us and our future generations. We should try and accomplish *kiddush Shem Shamayim* every day of our lives. We have very big shoes to fill. Let's take the fire that we see increasing every night of Chanukah and use it to enhance our lives. We will thus hopefully merit to greet *Mashiach* and return with him to *Eretz Yisrael*. May it happen in our day!

Purim, Prayer, and Pulling Together

As we approach Purim I would like to share with you one of the greatest stories I have ever heard. The Purim story unfolds gradually and ends with a crescendo of *geulah* (redemption); this story too ends with an incredible crescendo that can change your life's attitude forever.

Rabbi Moshe Plutchok is a *Maggid shiur* in Yeshiva Derech Chaim of Brooklyn. Like many who live in the city throughout the year, he and his family go to the mountains in Monticello in the summer. However, he sojourns in what is known as a "learning camp," located in Camp Morris. There they have a kollel where Rabbi Plutchok and other *rabbeim*, who teach in the various camps, learn in a *beis medrash* together in the afternoons; it is known as a *kollel mechanchim*.

One day a number of summers ago, Rabbi Plutchok saw a businessman walk into the *beis medrash* carrying an ArtScroll *Gemara*. The man sat down and learned with great enthusiasm. When he had a question he would go and ask others even if they were younger than he was, until he received a satisfying answer.

Rabbi Plutchok eventually got to talking with the man. The man told him that, unfortunately, he had advanced stage liver cancer. Rabbi

Plutchok was amazed, because this man came to the *beis medrash* every day with such a positive attitude and always learned with incredible *hasmadah* (diligence). "It's amazing to me," Rabbi Plutchok told him, "that although you have this terrible illness, you come here every day and are so upbeat about the learning."

"Rabbi," the man said, "I'll tell you the truth. The ArtScroll *Gemara* is carrying me. You see, I never went to a yeshivah. Now that the *Gemara* is in English, I am finally able to understand it. And if I don't understand something, I ask the rabbis here. It makes me feel very special. It makes me feel I can make a connection to the legacy of Torah and the Jewish people. That's what's carrying me."

One day, near the end of the summer, Rabbi Plutchok walked in to the *beis medrash* and saw this man sitting at the side of the room, looking sad. "Is everything okay?" he asked.

"No, Rabbi, not really," the man replied. "The illness is progressing and I was thinking, *What difference does it make if I learn? Who cares?* You and the others are all *talmidei chachamim*. Your learning makes a difference.

> "The illness is progressing and I was thinking, *What difference does it make if I learn? Who cares?* I'm not on your level, Rabbi. What's the difference if I learn?"

As for me, I don't understand everything it says even using the ArtScroll *Gemara*. When I ask my questions to the rabbis, I understand most of what they say, but not all. I'm not on your level, Rabbi. What's the difference if I learn? Who cares?"

Rabbi Plutchok felt terrible for the man, but, incredibly, just the night before he had heard an amazing story on a Jewish radio station. He decided to share it:

> There was a great symphony conductor, an Italian maestro named Arturo Toscanini, who led concerts all over the world. He was known as a complete perfectionist and had few peers.
>
> Toscanini had a biographer who would interview him periodically over the years as part of a major book he was writing. One evening, he called Toscanini and told him that he would be in town the next

night, and asked if he could come to the house to interview him. Toscanini answered that he would be doing something special that would require absolute concentration and he did not want to be interrupted. He told the man not to come.

"*Maestro*," the biographer asked, "what are you doing that's so special?"

"A concert is being played overseas. I used to be the conductor of that symphony orchestra, but I could not be there this year. So I am going to listen over shortwave radio, and hear how the substitute conductor leads the orchestra. I don't want any interruptions whatsoever."

"Maestro, it would be my greatest pleasure to watch how you listen to a concert played by an orchestra that you used to lead. I promise, I won't say anything. I'll sit on the other side of the room, quietly."

"You promise to be perfectly quiet?" Toscanini asked.

"Yes."

"Then you can come."

The next night, the biographer came and sat quietly at one side of the room while Toscanini sat at the other side and listened to the concert, which lasted almost an hour. Finally, when it ended, the biographer remarked, "Wow, wasn't that magnificent?"

Toscanini said, "Not really."

"Why not?"

"They were supposed to be 120 musicians, including 15 violinists. Only 14 of them showed up."

The biographer thought Toscanini was joking. How could he know from 6,000 miles away, over shortwave radio, that one of the violinists had not played? The biographer had his doubts, but didn't want to contradict the Maestro, so he left quietly.

The next morning, though, he was overwhelmed by curiosity and had to find out for himself, so he called the concert hall overseas, asked for the music director, and inquired as to how many musicians were supposed to have been in the performance the night before, and how many actually played. The director told him that they were supposed to have 120 musicians, including 15 violinists, but only 14 showed up.

The biographer was amazed! He returned to Toscanini and said, "Sir, I owe you an apology. I thought you were just making *it up the other night. But please, tell me, how could you know that one violinist was missing?"*

"There is a great difference between you and me," Toscanini answered. "You are a part of the audience, and to the audience everything sounds wonderful. But I am the conductor, and the conductor has to know every note of music that has to be played. When I realized that certain notes were not being played, I knew without a doubt that one of the violinists was missing."

Rabbi Plutchok now turned to the man and said, "Maybe to human beings it doesn't make a difference if you learn, but to the Conductor of the World Symphony — Who knows every note of music that is supposed to be played, Who knows every word of Torah that is supposed to be learned, every line of *tefillah* that is supposed to be prayed — to Him it makes a difference!" The man embraced Rabbi Plutchok and could not thank him enough for these words of *chizuk*.

That winter, Rabbi Plutchok met the son of this man and asked how his father was doing. The son told him that his father had passed away. However, he added, "Ever since my father returned from the bungalow colony, every time he opened that *Gemara* he would say, "I am performing for the Conductor of the World Symphony!"

That is why we are on this world. We each have our own potential to fulfill. You do not have to be like me and I do not have to be like you. We are all different, but each of us is part of a great symphony called *Klal Yisrael*, and if we don't perform the music that we can perform — the Torah that we can learn, the *chessed* that we can do, the *tefillah* that we can pray — it makes a difference to the Conductor of the World Symphony because He knows our potential and He notices everything.

We are coming close to that great holiday of Purim — a time of song, joy, and festivity. Let's remember the greatest joy: knowing that we each play for the Conductor of the World Symphony. Again, I don't have to be like you and you don't have to be like me. However let's each fulfill our potential. To the Conductor, it makes a difference. Every line that we learn, every word that we *daven*, every *chessed* that we do: He hears it and He records it.

Yom Ki-Purim

Purim is one of the most festive holidays of the year. If we were to consider which of the holidays is the most unlike Purim, we would surely agree that it is Yom Kippur. Indeed, Yom Kippur is the day when we fast and avoid all physical pleasures. The entire day is spent in prayer. Purim is just the opposite: singing, dancing, eating, drinking, and being happy. Of course, we pray, but it essentially totally the opposite.

Yet, the Arizal says that the name "Yom Kippur" means *"Yom Ki-Purim"* — it is *a day like Purim*. How could the holiest, most sincere, most awesome day of the year be like Purim? What aspects can possibly be the same?

Let me share with you an experience and an insight I heard on a summer trip in 2010 when I had the *zechus* to lead over a hundred people on a tour of Jewish holy and historical places in Spain. It was there in 1492 that the Inquisition took place, where Jews were tortured and killed for keeping Torah. My dear friend Rav Menachem Nissel of Israel, who came to lead the tour with me, explained the following. To escape the Inquisition many Jews became Conversos. These were Jews who on the outside looked as though they had converted to Christianity, but at night, when nobody saw, they kept the Torah. They were Jews in hiding. Who was the hero to all the Conversos? Who was the one, in the entire *Tanach*, to whom they looked up? It was Queen Esther.

Why Queen Esther? It is because, as the *Megillah* tells us, Esther in a sense was also a "converso." She did not tell anyone of her people or her birthplace (see *Megillas Esther* 2:10). Nobody knew she was a Jew. To the world she appeared to be a gentile, but at night when no one was around, she was able to be a religious Jew. Therefore, to the Conversos, Queen Esther was the hero to whom they related.

> **Queen Esther was the hero to all the Conversos because, the *Megillah* tells us, she did not tell "of her people or of her birthplace."**

The Avudraham, a Sefardic *Gadol*, notes that during the prayers of Yom Kippur, as well as of Rosh Hashanah, there is one word that we keep saying over and over: וּבְכֵן, which means "*and in this manner.*" We repeat this word in our Rosh Hoshanah and Yom Kippur prayers numerous times, וּבְכֵן תֵּן פַּחְדְּךָ, *And in this manner [Hashem], put Your awe over all creation;* וּבְכֵן תֵּן כָּבוֹד ... לְעַמֶּךָ, *And in this manner [Hashem], grant honor to Your people;* וּבְכֵן צַדִּיקִים, *And in this manner may the righteous....* Why do we repeat וּבְכֵן over and over on the High Holy Days?

The Avudraham says a remarkable thing and connects this phrase to Purim. We know the story. There was a terrible decree against the Jews. Mordechai told Esther to go to the king, Achashveirosh, and tell him to please save the Jews. Esther replied that she couldn't go in to the king uninvited, for anyone who did so could be put to death (see *Megillas Esther* 4:11).

Mordechai answered, "If you persist in keeping silent at a time like this, relief and deliverance will come to the Jews from another place" (ibid. 4:14).

Queen Esther was frightened. She knew she had no permission, but she decided she would heed Mordechai. So she said, "Assemble all the Jews ... and fast for me; do not eat or drink for three days, night and day ... וּבְכֵן, *and in this manner I will come to the king* (ibid. 4:16). What is the significance of her choice of the word וּבְכֵן?

As is well known, *sefarim kedoshim* (sacred books) write that every mention in the *Megillah* of the word הַמֶּלֶךְ, "the king," is not just a reference to Achashveirosh, but to the King of kings, Hashem Himself. Therefore, in essence Queen Esther was saying וּבְכֵן — "and in this manner" — in this state of trepidation and humbleness — I will go [to Hashem]. I don't have enough *zechusim* to approach the King, but nevertheless in this frightened state I will go."

The Avudraham says that that is what we say on Rosh Hashanah and Yom Kippur — וּבְכֵן ... וּבְכֵן ... וּבְכֵן. "In this manner," just as

Esther did when she went to the King — although she was frightened and felt that she did not deserve to enter — that's how we approach Hashem on Rosh Hashanah and Yom Kippur. We come "וּבְכֵן," *in this manner* with fear and trepidation, praying that we do merit to enter the Holy chambers of Hashem.

What happened to Esther? The king saw her, and she found favor in his eyes. He stretched out his שַׁרְבִיט הַזָּהָב, his golden scepter, and said, "Queen Esther… what is your petition? [Even if it be] unto half the kingdom, it shall be granted you" (ibid. 5:3).

Purim is a time when וּבְכֵן was answered. Even though she was hesitant and frightened, she went in and her prayers were answered. That's what the Arizal means by saying, "Yom Kippur is a *Yom Ki-Purim.*" We want Yom Kippur to be like Purim — to be a day when our prayers (וּבְכֵן) are answered.

Isn't that incredible?

Connecting to Those in Need

The Rambam tells us the Purim is a day of *tefillah*, of prayer. In fact, Purim is a day of celebration, because our *tefillos* were answered. The Rambam tells us another important thing: "It's more important to give presents and money to poor people than to have a big *seudah.*"

On Purim we celebrate a festive *seudah* with food, drink, song, and even dance. However the most important thing is to give to others who have less than we have and to invite them to join us. Many people do not have a place for the *seudah* on Purim. Nobody should be eating alone on Purim! We all have to share and celebrate together. There is no greater *simchah* in Hashem's eyes than when He sees that people reach out to those less fortunate than they. Look up and see the vital Rambam in *Hilchos Megillah* 2:17, about helping the poor and the unfortunate rather than celebrating with a *seudah* alone on Purim. It will structure your priorities.

If that is the case, then Purim is a time not only of reading the *Megillah* and of prayer, but it is also a time when we make a connection to others. Purim indeed is a day of *tefillah*, but it is also a day characterized by אִישׁ לְרֵעֵהוּ, *each man to his friend* (see *Megillas*

Esther 9:22). Purim is a day we have to think about others. That's really what it's all about.

Davening Lessons in the Megillah

At the end of the *Megillah* (9:25), when it is recounting the whole story, it says, ... בְּבֹאָהּ לִפְנֵי הַמֶּלֶךְ אָמַר עִם הַסֵּפֶר יָשׁוּב מַחֲשַׁבְתּוֹ הָרָעָה עַל רֹאשׁוֹ, *When she appeared before the king, he commanded by means of letters that [Haman's] wicked scheme ... should recoil on his own head.*

The Vilna Gaon uses this *pasuk* to teach an important lesson: It is imperative to *daven* from a *siddur*. בְּבֹאָהּ לִפְנֵי הַמֶּלֶךְ — when you go in front of the King, when you *daven* to the King [Hashem] — אָמַר עִם הַסֵּפֶר, say the words in the *siddur* (lit., book). יָשׁוּב מַחֲשַׁבְתּוֹ הָרָעָה — that will turn away your evil thoughts.

Don't *daven* by heart, because when you do your body is in one place but your mind is off someplace else. Many times you skip words. Always carry a small *siddur* with you. Never *bentch* by heart. If you *daven* by heart you will find that your mind wanders. You are going to think about family problems, sports, or the recession as you *daven*. When you look at the words in the *siddur*, it adds greatly to the concentration.

If we blend the lessons of *davening* with the Purim lesson of being concerned for others, we then realize that one of the most important things we should be doing when we pray *Shemonah Esrei* is thinking about the needs of other people.

I once performed a *bris* in Merrick, Long Island, for a family that was not religious. Afterward, I went into the kitchen to wash my hands and I saw a woman crying. I didn't know why she was crying, but my heart went out to her.

"Is there anything I can do?" I asked.

"No, Rabbi, I don't want to talk about it."

"It could help to talk it out," I said.

Finally, she told me. "This is the third time that you are in this house. The mother of the baby is my best friend. She has three boys. But I have none. What

> **"This is the third time that you are in this house. She has three boys. But I have none. What does G-d want from me?**

does G-d want from me? Why don't I have any children?" And she burst into tears again.

I shared with her a teaching of *Chazal* (*Bava Kamma* 92b), "If a person has a problem, find somebody else with the same problem and pray for them, and you will be answered first." If a girl is looking for a *shidduch* she should *daven* for a girl her age who is also looking for her marriage partner. Do you need a job? *Daven* for someone else who needs a job. Are you looking to have a child? *Daven* for someone in the same situation and you will be answered first.

I told her to give some *tzedakah*, and that I would put her name on a *Tehillim* list. Then I forgot about it.

A year later I got a call from a woman whose name I didn't recognize. "Rabbi Krohn," she said, "do you remember who I am? I'm the woman from Merrick. I want you to know that ever since I saw you at my friend's *bris*, I found out about a friend of mine with the same problem and have been praying for her since that day. And today I had a boy."

"Mazal tov! You made my day!" I said.

Then she said words that I will never forget. "Rabbi, I may have made your day, but you made my life."

Was it my advice? Of course not. It was the advice of the holy *Chazal*. As we approach Purim, let's remember that Queen Esther was answered at this time of the year. This is the time to pour out our hearts and take it upon ourselves to improve our *davening*. Be sensitive to the needs of other and make sure to *daven* for them.

Ish L'rei'eihu

After the Torah records the song that Moshe sang at the Red Sea (the *Az Yashir*) it says, וַתִּקַּח מִרְיָם הַנְּבִיאָה אֲחוֹת אַהֲרֹן אֶת הַתֹּף בְּיָדָהּ וַתֵּצֶאןָ כָל הַנָּשִׁים אַחֲרֶיהָ בְּתֻפִּים וּבִמְחֹלֹת, *Miriam the prophetess, sister of Aharon, took the drum in her hand and all the women went forth after her with drums and with dances* (*Shemos* 15:20).

The *Bnei Yissachar, Av, Maamar 4*, asks: Why is it the custom of people all over the world to dance in a circle?

He answers: It is because in a circle nobody is in the front and nobody is in the back. Everybody is equal.

That is the message of Purim. אִישׁ לְרֵעֵהוּ — *send gifts, each man to his friend*. My son R' Avrohom Zelig once pointed out that the *gematria* of אִישׁ is 311. The *gematria* of לְרֵעֵהוּ is also 311. This shows that each of us is both an individual with a unique role — an אִישׁ — but at the same time we are all part of a whole, of *Klal Yisrael,* and we must be concerned for each other.

That is the essence of the story we started with. Each of us performs for the Conductor of the World Symphony. We should never forget who we are and what we can accomplish, but we must also know that we are all in this together as one harmonious symphony — אִישׁ לְרֵעֵהוּ. That is the inspiring song of Purim.

Indices

Index of Personalities

Note: Included in this index are those historical personalities who played a role (or made a comment about) the stories which appear in this book. Excluded are most fictionalized names, minor characters, and narrators of the commentaries cited in the text. Page numbers indicate the first page of the story in which the person appears.

All titles have been omitted from this index to facilitate finding names.

Abraham, R' Yehuda   99
Adler, Mrs. Ella   61
Adler, Yanky   61
Alkabetz, Rav Shlomo HaLevi   215
Alter, R' Betzalel   71
Alter, Rabbi Yehudah Leib (Sefas Emes)   71
Alter, Rav Avrohom Mordechai (Imrei Emes)   71, 205
Arizal   215, 259
Ashkenazi, Harry   187
Astor, R' Yaakov   1
Avudraham   259
Baal Shem Tov   99
Babad, Binyomin   119
Benes, R' Hirsch   251
Benisch, Mrs. Pearl   233
Binik, Rabbi Moshe   21
Birnbaum, Rav Michel   187
Bluzhever Rebbe   241
Borger, Shmuel   21
Brander, Rabbi Sheah   21
Braunstein, Mr & Mrs. Jack   225
Braunstein, Rebbetzin Zehava   129
Brisker Rav, see Soloveitchik, Rav Velvel
Chalak, Chananya   31
Chazon Ish   91, 119
Chodosh, Rav Moshe Mordechai   205

Chortkover Rebbe, see Friedman, Rav Yisroel
Chozeh of Lublin   129
Cohen, Rav Dovid   53, 61, 81, 197, 225
Cohen, Rav Shaya   61
Cooper, Dr. Menachem   21, 177
Dessler, Rabbi Eliyahu   21
Drian, Rav Dovid   21
Dushnitzer, R' Elya   91
Ehrentreu, Rav Chanoch   197
Elyashiv, Rav   31, 233
Epstein, Rav Zelik   251
Faskowitz, Rabbi Moshe   177
Feinstein, Rav Elya Pruzhiner   177
Feinstein, Rav Moshe   139, 177, 187
Feinstein, Rav Reuven   139
Fishman, Rabbi Dovid   167
Flesch, Rabbi Moshe David   71
Fogel, Reb Meir   21
Frand, Rabbi Yissachar   45, 91, 129, 147
Freidenson, Mrs. Gittel   225
Freidenson, Rabbi Yosef   71, 225
Freifeld, Rabbi Shlomo   129
Friedman, Rabbi Avraham Peretz (Cary)   81, 147, 157, 187
Friedman, Rav Yisroel (Chortkover Rebbe)   71, 119
Galinsky, Rav Yaakov   99, 233

Gerrer Rebbe   81, 241
Gifter, Rav Mordechai   2
Ginzberg, Rabbi Aryeh   167, 197, 206
Glazer, Rabbi Eli   81
Goldberg, Tzvi   81
Goldman, Dr. Abba   147
Goldstadt, Akiva   225
Goldvicht, R' Chaim Yaakov   91
Gordon, Rav Lazer   197
Graydin, Rabbi Boruch   177
Grodzensky, Rav Avraham   21
Grodzensky, Rav Chaim Ozer   61
Groner, Rebbbetzin Nechama Doba   31
Gross, Rabbi Yisroel (Jerry)   81
Gurwitz, Rav Avrohom   251
Halpern, Reb Shimshon   129
Harris, Dov   119
Heiman, R' Shlomo   233
Heller, Rav Yehoshua   197
Hendrik, Prince of Netherlands   53
Herman, Mrs. Yetta   21
Heshel, Rabbi Avrohom Yehoshua (Kapishnitzer Rebbe)   99
Hirsch, Rabbi Samson Raphael   71, 81, 119, 139
Homburger, Shmuel (Sammy)   119
Hutner, Rabbi Yitzchok   45
Ibn Gabirol, Rabbi Shlomo   21, 61
Imrei Emes, see Alter, Rav Avrohom Mordechai
Jakobovits, Rabbi Immanuel   2
Juliana, Queen of Netherlands   53
Kahaneman, Rabbi Yosef (Ponevezher Rov)   2, 251
Kahn, Albert   167
Kahn, Avraham   119
Kahn, Mrs. Gital   167
Kamenetsky, Rabbi Shmuel   139
Kamenetsky, Rav Yaakov   2, 45, 107, 251
Kanievsky, Rav Chaim   215

Kanievsky, Rav Yaakov Yisrael (Steipler Gaon)   21, 61, 215, 233
Kapishnitzer Rebbe, see Heshel, Rabbi Avrohom Yehoshua
Karliner, Rav Aharon (Stoliner Rebbe)   81
Karo, Rav Yosef   215
Katz, R' Lazar HaKohen   241
Katz, Rav Moshe   53
Katz, Rav Yaakov Tzvi   53
Klausenberger Rebbe   31
Klein, Dr. Hindy   167
Kleinbart, Yidel   45
Kodinover, Rav Aaron   129
Kohn, Mrs. Sarah Rivkah   31, 119
Kornfeld, Rev Pinchus   215
Kotler, R' Shneur   225
Kotler, Rabbi Aaron   129, 225
Kramer, Alex   251
Kramer, Chananya   129
Krohn, Rabbi Kolman   31
Krohn, Mrs. Hindy   81, 107, 177, 251
Krohn, Rabbi Avrohom Zelig   2, 21, 31, 81, 251, 259
Lazersohn, Rabbi Avrohom Yosef   31
Lehrer, R' Byrech   45
Leiner, R' Mordechai   241
Lesser, R' Dov   225
Levenson, Tzvi Hirsch   71
Levenstein, Rav Chatzkel (Mashgiach of Ponevezh)   81, 107, 119
Levin, Reb Itcha Meyer   21
Levine, Rav Aryeh   119
Lopian, Rav Elya   21, 139
Lorincz, Rabbi Shlomo, and Mrs. Lorincz   21, 119
Lutzker Rov, see Sorotzkin, Rav Zalman
Maggid of Jerusalem, see Rabbi Sholom Mordechai
Mandel, David   167
Mandelbaum, Rav Naftali Yehuda   119
Marmorstein, Rabbi Avrohom   177

Mashgiach of Ponevezh, see
  Levenstein, Rav Chatzkel
Meletzky, Rabbi Chaikel 61
Meltzer, Rav Isser Zalman 119
Miller, Rabbi Avigdor 157
Mitnick, Rabbi Yitzchak 21
Mullen, Dr. David 187, 197
Munk, Rabbi Yechiel Aryeh 147
Munkaczer Rebbe, see Spira, Rav Tzvi
  Hirsch
Nanie, Mrs. Anna 241
Neugroschel, Rav Mordechai 53
Nissel, Rav Menachem 259
Pam, Rav Avraham 31, 107
Pasternack, Irwin 205
Pearl, Rabbi Avi 129
Perlstein, Max 119
Perr, R' Menachem 225
Perr, R' Yechiel 225
Pfeiffer, Chaviva 177
Pfeiffer, Dr. Julius 147
Pfeiffer, Fred 147
Pincus, Rabbi Heshy 205
Plotzker, Rabbi Binyomin 129
Plutchok, Rabbi Moshe 259
Ponevezher Rov, see Kahaneman,
  Rabbi Yosef
Portugal, Rav Eliezer Zusia (Skulener
  Rebbe) 31
Pruzhiner, Reb Elya (Feinstein) 177
R' Menachem Mendel of Riminov 91
Rappaport, Rav Mendel 197
Rebbe R' Elimelech of Lizhensk 71,
  91, 107, 187
Reichner, Mrs. Faigy 241
Reichner, Reb Yosef Yisroel 241
Reisman, Rabbi Yisrael 119, 129
Reisman, Rebbetzin Esther 119
Rema 233
Roberts, Rabbi Matis 157
Rotenberg, Rebbetzin Chana 233
Rothman, Rabbi Berel 177
Rothman, Rav Chaim Meir 53

Rothschild, Michael 21
Salant, Rav Shmuel 187
Salanter, R' Yisrael 91, 147
Salomon, Rav Mattisyahu 31, 129,
  215
Salomon, Yaakov 21, 119, 147
Sarna, Rav Chatzkel 21, 71
Schachter, Rabbi Fishel 71
Schenirer, Sarah 71, 233
Scherman, Rabbi Nosson 21, 177
Schild, Dovid 177
Schonberger, Reb Avrohom 251
Schwab, Rav Shimon 2, 31, 107
Schwadron, Rabbi Sholom
  Mordechai 2, 21, 31, 61, 81, 91,
  99, 119, 187, 233
Sefas Emes, see Alter, Rabbi Yehudah
  Leib
Segal, Rabbi Yehudah Zev 21, 91,
  233
Shapiro, R' Yitzchok Aron 205
Shapiro, Rav Meir 71
Shkop, R' Shimon 233
Shmulevitz, Rav Chaim 241
Shteinman, Rav Aaron Leib 31
Shternbuch, Rabbi Asher 31
Shternbuch, Rebbetzin Devorah 31
Silver, Rabbi Chaim 205
Skulener Rebbe, see Portugal, Rav
  Eliezer Zusia
Slonimer Rebbe 215
Soloveitchik, R' Chaim 233
Soloveitchik, Rav Velvel (Brisker
  Rav) 45
Sorotzkin, Michoel 187
Sorotzkin, Rav Boruch 187
Sorotzkin, Rav Zalman (Lutzker
  Rov) 21
Spira, Rav Tzvi Hirsch (Munkaczer
  Rebbe) 53
Steinberg, Avraham 119
Steipler Gaon, see Kanievsky, Rav
  Yaakov Yisrael

Stoliner Rebbe, see Karliner, Rav Aharon

Sullenberger, Chesley Burnett III   31

Tajtelbaum, Mendy   81

Tajtelbaum, R' Yitzchok Dovid   81

Teitelbaum, Rabbi Eli   129

Teitelbaum, Rav Yaakov   119, 233

Toscanini, Arturo   259

Trager, Rabbi Yehuda   21

Tress, Reb Elimelech   21

Tropp, R' Naftali   233

Tur (Rav Yaakov ben Rav Asher)   21

Tyberg, Moshe   119

Tyri, Rabbi Shmuel   53

Vilna Gaon   91, 205

Volozhiner, Rav Chaim   119

Volozhiner, Rav Yitzchok   119

Wallenberg, Raoul   251

Wasserman, Rabbi Simcha   31, 205

Wasserman, Rav Elchonon   31, 71, 205

Weisfish, Rabbi Eliyahu   215

Werner, Rav Abba   197

Wikler, Dr. Meir   61, 157, 167

Wilhelmina, Queen of Netherlands   53

Winder, Rabbi Yehudah   107

Wolbe, Rabbi Shlomo   21

Zakheim, Mrs. Faygie   167

Zimmerman, Rabbi Dr. Phillip   187

Zlotowitz, Rabbi Meir   21, 197

Zwick, Rabbi Moshe   225

Index of Sources

Scriptural and Talmudic Index for all eight Maggid books.

Note: **MS** indicates *The Maggid Speaks*; **AMT** indicates *Around the Maggid's Table*; **FM** indicates *In the Footsteps of the Maggid*; **MJ** indicates *Along the Maggid's Journey*; **EM** indicates *Echoes of the Maggid*; **PM** indicates *Perspectives of the Maggid*, and **RM** indicates *Reflections of the Maggid*; **SM** *In the Spirit of the Maggid*.

Page numbers reflect the page on which stories begin.

Tanach

Bereishis 1:1 **EM** 140
Bereishis 1:2 **EM** 291
Bereishis 1:4, 10, 12, 18, 21, 25, 31 **EM** 102
Bereishis 1:5 **PM** 205
Bereishis 1:7 **EM** 102
Bereishis 1:12 **EM** 102
Bereishis 1:16 **SM** 315
Bereishis 1:28 **PM** 129
Bereishis 2:7 **MS** 265
Bereishis 2:16-17 **MS** 229
Bereishis 2:18 **PM** 147
Bereishis 2:19 Rabbeinu Bechaya **FM** 143
Bereishis 2:21 **PM** 147, 241
Bereishis 3:9 **MJ** 269
Bereishis 3:19 **PM** 45, 91
Bereishis 4:6-7, 8 **PM** 61
Bereishis 4:7 **PM** 147
Bereishis 5:1-**SM** 300,301
Bereishis 5:3-32 **RM** 255
Bereishis 4:4 **PM** 61 (see Kli Yakar) **MS** 140 **MJ** 102
Bereishis 4:13 **RM** 147
Bereishis 6:16 **EM** 213 **RM** 274 (Rashi)
Bereishis 11:32 (Rashi) **PM** 177
Bereishis 12:1 **PM** 129
Bereishis 12:2 **PM** 119

Bereishis 12:5 **SM** 301
Bereishis 14:13 **EM** 284
Bereishis 14:20 **RM** 263
Bereishis 17:9 **RM** 161
Bereishis 17:11 **MS** 260 **RM** 161
Bereishis 17:27 **MJ** 245
Bereishis 18:1-8 **MS** 89
Bereishis 18:12 **PM** 147
Bereishis 18:13 and Rashi **PM** 147
Bereishis 18:19 **MS** 52
Bereishis 19:27 **FM** 146 **SM** 175
Bereishis 21:1 **EM** 39
Bereishis 21:19 **PM** 129
Bereishis 22:1 (see Rashi, Ramban, Rabeinu Bechaya) **SM** 123
Bereishis 22:5 **EM** 168
Bereishis 23:3 Ohr HaChaim **AMT** 131
Bereishis 24:2 (See Kli Yakar) **EM** 306 **PM** 91
Bereishis 24:65 (see Haamek Davar) **PM** 147
Bereishis 26:12 **EM** 19 **RM** 263
Bereishis 27:20 **MJ** 117
Bereishis 27:29 **FM** 237
Bereishis 27:33 **FM** 237
Bereishis 28:15 **MJ** 250
Bereishis 28:22 **RM** 263
Bereishis 29:31 **EM** 272

Bereishis 29:35 **PM** 53
  RM 82 (See Sforno)
Bereishis 30:1 (see Ramban)
  PM 147
Bereishis 30:2 **PM** 147
Bereishis 30:25 **MJ** 115 **RM** 247
Bereishis 32:5 **PM** 45
Bereishis 32:24 **EM** 274
Bereishis 32:28-30 **MS** 238
Bereishis 32:35 (see Kli Yakar)
  SM 292
Bereishis 34:7 **AMT** 58
Bereishis 35:22 **MJ** 119
Bereishis 37:2 **EM** 168
Bereishis 37:3 **RM** 257
Bereishis 37:11 **MJ** 40 **PM** 215
  RM 172
Bereishis 37:24 (Rashi) **EM** 285
Bereishis 37:25 **PM** 81 **RM** 257
Bereishis 37:33 **PM** 99
Bereishis 41:9 **FM** 236
Bereishis 42:1 **MJ** 259 **PM** 99
Bereishis 42:24 **SM** 154
Bereishis 44:17 Rabbeinu Bechaya
  MJ 83
Bereishis 44:18 **AMT** 88
Bereishis 44:30 **RM** 231
Bereishis 44:34 **EM** 135
Bereishis 45:5 **MJ** 83
Bereishis 45:24 **EM** 150 **SM** 114
Bereishis 45:28 **PM** 71 **SM** 182
Bereishis 49:10 **PM** 53 **EM** 95
Bereishis 46:29 Rashi **MS** 25
Bereishis 49:4 **MJ** 118, 119
Bereishis 49:10 **EM** 95
Bereishis 50:17 Rabbeinu
  Bachaya **MJ** 83 **PM** 197
Bereishis 50:20-21 **PM** 197
Bereishis 50:21 **MJ** 83

Shemos 1:15, 17 **EM** 208
Shemos 1:20,21 **SM** 265
Shemos 1:22 **EM** 207

Shemos 2:6 **RM** Intro (See Baal
  HaTurim)
Shemos 2:15 **FM** 32 **MJ** 33
Shemos 2:20 **MJ** 33
Shemos 3:2 **PM** 99
Shemos 3:4 **PM** 119
Shemos 3:7 **PM** 167
Shemos 6:9 **MJ** 47
Shemos 7:2 **RM** Intro (Rashi)
Shemos 8:2 **PM** 61
Shemos 10:22 **FM** 171
Shemos 12:19 **EM** 255
Shemos 12:36 **AMT** 35
Shemos 12:42 **RM** 268
Shemos 13:16 **MJ** 213
Shemos 13:18 (Rashi) **EM** 298
Shemos 13:19 **MS** 260
Shemos 15:2 **AMT** 21
Shemos 15:20 **PM** 259
Shemos 16:1 (Rashi) **EM** 298
Shemos 16:31 **FM** 14
Shemos 17:9 **RM** 80 **SM** 32
  (Rashi)
Shemos 18:1 (Rashi) **MS** 221
Shemos 19:2 **RM** 257 (and Rashi)
Shemos 19:12 **EM** 308
Shemos 20:6 **RM** 271 (Ohr
  HaChaim) **PM** 241 (Ohr HaChaim)
Shemos 20:7 **MS** 211
Shemos 20:13, 14 **PM** 91
Shemos 20:15 **PM** 3
Shemos 22:21 (see Rambam and
  Rashi) **PM** 167
Shemos 22:24 **SM** 151
Shemos 23:2 **MJ** 65
Shemos 23:7 **PM** 53 **EM** 161
Shemos 25:8 **MJ** 205
Shemos 25:8 Malbim **MJ** 205
  PM 225
Shemos 25:23 **FM** 173
Shemos 25:34 **EM** 259
Shemos 30:12 **RM** 179 (Baal
  HaTurim)

Shemos 31:1, 4 **MS** 201
Shemos 31:13, 17 **MS** 260
Shemos 31:14 **RM** 172
  PM (Torah Temimah) 215
Shemos 31:16,17 **SM** 92
Shemos 32:19 **FM** 239 **SM** 154
Shemos 33:22 **RM** 215
Shemos 34:3 **PM** 71
Shemos 34:7 **FM** 43
Shemos 34:9 **MJ** 72
Shemos 35:3 **EM** 171
Shemos 39:29 **PM** 61

Vayikra 1:1 **EM** 55
Vayikra 2:13 **RM** 259
Vayikra 3:16 **MS** 140
Vayikra 5:23 **AMT** 65
Vayikra 7:19 **FM** 256
Vayikra 10:3 **PM** 31 **SM** 318
Vayikra 16:30 **EM** 293 **PM** 215
Vayikra 18:5 **MJ** 158 **EM** 209
Vayikra 19:2 **AMT** 187
Vayikra 19:11, 13 **PM** 91
Vayikra 19:17 **MJ** 107
Vayikra 19:18 **MS** 49 **SM** 250
  MJ 81 **PM** 71 **RM** 275
Vayikra 19:22 **RM** 246
Vayikra 21:1-3 **RM** 159
Vayikra 21:14 **MJ** 55
Vayikra 23:16 **AMT** 266
Vayikra 23:27 **MJ** 131 **PM** 119
Vayikra 23:43 **RM** 140
Vayikra 26:17 **FM** 137
Vayikra 26:37 **RM** 13
Vayikra 19:17 Ituri Torah **MJ** 108

Bamidbar 1:2 **RM** 110
Bamidbar 1:45 **RM** 86
Bamidbar 6 **RM** 235
Bamidbar 8:2 **SM** 228
Bamidbar 9:23 **RM** 260
Bamidbar 13:16 **MJ** 172
Bamidbar 13:33 **MJ** 57

Bamidbar 15:24 **EM** 249
Bamidbar 15:39 **AMT** 256
Bamidbar 15:41 **RM** 265
Bamidbar 23:9 **RM** 276
Bamidbar 23:10 **MJ** 264
Bamidbar 23:23 **RM** 67 (Rashi)
Bamidbar 23:24 **RM** 262
Bamidbar 25:12 **MJ** 105
Bamidbar 31:2 **FM** 32
Bamidbar 31:6 **FM** 32

Devarim 2:3 **MJ** 259
Devarim 3:25 **RM** 86
Devarim 4:9 **MJ** 220
Devarim 4:15 **MJ** 132 **PM** 119
Devarim 5:6-18 **SM** 67
Devarim 6:5 **MS** 247 **PM** 71
  SM 293 **AMT** 153 **SM** 293
Devarim 6:7 **MJ** 67, 99 **PM** 233
Devarim 7:26 **MS** 159
Devarim 8:8 **FM** 169
Devarim 8:10 **PM** 81
Devarim 8:12 **PM** 99
Devarim 9:17 **SM** 154
Devarim 10:2 **FM** 239
Devarim 10:12 see Daas Zekeinim
  PM 129
Devarim 11:26-28 **SM** 304
Devarim 11:27 see Daas Zekeinim
  SM 303
Devarim 14:22 **EM** 258 **RM** 263
Devarim 15:7 **PM** 99 **RM** 137
Devarim 16:11 **FM** 134
Devarim 16:19 **FM** 235
Devarim 17:11 **EM** 258
Devarim 18:15 **FM** 221
Devarim 21:1-9 **MJ** 53
Devarim 22:1-4 **MJ** 122
Devarim 22:1 **FM** 61
Devarim 22:3 **FM** 61 **PM** 225
Devarm 22:10 **FM** 142
Devarim 22:11 **AMT** 173
Devarim 24:14 **PM** 91

Devarim 25:3 **AMT** 266
Devarim 25:18 **MJ** 254
Devarim 27:18 **MS** 152
Devarim 27:26 Ramban **EM** 184
Devarim 28:17 **EM** 79
Devarim 28:19 **EM** 79
Devarim 28:21 **EM** 79
Devarim 28:47 **FM** 37 (Me'am
  Loez) **PM** 147
Devarim 29:6 **EM** 292
Devarim 28:57-61 **SM** 96
Devarim 29:9 **SM** 97
Devarim 29:28 **MJ** 60
Devarim 30:2 **PM** 215
Devarim: 31:9 **RM** 131
Devarim 31:21 **EM** 267
Devarim 32:2 Torah Temimah
  FM 266
Devarim: 32:7 **RM** 222
Devarim 32:15 **PM** 81
Devarim 34:5 **FM** 261
Devarim 34:6 **RM** 159
Devarim 34:12 **SM** 153, 170

Yehoshua 1:1 Radak **FM** 259

Shoftim 3:20 **FM** 159
Shoftim 4:17 **MJ** 33
Shoftim 4:21 **MJ** 33
Shoftim 5:8 **EM** 235
Shoftim: 13:8 **RM** 235
Shoftim: 13:13 **RM** 235
Shoftim: 13:14 **RM** 235

Shmuel I 1:1 **EM** 39
Shmuel I 2:2 **EM** 39
Shmuel I 16:7 **MJ** 100

Shmuel II 19:1, 5 **PM** 241

Melachim I 18:36 **RM** 196
Melachim II 23:25 **EM** 184

Yeshayahu 2:3 **PM** 225
Yeshayahu 8:17 **EM** 267
Yeshayahu 25:8 **MJ** 107
Yeshayahu 27:13 **PM** 205
Yeshayahu 29:13 **AMT** 137
Yeshayahu: 30:20 **RM** 67
Yeshayahu 38:16 **SM** 189
Yeshayahu: 40:31 **RM** 271
Yeshayahu 41:6 **EM** 208
Yeshayahu 43:22 **MS** 249
Yeshayahu 49:3 **AMT** 28
Yeshayahu 55:6 **MS** 242 **EM** 302
Yeshayahu 58:7 **FM** 61
Yeshayahu 61:10 **SM** 248
Yeshayahu 62:5 **SM** 248

Yirmiyahu 2:13 **MS** 250
Yirmiyahu 9:8 **EM** 161
Yirmiyahu 12:11 **MS** 250
Yirmiyahu 17:13 **AMT** 267
Yirmiyahu 23:29 **MJ** 48
Yirmiyahu: 24:6 **RM** 86
Yirmiyahu: 31:15 **RM** 67
Yirmiyahu 31:21 **PM** 147
Yirmiyahu Perek 32 **MS** 185

Yechezkel 1:3 **AMT** 252
Yechezkel 11:9 **MJ** 63
Yechezkel 16:6 **AMT** 107 **SM** 317
Yechezkel 36:25 **AMT** 267

Hoshea 10:12 **EM** 62

Amos 2:6 **SM** 85

Ovadiah: 1:18 **PM** 251 **RM** 247
  SM 295

Yonah 1:8,9 **EM** 283
Yonah 8:9 **PM** 45

Habakkuk 2:4 **EM** 165

Tzephaniah 3:6,7 **SM** 310

Chaggai 2:8 **EM** 304

Malachi 2:6 **EM** 19
Malachi 3:3 **RM** 276
Malachi 3:7 **PM** 233
Malachi 3:24 **AMT** 124

Tehillim 6:3 **FM** 77
Tehillim 8:5 **RM** 104
Tehillim 12 **FM** 77
Tehillim 15:22 **MS** 66
Tehillim 17:8 **RM** 103
Tehillim 19:8 **MJ** 258 **SM** 116
Tehillim 19:9 **SM** 296
Tehillim 19:11 **MJ** 94, 228
Tehillim 19:15 **PM** 1
Tehillim 20:2 **AMT** 110
Tehillim 20:8 **RM** 70
Tehillim 20:9 **RM** 70
Tehillim 24:3, 4 **EM** 127
Tehillim 24:4 **MS** 258
Tehillim 27:4 **EM** 295
Tehillim 27:5 **MJ** 198 **RM** 140
Tehillim 27:14 **SM** 307
Tehillim 30:6 **RM** 244
Tehillim 30:7 **AMT** 206
Tehillim 34:13-14 **MJ** 165 **EM** 140
Tehillim 34:15 **MS** 242 **EM** 102
Tehillim 36:8-11 **RM** 265
Tehillim 37:11 **EM** 19
Tehillim 37:23 **MS** 224 **RM** 100
Tehillim 41:2 **AMT** 73
Tehillim 49:17 **FM** 58
Tehillim 49:18 **FM** 58
Tehillim 50:23 **EM** 257
Tehillim 51:14 **MJ** 162
Tehillim 51:17 **SM** 283
Tehillim 51:19 **EM** 155
Tehillim 55:15 **MJ** 156
Tehillim 55:23 **AMT** 218
Tehillim 61:7 (and Radak) **EM** 253

Tehillim 68:7 56
Tehillim 69:13 **AMT** 265
Tehillim 81:2 **RM** 207
Tehillim 84:5 **RM** 244
Tehillim 90:10 **SM** 17
Tehillim 90:12 **PM** 71
Tehillim 91 **MJ** 165
Tehillim 92:6 **FM** 82
Tehillim 92:6-7 **MS** 233
Tehillim 92:7 **AMT** 194
Tehillim 93:4 **EM** 87
Tehillim 94:1-2 **MS** 237
Tehillim 97:11 **SM** 232
Tehillim 100 **MS** 77
Tehillim 100:2 **FM** 266
Tehillim 102:1 **AMT** 25
Tehillim 104:24 **AMT** 233
Tehillim 111:5 **PM** 99
Tehillim 112:5, 6 **EM** 142
Tehillim 116:3,4 **PM** 129 **SM** 148
Tehillim 116:8 **SM** 87
Tehillim 116:13 **PM** 129 **SM** 148
Tehillim 116:16 **FM** 260 **EM** 119
  RM 19
Tehillim 118:1 **SM** 233
Tehillim 118:1 **SM** 48
Tehillim 118:5 **SM** 234
Tehillim 118:17 **EM** 100 **RM** 255
Tehillim 118:25 **FM** 260 **EM** 182
Tehillim 119:60 **PM** 21
Tehillim 119:162 **SM** 296
Tehillim 119:64 **SM** 13
Tehillim 119:176 **MJ** 232
Tehillim 121:1 **PM** 139 (see Midrash
  PM 205
Tehillim 121:1-2 **AMT** 206
Tehillim 121:5 **PM** 53
Tehillim 121:7 **MJ** 208
Tehillim 121:15 **EM** 304
Tehillim 126:5 **FM** 148
Tehillim 137:1 **PM** 251
Tehillim 137:1,4,5,7 **SM** 85
Tehillim 142 **PM** 233

Tehillim 144:7   **SM** 295   **PM** 251
Tehillim 144:15   **RM** 244
Tehillim 145:9   **RM** 207
Tehillim 145:16   **RM** 244
Tehillim 145:16,17   **SM** 316
Tehillim 145:18   **EM** 162
Tehillim 145:19   **PM** 251
Tehillim 146:3   **SM** 314
Tehillim 146:8   **RM** 149
Tehillim 146:9   **RM** 149
Tehillim 147:3,4   **SM** 315
Tehillim 150:6   **PM** 53   **RM** 82

Mishlei: 1:5   **RM** 110
Mishlei: 1:8   **RM** 32
Mishlei: 1:9   **RM** 253
Mishlei 3:2   **MJ** 208
Mishlei 3:9   **SM** 247
Mishlei 3:15   **EM** 235   **SM** 110
Mishlei: 3:17   **RM** 89
Mishlei 3:18   **SM** 311
Mishlei 4:25   **MS** 155
Mishlei 10:2   **MS** 164   **MJ** 92
   SM 230
Mishlei 10:8   **AMT** 35
Mishlei 11:4   **MJ** 164   **SM** 231
Mishlei 12:18   **AMT** 276
Mishlei 15:1   **AMT** 78   **MJ** 98
   PM 61   **RM** 117
Mishlei 15:27   **AMT** 136
Mishlei 16:5   **MS** 159
Mishlei 18:23   **SM** 269
Mishlei 19:21   **AMT** 220   **SM** 304
Mishlei 20:24   **EM** 51   **PM** 197
Mishlei 20:27   **SM** 267   **SM** 91
Mishlei 21:21   **AMT** 96
Mishlei 22:6   **FM** 196   **EM** 270
Mishlei 22:9   **EM** 246
Mishlei 27:2   **FM** 253
Mishlei 27:21   **EM** 19
Mishlei 28:14   **FM** 226
Mishlei 30:10   **SM** 208
Mishlei 31:10-31   **AMT** 274

Mishlei 31:20   **MJ** 128

Iyov 5:7   **AMT** 260
Iyov 22:28   **AMT** 209
Iyov 23:13   **SM** 157
Iyov 29:34   **EM** 19
Iyov 31:32   **AMT** 54
Iyov 38:4   **EM** 291
Iyov 41:3   **AMT** 144   **PM** 241
Ivov 42:10   PM 119

Daniel 2:21   **AMT** 253   **RM** 116
Daniel 12:3   **MJ** 43

Ezra 10:44   **MJ** 245

Shir HaShirim 1:4   **SM** 296
Shir HaShirim 3:10   **MJ** 66
Shir HaShirim 5:1-7   **MS** 266
Shir HaShirim 7:11   **EM** 260

Eichah 1:3   **EM** 255
Eichah 1:12   **EM** 300
Eichah 3:31, 32   **MJ** 171   **PM** 225
Eichah 5:21   **PM** 233

Koheles 1:2   **MS** 250
Koheles 3:1   **FM** 82
Koheles 3:1,4   **SM** 282   **SM** 282
Koheles 4:12   **FM** 13
Koheles 7:2   **FM** 175
Koheles 7:29   **MS** 230
Koheles 9:8   **RM** 259
Koheles 10:19   **EM** 305
Koheles 11:1   **FM** 31   **MJ** 92
Koheles 12:13   **MS** 250

Esther 1:6   **RM** 257
Esther 1:7   **MJ** 254
Esther 2:10   **PM** 259
Esther 3:9   **MS** 162
Esther 4:5   **MJ** 254
Esther 4:11   **PM** 259

Esther 4:14 **PM** 259
Esther 4:16 **PM** 259
Esther 5:3 **PM** 259
Esther 7:8 **FM** 128
Esther 8:16 **MJ** 255
Esther 9:25 **MJ** 125 **PM** 259
  SM 313

Medrashim
Bereishis Rabbah 2:4 **RM** 234
  PM 251
Bereishis Rabbah 4:6 **EM** 102
Bereishes Rabbah 14:9 **PM** 53
  RM 82
Bereishes Rabbah 17:5 **PM** 241
Bereishes Rabbah 17:6 **PM** 147
Bereishis Rabbah 20:1 **EM** 285
Bereishis Rabbah 20:12 **EM** 296
Bereishis Rabbah 21:14 **PM** 129
Bereishis Rabbah 22:13 **PM** 215
Bereishis Rabbah 42:8 **EM** 284
  PM 45 **RM** 36
Bereishes Rabbah 44:7 **RM** 36
Bereishis Rabbah 67:3 **FM** 237
Bereishis Rabbah 68:4 **FM** 79
Bereishis Rabbah 71:7 **PM** 147
Bereishis Rabbah 94:3 **PM** 71
  SM 182
Tanchuma Bereishis 9 **MJ** 102
  PM 61
Tanchuma Lech Lecha 8 **FM** 258
Tanchuma Toldos 5 **MJ** 259

Shemos Rabbah 1:27 **PM** 119
Shemos Rabbah 4:2 **MJ** 33
Shemos Rabbah 14:3 **FM** 171
Shemos Rabbah, 15:12, 17:3,
  19:5 **SM** 317
Shemos Rabbah 21:6 **MS** 224
Shemos Rabbah 35:6 **AMT** 176
Tanchuma Ki Sisa 31 **PM** 71

Vayikra Rabbah 2:8 **AMT** 252

Vayikra Rabbah 9:3 **MJ** 115
Vayikra Rabbah 9:9 **SM** 163
Vayikra Rabbah 11:8 **PM** 31
  RM 75
Vayikra Rabbah 15:9 **RM** 234
Vayikra Rabbah 27:2 **PM** 241
Vayikra Rabbah 30:14 **FM** 120
Vayikra Rabbah 32:2 **EM** 87
Tanchuma-Tazriah 11 **RM** 234

Bamidbar Rabbah 14:2 **PM** 241
Bamidbar Rabbah 21:2 **PM** 147
Bamidbar Rabbah 22:8 **FM** 173
Bamidbar Rabbah 142 **AMT** 14:2
Tanchuma Bamdibar 22:8 **PM** 99
Tanchuma Matos Chapter 3 **FM** 32

Devarim Rabbah 2:31 **MJ** 40
Tanchuma Nitzavim 1 **PM** 157
Tanchuma Ha'Azinu 7 **SM** 267

Koheles Rabbah 1:7:5 **AMT** 253
  RM 116
Koheles Rabbah 1:13 **PM** 91

Esther Rabbah 8:5 **MJ** 254
Esther Rabbah 2:11 **MJ** 254
Esther Rabbah 10:11 **MJ** 259

Shir Ha'Shirim Rabbah 1:1:4:3
  SM 296
Shir Hashirim Rabbah 4:2 **EM** 129
Shir Hashirim Rabbah 5:2:2
  RM 268

Yalkut Shimoni-Bo 187:11 **RM** 207
Yalkut Shimoni Mishlei 31 **FM** 57

Ruth Rabbah 2:9 **FM** 159

Eichah Rabbah 1:28 **EM** 255

Medrash Eileh Ezkarah **MJ** 83

Zohar, Tzav 31b **SM** 233

Mishnah and Talmud
Berachos 3b **AMT** 157
Berachos 4b **SM** 316
Berachos 5a **MJ** 163 **SM** 306
Berachos 5b **FM** 161
Berachos 6b **FM** 146, 163
  RM 196 **SM** 175
Berachos 6b Rabbeinu Yonah and
  Shiltei HaGiborim **FM** 147
Berachos 7b **FM** 16,34
  EM 150 **RM** 67 **SM** 267
Berachos 8b **MS** 228
Berachos 8b Rashi **EM** 87
Berachos 9b **AMT** 47
Berachos 10a **AMT** 214
Berachos 10a Rashi **EM** 39
Berachos 12a **MJ** 61
Berachos 13b **EM** 295 **PM** 45
Berachos 16b **MJ** 262
Berachos 17a **MJ** 253 **RM** 110
Berachos 26a **FM** 128
Berachos 28b **AMT** 90, 130
Berachos 30a **RM** 171
Berachos 30b **MJ** 35
Berachos 32a **EM** 296
Berachos 33a **RM** 13
Berachos 35b **PM** 91
Berachos 47b **RM** 175
Berachos 54a **FM** 97 **MJ** 61
Berachos 55a **MS** 153 **FM** 173
  RM 116
Berachos 60a **FM** 226
Berachos 60b **RM** 185
Berachos, Meiri (Intro.) **SM** 309

Yerushalmi Berachos 5:2 **SM** 295

Yerushalmi Peah 1:1 **AMT** 277
Tosefta Peah 3:13 **AMT** 134

Bikkurim 3:3 **EM** 150

Shabbos 10a **MS** 76
Shabbos 21b **FM** 116
Shabbos 22a **EM** 285
Shabbos 23b **AMT** 94 **RM** 145
Shabbos 31a **AMT** 171 **EM** 298
  FM 170 **PM** 91, 107
Shabbos 31b **RM** 260
Shabbos 32a **AMT** 222 **EM** 227
  RM 104 **RM** 177 **SM** 97
Shabbos 35b Rashi **PM** 251
Shabbos 49a Tosafos **MS** 160
Shabbos 49b **RM** 260
Shabbos 67a **EM** 265
Shabbos 87a **SM** 67
Shabbos 89b see Rashi **SM** 67
Shabbos 92b **AMT** 227
Shabbos 104a **FM** 90 **RM** 268
Shabbos 118b **PM** 205
Shabbos 119a **AMT** 43
Shabbos 127a **AMT** 227
Shabbos 130a **FM** 164 **RM** 161
Shabbos 133b **MJ** 107
Shabbos 146a **FM** 111
Shabbos 151b **PM** 99
Shabbos 153b **AMT** 227
Shabbos 156b **FM** 243

Eruvin 13b **RM** 67
Eruvin 21b **FM** 131
Eruvin 22a **MS** 264
Eruvin 34a **MJ** 218
Eruvin 41b **MJ** 140
Eruvin 54a **PM** 233
Eruvin 55a **FM** 232
Eruvin 65a **MS** 166
Eruvin 65b **AMT** 82 **MJ** 200

Pesachim 50b **EM** 260
Pesachim 65b **RM** 257
Pesachim 88b **FM** 259
Pesachim 116b **MJ** 269

Pesachim 118b **AMT** 271
Pesachim 119b **PM** 129 **SM** 147

Yoma 4b **EM** 55
Yoma 9b **FM** 52 **EM** 272
Yoma 23a **AMT** 263
Yoma 37a **RM** 239
Yoma 38b **SM** 133
Yoma 44a **EM** 285
Yoma 52a **EM** 259
Yoma 69b **EM** 87
Yoma 74b **EM** 180
Yoma 75a **FM** 14
Yoma 85b **MS** 139
Yoma 86a **EM** 158 **RM** 51

Succah 11b **FM** 60
Succah 41a **FM** 171
Succah 56b **EM** 234

Beitzah 15b **AMT** 213

Rosh Hashanah 16a **MS** 184 **PM** 99
Rosh Hashanah 17a **EM** 70, 287
Rosh Hashanah 17b **FM** 43
Rosh Hashanah 18a **EM** 302

Taanis 7a **AMT** 270 **SM** 297
Taanis 8b **PM** 107
Taanis 8b-9a **RM** 263
Taanis 9a **FM** 133 **EM** 258
Taanis 10b **EM** 150
Taanis 21a **AMT** 238
Taanis 23a **FM** 271
Taanis 25b **FM** 43 **EM** 287
  PM 187
Taanis 26b **FM** 267
Taanis 29a **FM** 267
Taanis 31a **MJ** 225

Megillah 3a **RM** 51
Megillah 6b **FM** 213
Megillah 13b **FM** 69

Megillah 14a **MS** 186
Megillah 16b **MJ** 255
Megillah 17b **AMT** 130
Megillah 24b **EM** 296
Megillah 24b Rashi **EM** 293
Megillah 27b-28a **RM** 265
Megillah 28a **PM** 99

Moed Katan 5a **EM** 257
Moed Katan 9a **MJ** 116
Moed Katan 27b **RM** 259

Chagigah 9b **MJ** 221
Chagigah 12a **EM** 291

Yevamos 62b **FM** 62 **MJ** 144
Yevamos 62b, Maharal Chiddushei
  Aggados **MJ** 144 **RM** 110
Yevamos 62b **SM** 77
Yevamos 63a **EM** 162 **RM** 13
  SM 162, 310
Yevamos 69a **EM** 60
Yevamos 79a **AMT** 73
Yevamos 87b **SM** 231
Yevamos 97a **EM** 260
Yevamos 121b **MS** 114 **AMT** 86

Kesubos 8b **MJ** 251 **PM** 45
Kesubos 17a **RM** 88
Kesubos 21a **RM** 165
Kesubos 30a **MS** 175
Kesubos 50a **MJ** 129
Kesubos 67a **AMT** 86
Kesubos 77b **FM** 237
Kesubos 105a **EM** 19
Kesubos 105b **FM** 91, 235
Kesubos 107b **MS** 68

Nedarim 39b **FM** 66
Nedarim 49b (Meiri) **PM** 107
Nedarim 64b **MS** 243
Nedarim 81a **EM** 43

Sotah 2a **MS** 39 **RM** 268 **SM** 140
Sotah 7b **MS** 75
Sotah 8b **EM** 305 **PM** 241
Sotah 10b **AMT** 62
Sotah 12a **EM** 207
Sotah 13a **AMT** 34
Sotah 14a **RM** 159 **RM** 198
Sotah 17a **MJ** 104
Sotah 21a **FM** 27
Sotah 38b **EM** 246
Sotah 47a **AMT** 51 **EM** 75
  RM 239
Sotah 49b **PM** 139
Yerushalmi Sotah 7:4 **EM** 183

Gittin 7a **FM** 132 **PM** 107
Gittin 14b **AMT** 131
Gittin 52a **RM** 172
Gittin 55b **FM** 226
Gittin 56a **AMT** 115
Gittin 62a **FM** 243
Gittin 90b **PM** 167

Kiddushin 1:9 **RM** 265
Kiddushin 2a **MS** 180
Kiddushin 2b **MJ** 273
Kiddushim 26a **MJ** 67
Kiddushin 30b **MJ** 65 **PM** 167
Kiddushin 31a **RM** 246
Kiddushin 32b **RM** 75
Kiddushin 33a **FM** 224 **EM** 150
Kiddushin 38a **FM** 266
Kiddushin 39b **RM** 243
Kiddushin 82a **PM** 91
  (Maharsha) **PM** 107
Kiddushin 82b (Maharsha) **PM** 107
Yerushalmi Kiddushin 4:12 **PM** 81

Bava Kamma 17a **AMT** 270
Bava Kamma 35a **RM** 166
Bava Kamma 92a **FM** 99 **PM** 107,
  119
Bava Kamma 92b **FM** 32 **PM** 259

Mishnah Bava Metzia 2:11 **FM** 199
Bava Metzia 21b **EM** 235, 237
Bava Metzia 24a **MJ** 237 **PM** 225
Bava Metzia 29b **MS** 68 **PM** 91
Bava Metzia 30a **FM** 61
Bava Metzia 38a **MJ** 272
Bava Metzia 58b **AMT** 60 **FM** 140
Bava Metzia 2:11 **RM** 231
Bava Metzia 107b **MS** 168 **PM** 119

Bava Basra 8a **MJ** 43
Bava Basra 8b **RM** 241
Bava Basra 9a **AMT** 170 **SM** 269
Bava Basra 10a **MS** 243
Bava Basra 11a **RM** 259 **SM** 269
Bava Basra 21a **MJ** 205
Bava Basra 22a **FM** 141
Bava Basra 25 **PM** 91
Bava Basra 25a **PM** 225
Bava Basra 29a **RM** 80
Bava Basra 29b **AMT** 261
Bava Basra 74a **FM** 156
Bava Basra 91a **RM** 19
Bava Basra 103b, 104b, 205b
  MJ 220
Bava Basra 121b **MJ** 225

Mishnah Sanhedrin 10:1 **MS** 137,
  138, 263
Sanhedrin 19b **AMT** 100
Sanhedrin 20a **RM** 226
Sanhedrin 22b **PM** 31
Sanhedrin 27b **RM** Intro p.13
Sanhedrin 32b **FM** 262
Sanhedrin 37a **AMT** 183
Sanhedrin 38b **MS** 229 **EM** 241
Sanhedrin 59b **PM** 45
Sanhedrin 88b **MJ** 266
Sanhedrin 89a **AMT** 115
Sanhedrin 90a **MS** 137, 138, 263
Sanhedrin 96a **FM** 159
Sanhedrin 97b **MS** 67 footnote

Sanhedrin 98b **MS** 258
Sanhedrin 99a **EM** 291 **RM** 229
  (See Rashi)
Sanhedrin 99b **AMT** 260
Sanhedrin 100b **EM** 131
Sanhedrin 104b **EM** 300
Sanhedrin 107a **SM** 140

Makkos 10b **MJ** 134
Makkos 22b **AMT** 161, 266
  FM 180

Shevuos 39a **AMT** 186 **RM** 13
Shevuos 45a **RM** 166
Yerushalmi Shevuos 1:5 **MS** 77
  (footnote)

Avodah Zara 3a **PM** 215
Avodah Zara 10b **SM** 157
Avodah Zara 17b **FM** 150
Avodah Zara 25a **MJ** 264
Avodah Zara 39b **FM** 35
Avodah Zara 54b **RM** 159

Kallah Rabbasi Perek 2 **MS** 178

Mishnah Avos 2:15 **PM** 61
Avos 1:1 **RM** 113
Avos 1:4 **MS** 20, 24 **EM** 155
Avos 1:5 **FM** 126 **PM** 139
Avos 1:6 **AMT** 271
Avos 1:12 **EM** 19
Avos 1:15 **AMT** 55
Avos 2:1 **MS** 253 **RM** 155
Avos 2:4 **MS** 206 **MJ** 113
Avos 2:5 **FM** 229
Avos 2:10 **SM** 303
Avos 2:21 **MS** 56
Avos 3:1 **AMT** 121 **MJ** 222
Avos 3:10 **MJ** 220
Avos 3:11 Tiferes Yisrael 72 **FM** 140
Avos 4:1 **MS** 48 **AMT** 128
  RM 271

Avos 4:2 **FM** 159 **RM** 177
Avos 4:11 **AMT** 249
Avos 4:12 **SM** 32
Avos 4:15 **RM** 80
Avos 4:20 **EM** 102
Avos 4:21 **FM** 265 **MS** 248, 261,
  264
Avos 5:20 **MS** 178
Avos 5:22 **MJ** 243
Avos 5:22 **RM** 86
Avos 5:23 **PM** 21
Avos 5:26 **FM** 25
Avos 5:30 Bartenura **SM** 123
Avos 6:6 **FM** 62 **EM** 67

Avos D'Rav Nosson 1:4 **RM** 113

Horayos 12a **MJ** 268
Horayos 14a **FM** 220

Zevachim 13b **EM** 235, 237

Menachos 13b **EM** 235, 237
Menachos 20b Tosafos **EM** 299
Menachos 29b **PM** 233
Menachos 43b **MS** 165 **PM** 129
  SM 13
Menachos 44a **SM** 189
Menachos 99a **FM** 238

Chulin 92a **MS** 67 footnote

Bechoros 58b **AMT** 275

Arachin 16a **EM** 285

Kereisos 14a **MJ** 244

Tamid 32a **FM** 245 **MJ** 34

Keilim 2:1 **EM** 155

Niddah 45b **FM** 42 **PM** 241

Niddah 70b **PM** 91   107

Rambam

Rambam Hilchos Chometz U'Matzah
8:2 **RM** 260

Hilchos Megillah 2:17 **PM** 259

Rambam Hilchos Sefer Torah 7:1
RM 131

Rambam Hilchos Shmittah
V'yovel 5:13 **RM** 159 **PM** 21

Rambam Hilchos Talmud Torah 1:8
FM 94

Rambam Hilchos Teshuvah 2:1
SM 40

Rambam Hilchos Teshuvah 2:9
FM 185 **EM** 70 **MJ** 146

Rambam Hilchos Teshuvah 2:11
MS 139

Rambam Hilchos Teshuvah 3:4
MS 241

Rambam Hilchos Teshuvah 7:3
PM 241

Rambam Hilchos Teshuvah 7:4
EM 291

Rambam Huchos Lulav 8:15 **FM** 38

Rambam Hilchos Geirushin 2:20
AMT 28

Rambam Hilchos Issurei Mizbei'ach
7:11 **MS** 140

Rambam Hilchos Melachim 11:3
FM 241

Rambam Pirush Hamishnayos Maakos
3:16 **RM** 265

Shulchan Aruch

Orach Chaim 6:2 Darchei Moshe
MJ 205, 209

Orach Chaim 8:2 **FM** 148

Orach Chaim 8:2 Mishnah Berurah 4
FM 150

Orach Chaim 28 Mishnah Berurah
Note 9 **FM** 165

Orach Chaim 44:1 **MS** 160

Orach Chaim 46:3 **MS** 165

Orach Chaim 51:7 Mishnah Berurah
note 19 **EM** 150

Orach Chaim 51:7 **SM** 316

Orach Chaim 51 B'eer Hativ note 7
EM 150

Orach Chaim 61:3 **SM** 158

Orach Chaim 90 **FM** 157

Orach Chaim 90:19 **SM** 175

Orach Chaim 92:2 **AMT** 124
FM 180

Orach Chaim 115 (Tur) **PM** 233

Orach Chaim 123 Mishnah Berurah
Note 2 **FM** 159

Orach Chaim 124:7 **RM** 147

Orach Chaim 124:7 Mishnah
Berurah note 26 **RM** 147

Orach Chaim 125:1 **FM** 222

Orach Chaim 128:6 **EM** 73

Orach Chaim 128:45 **EM** 73

Orach Chaim 128 Mishnah Berurah
note 172 **EM** 73

Orach Chaim 135 Mishnah Berurah
28 **FM** 231

Orach Chaim 142:6 Mishnah
Berurah **EM** 256

Orach Chaim 167:5 **RM** 259

Orach Chaim 218:6 **FM** 200

Orach Chaim 223 Mishnah Berurah
Note 2 **MJ** 62

Orach Chaim 230:4 **SM** 290

Orach Chaim 230:5 **RM** 185

Orach Chaim 233:1 **FM** 127

Orach Chaim 248:3 Mishnah Berurah
Note 20 **MJ** 136

Orach Chaim 257:8 and Mishnah
Berurah note 49 **SM** 195

Orach Chaim 262:5 **RM** 172

Orach Chaim 271:4 **RM** 55

Orach Chaim 271 Mishnah Berurah
Note 41 **FM** 169

Orach Chaim 272:9 **RM** 55

Orach Chaim 316:10 **RM** 207

Orach Chaim 405 **MJ** 140

Orach Chaim 425:2 Mishnah
Berurah note 10 **SM** 248

Orach Chaim 426:2 **MJ** 154

Orach Chaim 428:6 Mishnah Berurah
note 17 **EM** 79

Orach Chaim 428:8 **SM** 248

Orach Chaim 490:9 **MS** 265

Orach Chaim 494:3, Shaarei Teshuva
note 7 **RM** 131

Orach Chaim 547:1 **EM** 289

Orach Chaim 554:1 **SM** 296

Orach Chaim 581:1 Mishnah Berurah
7 **AMT** 34

Orach Chaim 581:4 **RM** 198

Orach Chaim 581:4 Mishnah
Berurah note 27 **RM** 198

Orach Chaim 583:1 **MJ** 268

Orach Chaim 602:4 **MJ** 154

Orach Chaim 606:1 Mishnah Berurah
note 11 **PM** 197

Orach Chaim 626 **RM** 140

Orach Chaim 633:2 **RM** 140

Orach Chaim 638 Mishnah Berurah
Note 24 **FM** 136

Orach Chaim 639:1 **EM** 155

Orach Chaim 649:5 **MJ** 160

Orach Chaim 651:5 **FM** 120

Orach Chaim 678:1 **AMT** 95

Orach Chaim 694:3 **MS** 162

Choshen Mishpat 259 **RM** 156
PM (259:3) 225

Even HaEzer 61:1 **MJ** 167

Yoreh Deah 53:2 **FM** 68

Yoreh Deah 115:1 **FM** 35

Yoreh Deah 179 **MJ** 268

Yoreh Deah 240:2 **PM** 139

Yoreh Deah 242:16 **MJ** 116

Yoreh Deah 244:8 **RM** 268

Yoreh Deah 249:1 **MJ** 129

Yoreh Deah 249-251 **MS** 52

Yoreh Deah 263:1 **RM** 161

Yoreh Deah 268:2 **FM** 111
SM 197

Yoreh Deah, Tur 286; Darchei
Moshe **EM** 19

Yoreh Deah 336 **EM** 266

Yoreh Deah 336 (Birkei Yosef)
SM 290

Yoreh Deah 342 **MJ** 242

Yoreh Deah 351:2 **FM** 155

Yoreh Deah 362:2 **AMT** 131

Chayei Adam 155:4 **SM** 207

Tefillos

Aleinu prayer **SM** 238

Ashamnu prayer **SM** 286

Ashrei **PM** 107

Bareich Aleinu **PM** 45, 107

Baruch She'amar **PM** 31

Birchas HaMazon **PM** 81, 107, 129,
139, 233, 259

Birchas Hashachar **SM** 210

Birkas Hatorah prayer **SM** 297

Birkas Hatorah **SM** 114

Birkas Rosh Chodesh prayer **SM** 108

Borei Nefashos prayer **SM** 50

Kol Nidrei prayer **PM** 119

Kriyas Shema **PM** 61, 71, 107, 187

Lechah Dodi **PM** 215

Modeh Ani **PM** 53

Ne'ilah **PM** 99

Ribon Kol Haolamim prayer **SM** 90

Shalom Aleichem prayer **SM** 90

Selichos prayers **PM** 233

Shema Koleinu prayer **PM** 61, 107

Shemoneh Esrei prayer **PM** 31, 45,
61, 99, 107, 119, 233, 259
SM 288, 295, 312, 315

Shemoneh Esrei prayer of Mussaf of
Yom Kippur **PM** 205

Sheva Brochos prayer **SM** 160

U'Nesaneh Tokef prayer **SM** 14, 46
Vayivarech David prayer **PM** 107
Yizkor **PM** 251

Shimusha Shel Torah 228 **SM** 300

Other Sources
Ahavas Chessed 2:4 **FM** 150
Alei Shur Vol. 2, Ch. 12, Vaad 5
  PM 21
ArtScroll Bris Milah 35, 39 **MS** 238
ArtScroll Bris Milah 77, 97
  RM 239
ArtScroll Bris Milah 84 **MS** 260
Atarah Lamelech p. 120 **RM** 271
B'derech Eitz HaChaim p. 53
  MJ 72
Birchas Cheretz, Parashas Va'eira
  PM 61
Bnei Yissachar, Av, Maamar 4
  PM 259
Chayei Adam 155:4 **SM** 207
Daas Torah, Bereishis-p.11 **SM** 170
Divrei Eliyahu (Bava Basra 11a)
  SM 269
Divrei Eliyahu p.96 **SM** 176
Eliyahu Rabbah 25 **MJ** 262 **PM** 233
Emes L'Yaakov, Bereishis 3:14
  PM 21
Gesher HaChaim 14:20 **FM** 175
Guardian of Jerusalem p. 210-211
  RM 143
Igeres HaRamban **MS** 206 **SM** 298
Igros Moshe Y.D. 2:122 Bris Milah
  (Artscroll) p.45 **SM** 231
Igros Moshe YD Volume2:122, OC
  Volume 4:66 **SM** 267
Igros U'Michtavim, Letter 94 (Rabbi Y.
  Hutner) **PM** 45
Inspiration and Insight Volume 2 p. 91
  RM 13
Kad Hakemach, Emunah **EM** 162
Kovetz He'Aros 6:6 **SM** 292

Kovetz Maamarim V'Agados Volume 1,
  252 **SM** 293
Leket Kemach Hachodosh vol. III Intro
  EM 95
Leket Kemach HaChadash, hakdamah
  PM 53
Lev Eliyahu, Vol. 3, p 337-339, 276)
  PM 139
Maaseh Avos Siman L'Bonim Volume
  3, p. 105 **RM** 172
Maaseh Rav no. 248 **EM** 162
Maayan Bais Hashoevah Shemos
  5:22 **RM** 244
Maayan Bais Hashoevah Haftarah
  Naso p. 310 **RM** 235
Meir Einei Yisrael Volume 4 p. 503
  RM 94
Meishiv Davar No. 48 **FM** 231
Meshech Chochmah (Bereishis 2:16)
  PM 81
Mesillas Yesharim Chapter 1 **FM** 216
Mesillas Yesharim Chapter 13
  PM 81
Michtav Me'Eliyahu p.187 **MJ** 269
Michtav Me'Eliyahu Volume 1,
  p. 140 **RM** 92
Michtav Me'Eliyahu Volume 4,
  p. 246 **RM** 110
Mishnas Rav Aharon Volume 1 p. 84,
  92 **RM** 274
Mishnas Rav Aharon Volume 1,
  p. 88 **PM** 129
Mishnas Rav Aharon Vol. 3, p.15
  FM 62
Mishnas Rav Aharon Vol. 3, p. 54
  MJ 205 **PM** 225
Mishnas Rav Aharon Vol 3, p. 176
  EM 148
Moreshes Avos, Devarim p.140
  MJ 72
Nefesh HaChaim Intro **EM** 49
  PM 119
Ner Mitzvah p. 12 n. 60 **PM** 187

Nesivas Sholom Vol. 2, p. 125
  MJ 51
Nesivos Olam (Nesiv Ha'Avodah
  Chapter 7) **SM** 33
Ohr Yechezkel, p. 327 **PM** 81
Ohr Yechezkel Vol.3 p. 288 **FM** 171
Ohr Yechezkel Vol. 4, p. 101
  PM 119
Olelos Ephraim Tehillim 24:3 **EM** 127
Orchos Tzaddikim, Shaar 15 Hazrizus
  PM 21
Otzros Hatorah, Elul Chapter 8:251
  SM 306
Pachad Yitzchok, Purim Chapter 18
  SM 32
Pesikta Rabbasi 9:2 **MJ** 259
Pirkei D'Rav Eliezer 29 **AMT** 139
Rabbenu Bechaya, Shulchan Shel
  Arbah **PM** 81
Rabbi Schwab on Prayer
  179,180 **SM** 316
Sefer Halkarim 4:33 **MJ** 222
Sefer Chassidim 210 **RM** 265
Sefer Chassidim 254 **RM** 94
Sefer Chassidim 323 **PM** 99
Sefer Chassidim 324 **PM** 99
Sefer Chassidim 454 **PM** 99

Selichos Kodem Rosh Hashanah
  (Motzaei Shabbos) **MS** 77
Shaarei Teshuvah Shaar 3:71
  RM 100

She'elos Uteshuvos Maharatz Chayes
  #26 **RM** 198
Shemiras Halashon Shaar Hazechiran
  Ch. 10 **EM** 288
Sefer HaChinuch Mitzvah 33
  PM 139, 177
Sefer HaChinuch Mitzvah 430
  PM 107 **SM** 313
Shehasimchah B'me'ono p.76
  SM 140
Sichos Levi p.34 **MJ** 115
Sichos Mussar Maamer #7 (5731)
  RM 226
Sichos Mussar Maamer #8 (5731)
  RM 92
Taamei HaMinhagim No. 1034
  FM 175
Table for Two **PM** 147
Tanna D'vei Eliyahu 10:8 **EM** 235
Tanya Chapter 18 **RM** 51
Tehillim Treasury p. 149 **RM** 265
Terumas Hadeshen 2:57 **EM** 262
Toras Hamilachos Intro **EM** 119
Tuvcha Yabiu Volume 1, p. 311
  RM 172
Tuvcha Yabiu Volume 2, p. 247
  RM 145
Tzidkas HaTaddik **PM** 21, 187
Wisdom in the Hebrew Alphabet
  PM 147
Zeriyah U'Binyan B'Chinuch p. 35
  RM 237